FAITH, FORM, AND FASHION

Faith, Form, and Fashion

CLASSICAL REFORMED THEOLOGY
AND ITS POSTMODERN CRITICS

PAUL HELM

CASCADE Books • Eugene, Oregon

FAITH, FORM, AND FASHION
Classical Reformed Theology and Its Postmodern Critics

Copyright © 2014 Paul Helm. All rights reserved. Except for brief quotations in critical publications or reviews, no part of this book may be reproduced in any manner without prior written permission from the publisher. Write: Permissions, Wipf and Stock Publishers, 199 W. 8th Ave., Suite 3, Eugene, OR 97401.

Cascade Books
An Imprint of Wipf and Stock Publishers
199 W. 8th Ave., Suite 3
Eugene, OR 97401

www.wipfandstock.com

ISBN 13: 978-1-62564-591-3

Cataloging-in-Publication data:

Helm, Paul.

    Faith, form, and fashion : classical reformed theology and its postmodern critics / Paul Helm.

    x + 278 p.; 23 cm—Includes bibliographical references and index.

    ISBN 13: 978-1-62564-591-3

    1. Vanhoozer, Kevin J. 2. Franke, John R. 3. Philosophical theology. 4. Reformed Churches—Doctrines. I. Title.

BT40 H455 2014

Manufactured in the USA.

"Scripture quotations are from The Holy Bible, English Standard Version® (ESV®), copyright © 2001 by Crossway, a publishing ministry of Good News Publishers. Used by permission. All rights reserved."

To
Tony and Lynn Cannon

Human beings are, necessarily, actors who cannot become something before they have first pretended to be it; and they can be divided, not into the hypocritical and the sincere, but into the sane who know that they are acting and the mad who do not.

—W. H. Auden

Nothing is more familiar or characteristic among Christians than assertion. Take away assertions, and you take away Christianity.

—Martin Luther

Contents

Preface ix

Introduction 1

A. Classic Reformed Theology
1. The Form of Theology 11
2. Epistemology 39

B. Some New Proposals Considered
3. Nature and Narrative 71
4. Being and Doing 103
5. Speech Acts, Propositions, and Assertions 130
6. Propositions, Time, and Truth 155
7. Meaning and Reasoning 179
8. Foundationalism and Its Woes 206
9. Knowing and Believing 235

C. Conclusion
10. CRT and the Future 263

Bibliography 267
Index 273

Preface

This book is the result of thinking about systematic theology from the point of view of an analytic philosopher. In particular, of examining certain revisionist proposals regarding the nature of Christian doctrine and theology offered by theologians with a broadly Reformed outlook. I quickly came to the conclusion that these proposals, though sufficiently unclear to prevent serious implementation, would be disastrous if carried through consistently. They embody a series of philosophical errors, mostly of a fundamental and, dare I say it, of an elementary kind, as well as some regrettable errors of fact.

This study recognizes that there is an inevitable intertwining of theology and philosophy at the systematic theological level. The ordering of theological claims, and an understanding of the claims themselves, requires the use of philosophical tools. My concern is that the great tradition of Reformed theologizing—benefitting from the catholic conciliar and creedal tradition, and from the theological brilliance of Augustine, reworked in late medievalism and refreshed by the renewed exegetical effort flowing from the Reformation—should not be rejected due to ignorance of the tradition, or by an appeal to jejune intellectual considerations that are destined to pass and no doubt shortly to be replaced by a new wave.

It is a concern to uphold this tradition, not as a museum piece, but as an essential part of the life of the church, that I hope prevents this study from being merely negatively critical.

Earlier published outings from which I have borrowed are:

"Does the Authority of a Tradition Exclude the Possibility of Change?" In *Identity and Change in the Christian Tradition*, edited by Marcel Sarot and Gijsbert van den Brink. Frankfurt am Main: Lang, 1999.

"The Perfect Trustworthiness of God." In *The Trustworthiness of God*, edited by Paul Helm and Carl Trueman. Leicester, UK: Apollos, 2002.

"No Easy Task: John R. Franke and the Character of Theology." In *Reforming or Conforming*, edited by Gary L. W. Johnson & Ronald L. Gleason. Wheaton, IL: Crossway, 2008.

"B. B. Warfield's Path to Inerrancy: An Attempt to Correct Some Misunderstandings." *Westminster Theological Journal* 72/1 (2010) 23–42.

"Grace Builds upon Nature: Philosophy and the Future of Theology." In *Theology and the Future: Evangelical Assertions and Explorations*, edited by Trevor Cairney and David Starling, London, Bloomsbury T & T Clark, 2014.

Much of the material now published has been used in the course of teaching in various places, and I thank the students both for their interest and their patience. I am especially grateful to my friends Oliver Crisp and James Dolezal, among others, and especially to the ever-meticulous Mark Talbot, for helpful suggestions and encouragement of various kinds. But first and foremost I thank my wife Angela for her marvelous support during the somewhat difficult time in which this work was completed.

Cold Aston,
Gloucestershire, UK

Introduction

This book is about the form of Reformed theology, about its metaphysical and epistemological character, and about its method or methods. By "Reformed theology" is understood a theology that endeavors to express and to be faithful to Scripture while standing in the tradition of the ecumenical creeds, the confessions of faith of the early generations of the Reformed era, and subsequent Reformed Orthodoxy. It professes that faith through successive cultures, the Enlightenment, Romanticism, Modernism, and so on. Its articulation has two aspects: the development of its intentions to be consistent with and faithful to Scripture and the creeds, and to express the nature of our knowledge of God and of ourselves that Scripture conveys.

This is a tradition of "catholic Protestantism," as Oliver Crisp has argued. And as Richard Muller and others have convincingly shown, this theology was worked out with great sophistication in the era of Reformed Orthodoxy. Muller has demonstrated that within Reformed Orthodoxy there are various strands of theological thought having a basic unity, and with a somewhat eclectic attitude to philosophy, and thus to the relations between theology and philosophy. The names of French theologians such as John Calvin and Theodore Beza, of Italians such as Jerome Zanchius and Francis Turretin, English Puritans such as Stephen Charnock and John Owen, Scots such as Robert Rollock and Samuel Rutherford, and Dutch theologians such as Peter Van Maastricht and Gisbert Voetius are representative of numerous other theologians whose views are so carefully examined and collated by Muller.[1] The work of Jonathan Edwards and the Baptist theologian John Gill, were indebted to this orthodoxy. In the nineteenth century the theology of the Hodges and B. B. Warfield at Princeton, W. G. T. Shedd of Union Theological Seminary, New York, Scottish theologians such as William Cunningham and George Smeaton, and in the early years of the twentieth century, Herman Bavinck of the Free University of Amsterdam,

---

1. See Muller, *Post-Reformation Reformed Dogmatics*.

and many others continue in this tradition. I shall refer to this tradition as Classical Reformed Theology (CRT).

To think of the identity of Reformed theology in these terms may seem somewhat arbitrary. There are other ways of cutting the cake, no doubt. But I think it is fairly clear that these other ways are more amorphous and harder to handle. For example, B. A. Gerrish discusses Reformed theological identity in broadly institutional terms, the continuous theological output of what Friedrich Schleiermacher called "the Reformed school," and he allows this school to embrace profound differences in theological and philosophical outlook. The fact that Calvin and Schleiermacher each manifest an intense interest in religion is allowed to prevail over the very different conceptions each had of it.[2] The great advantage of taking one's lead from the creedal and confessional tradition and its numerous exponents is that it provides a body of thinking in the considerable body of theological literature, which one can, so to speak, nail down, describe, and evaluate using the usual academic tools.

But it would be mistaken to think of CRT as monochrome. As Muller has also shown,[3] CRT provides a rich as well as a somewhat diverse heritage, and an eclectic attitude towards philosophy. Yet although they occasionally differ among themselves about method, and on doctrinal detail and emphasis, theologians of this tradition exhibit a remarkable harmony in their general theological outlook. It is the parameters and presuppositions of this outlook that will concern us here, not the discussion of particular doctrines except as these exemplify that tradition is some respect. Standing to one side of this confessional tradition, though remaining under a wider umbrella of Reformed theology, are revisionist theologians such as Schleiermacher and Barth. Their thought by and large falls outside this book. Such revisionists recognize an indebtedness to the philosophy of Immanuel Kant,[4] whereas as a general rule the intellectual currents of confessional orthodoxy flow from the medieval theologians, and more recently show some indebtedness to Thomas Reid.

Of course a tradition is always open to revision, especially one that stresses human sin and fallibility as much as the Reformed faith does.

---

2. See for example, Gerrish, *The Old Protestantism and the New: Essays on the Reformation Heritage*, especially chapter 12, and his *Continuing the Reformation: Essays on Modern Religious Thought*, Part Three.

3. For example, Muller, "*Ad fontes argumentorum*: The Sources of Reformed Theology in the Seventeenth Century."

4. Several of the essays collected together in McCormack, *Orthodox and Modern: Studies in the Theology of Karl Barth*, clearly show Barth's indebtedness to the epistemology of Immanuel Kant.

Nevertheless, any responsible revision must always be undertaken for good reason, and in an intellectually thorough manner. Apart from such a reason, Reformed theology is confessed to be a legitimate expression of the permanent Christian gospel. The mantra *semper reformanda* is usually taken, without any discussion, to mean that those in the Reformed tradition should be active in seeking doctrinal revision and new departures in theology. However, the phrase was originally, "The church is reformed and always being reformed according to the Word of God." What it means is that the church should continually reform its life and witness by reference to the theological principles of the Reformation and, of course, of Scripture. It should be emphasized that what follows is not intended as a defense of the validity of CRT, either by historical precedent or by theological and other forms of reasoning. Rather it takes it as a given tradition, endeavoring to sketch its basic thrust and temper, and against it to measure more recent proposals to reconstruct it.

So this study is a reconsideration of some of the central intellectual presuppositions and working methods of that tradition, but one that, I hope, recognizes the differences within it, as well as what unites it. Its outlook is emphatically not confessional in the narrow sense, seeking to defend every jot and tittle of a Confession at all costs. It is written at a time when seriously intended questions about both its theological method and content are being raised from within that general tradition. The chief aim is not only to re-present the methodological outline of such theology, but to do so in a way that demonstrates that the arguments for a radical change in the method and outlook of CRT offered by "post-conservatives" and "post-foundationalists"[5] are weak and unconvincing. For CRT to be overturned, or relegated to the museum, the arguments for doing so will have to be considerably stronger than those currently available. So, I judge, anyone who wishes to retain the theological stance and method of CRT, and re-state it in the modern culture, may do so undeterred. He or she need not be discomfited by these new proposals, or fear that what they have to say has undermined or significantly skewed that great theological tradition.

To show this involves consulting and citing theologians from the CRT. I have tried to provide a representative range of these. But the bulk of the book is my own attempt to explain and defend its theological procedure in what I hope is a fresh and up to date way, and to do this in the light of current misunderstandings of CRT by the protagonists of new proposals that are intended to supplant it. Part of this project is a thesis about the

---

5. See Vanhoozer, *The Drama of Doctrine*, 278f. for Vanhoozer's post-conservative approach, and 291f. for his post-foundationalist outlook.

connection between manner and matter. Certain methods and results are intrinsic to CRT. This is not to say that there is one philosophical orthodoxy. But there has to be a philosophical outlook that ensures the objectivity of knowledge, for example. However, from the point of view of Reformed theology it does not matter what exactly the provenance of that outlook is provided that the philosophical tools are subordinate to the faith. As we shall see, there has in fact been a fairly eclectic approach to the sources of those philosophical tools that help to provide understanding for the faith. It is impossible to shed its theological methods and their presuppositions and to ensure the survival of Reformed theology in some other way. If you throw out the bathwater, then you throw out the baby as well.

I have chosen to focus upon the work of Kevin Vanhoozer[6] and John Franke[7] as exemplars of these new proposals because they are among the ablest and certainly the most prolific writers on theological method from the confessional Reformed stable. Each is often self-conscious about the fact. In his latest book *Remythologizing Theology*, Vanhoozer discusses not only how the theological metaphysics of theo-drama impacts upon features of classical Christian theism such as God as creator, his almightiness, his impassibility and his speech, but also upon distinctive features of Reformed theology such as the *pactum salutis* and the idea of effectual calling.

The revisionary proposals of such as Vanhoozer and Franke, considered together, have the following characteristics; they move away from the view of Christian theology as consisting of sets of truths. They advocate a decidedly conditional epistemology, qualified in terms of "context" or "perspective" and in Vanhoozer's case (less so in the case of Franke), *they think of theological construction in terms of the development of a kind of narrative* (following Von Balthasar), as a "theo-drama." In this they not only swim with a strong contemporary theological current, but also swallow a good deal of the postmodern attitude to metaphysics and epistemology. But other practitioners might easily have been chosen. For example, the Reformed theologian Michael Horton also exemplifies much of what Vanhoozer says. In his book *Covenant and Eschatology: The Divine Drama* there is, as the title of the work suggests, an emphasis upon drama. "Our goal all along will be to defend the definition of theology as *the church's reflection on God's performative action in word and deed and list own participation in the drama of redemption.*"[8] And there is the desire to engage in theology in

---

6. Besides Vanhoozer's *The Drama of Doctrine*, see, for example, his *Remythologizing Theology*,

7. Franke, *The Character of Theology: A Postconservative Evangelical Approach*.

8. Horton, *Covenant and Eschatology*, 4

a post-foundationalist mode. "The more that modern foundationalism is shaken off, the greater the openness to particular confessional theologies."[9] Chapter 9 of *Covenant and Eschatology* is entitled "Community Theater, Local Performances of the Divine Drama," and Horton rejects the attitude to Scripture that reckons it to be "a sourcebook of timeless truths," "timeless propositions," or timeless ideas.[10] So, plenty of common ground here: a suspicion of theology as "timeless truth," the rejection of foundationalism, and the preponderant stress on the dramatic and the performative. We might reasonably say that the theologians selected for attention here, Kevin Vanhoozer and John Franke, are representative of a wider contemporary wave. Together they exemplify, in an overlapping way, the effect of the postmodern attitude on Christian theology. It is this attitude that the book critically scrutinizes. It is hoped, though, that this scrutiny will be of interest in other traditions of the church on which post-conservatism and post-foundationalism are bearing down.

The discussion that follows does not have for its conclusion that post-foundationalism as a method of doing theology ought to be rejected. That's not the argument. Rather, the argument is that Vanhoozer and Franke are not consistent proponents of the main spine of Christian theology, but in trying to combine it with other positions they run into inconsistency. In the case of Vanhoozer his treatment of what he calls "propositonalist" theology is skewed to the point of caricature. As we shall see, properly understood both Scripture and Classic Reformed theology are consistent with the speech act emphasis on language that he favors. And so his critique of "propositionalism" is largely beside the point.

The chapters of the book contain a number of fresh discussions of the logical, metaphysical, and epistemological matters that undergird CRT and that bring into relief the weakness of the new proposals. Taken together they present a cumulative case that endeavors to show the weaknesses of the current postmodern and post-foundationalist proposals that preoccupy the Reformed segment of worldwide Christian theology. This case offers, I realize, a negative thesis, but it may be put positively: a Christian theologian who is attracted by the post-foundationalist "turn" in theology, either by its methods or by its theological conclusions, will find in those claims and conclusions no good reason to depart from the doctrinal pattern of CRT, though the responsibility remains on any systematic theologian to restate

---

9. Ibid.

10. See ibid., 30, 125, 240 respectively. Horton has more recently undertaken a systematic theology of a more conventional kind: *The Christian Faith: A Systematic Theology for Pilgrims on the Way*.

Christian doctrine in a contemporary manner as the cultural context warrants this.

Those who engage in issues of theological method must also become seriously engaged in philosophical questions and issues. This is because it is impossible to do systematic theology without having a view about the nature of divine and human reality, and about the sources of knowledge of God and of ourselves, and so to interact with the culture. Part of the problem with the proposals exemplified by John Franke and Kevin Vanhoozer is that they have not allowed themselves to be sufficiently philosophical. Key issues have been glossed over or left unclear, for the conceptual and philosophical side of things has not been sufficiently penetrating or sustained.

Each chapter of what follows sets out a distinctive argument or set of arguments. The first two chapters are intended to articulate and to defend the ontological and epistemological character of CRT, with particular stress being laid on its systematic character. This sets the stage for the critique. The arguments of the later chapters engage with the innovative proposals on a number of fronts. The aim is to show that the proposals, considered as offering appealing alternative methods, are almost without exception unconvincing, and in some respects confused. If this thesis is cogent then it follows that those who wish to share the theological outlook of CRT have good reason to reject the innovative proposals.

Chapter 1 sets out the parameters of classical Reformed theology, and particularly what is understood by its being *systematic* theology. The next chapter has to do with the epistemological bases of the theology, particularly with the issues of metaphysical realism, objectivity and certainty, and the relation between nature and grace. These two chapters set the scene. The next three chapters are, broadly speaking, concerned with what has been referred to as the narrative turn in theology. The "post-foundationalists" appeal to a general phenomenon that has had a considerable impact on how theology is currently understood and practiced. Here I shall have in mind Vanhoozer's idea of theo-drama and the theological proposals that he has recently drawn from it in his latest book, centering on the idea of God as a communicative agent. We shall look at the theological consequences of privileging narrative over systematic connectedness, and we shall provide an assessment of some of the arguments that are offered for making such a shift. So in chapter 3 we shall examine the logic of narrative, and the relation between being and doing. Which, in theology, comes first, logically speaking: the study of reports of activity, human and divine, or the study of the being and character of God and of humankind? In the next chapters, 4 and 5, we examine one source of unease that revisionists have with classical theology, that it is "propositionalist" and "rationalist" and "timeless." Broadly speaking these three chapters have to do with the metaphysical framework in which classic systematic reflection of the Christian faith does and should take place.

Then, in the second half of the examination of the new proposals, chapters 7 to 9, we shall consider certain epistemological issues, particularly the confusion between the *identification of* and the *identity* of God, the place of induction and deduction in theological reasoning, the much-publicized issue of "foundationalism," and the character of the knowledge and beliefs about God and ourselves that it is possible to have. Chapter 10 is a short conclusion.

CLASSIC REFORMED THEOLOGY

1

The Form of Theology

This chapter is devoted to outlining some of the essential features, the intellectual structures of Classical Reformed Theology (CRT). We shall not be chiefly concerned with the literary shape that a particular theologian chooses to give to his theology, though it might be worth saying a word or two about this to begin with.

Literary Shape

In his *Institutes*, John Calvin, one main fountain-head of Reformed theology, wrote what amounts to his systematic theology (though it has strong occasional elements in it), structuring it by the overarching claim that true wisdom consists in the knowledge of God and of ourselves. He announces this theme in the opening words of the book, and it controls the discussion of at least the first three books. It is only through Jesus Christ that we are brought to know God and ourselves. By contrast, others have preferred to follow the *loci* method. That is, they have constructed their work in the form of a series of discrete doctrinal topics, sometimes in a straightforwardly didactic way, sometimes in more polemical terms. And so Francis Turretin develops the *loci* method by *elencthus*, by questioning and answering. This method, both topical and catechetical, in which Christian theology is developed doctrine by doctrine, has come down to us as the dominant organizing principle. Instances of it can be found in Charles Hodge's *Systematic Theology*, in William Shedd's nineteenth-century *Dogmatic Theology*, and in the early twentieth century in such as Herman Bavinck and in the journal articles of B. B. Warfield, whose work has had a number of popular imitators, such as Louis Berkhof. Yet others, such as the Puritan

John Owen, have "systematized" by considering Christian theology from a variety of complementary standpoints, such as the Holy Spirit, justification, and so on. Calvin's own approach has rather dropped out of fashion; the only example I know of is the Southern Presbyterian Robert Breckinridge's work *The Knowledge of God*,[1] though no doubt there are others. Others have structured Christian theology in terms of the concept of the covenant and developed "covenant theology." Herman Witsius in his *Economy of the Covenants* is a prime example.[2] We shall consider the relation between systematic theology and covenant theology shortly.

Each approach has strengths and weaknesses. Having one main theme or concept, such as Calvin's *Institutes*, provides a synoptic or unifying approach that binds together the various doctrinal discussions. In addition, Calvin writes in the first or second person, the knowledge of God and of *ourselves*, adopting a more immediately personal style. Calvin is also able, through this structure, to link together doctrines that are linked in reality. So he discusses justification and sanctification together, treating them as two distinct but inseparable gifts, through his brilliant idea of Christ's two-fold grace. But the price he pays for this approach (despite his praiseworthy concern for "order") is the toleration of a kind of disorderliness. For example, though he deals with the fall of mankind at the beginning of Book II, he has in fact already introduced some effects or results of the fall before that, in his treatment of the perversion of the natural knowledge of God. This knowledge with which we are endowed, he says in Book I, chapter 4, is stifled and corrupted as a result of the fall. So the structure of the work is not that of a set of topics or steps, but more like a symphony, in which an initial theme is introduced and elaborated, and developed further as the work progresses. The old idea of systematic theology as a "body of divinity" underlines this organic character. And so the theme of the knowledge of God and of ourselves, introduced in the very first lines of Book I of the work, returns at the beginning of Book II, and again elsewhere.

Others, such as Turretin and Hodge and Bavinck and Berkhof, favor a topical or loci method. This is a step-by-step approach, in which each topic is penetratingly discussed. In Turretin, each topic is framed in terms of the controversies of his day. The obvious advantages of this approach are thoroughness and clarity. But the separation of topics can sometimes create misleading impressions. Take again the relation of justification and

---

1. Breckinridge, *The Knowledge of God, Objectively Considered, Being the First Part of Theology, Considered as a Science of Positive Truth, Both Inductive and Deductive*. In fact, however, this work is also topical in structure.

2. Witsius, *The Economy of the Covenant between God and Man Comprehending a Complete Body of Divinity*.

sanctification. In Turretin's and Hodge's treatments, these topics are deliberately separated, and this works against what needs to be said about the connectedness of the two. For while justification and sanctification are two distinct elements in God's saving purposes that are conceptually very different, they are nonetheless inseparably connected, as Calvin makes clear. Separating their treatment may suggest that they are only accidentally connected, even though efforts may be made to mitigate this impression.

Covenant Theology was developed within the Reformed community in the early years of the seventeenth century, by theologians such as Ursinus, Olevianus, Robert Rollock, John Preston, and John Ball. At least in Holland this development gave rise to a certain tension as it was seen to be less scholastic and exact than the dominant Reformed Orthodoxy, and not organized topically and controversially (i.e., in terms of the several doctrines of the Christian faith, and the analysis of doctrinal errors and their resolution). By contrast, the basic organizing principle of covenant theology is that of the unfolding economy of salvation, through a succession of developing covenants established between the Lord and his people. Such theology has a "redemptive historical" character. Though at first the scholastic and the covenant approaches were regarded as exclusive alternatives, hence the controversy, they were, in works such as that of Herman Witsius' *The Economy of the Covenants between God and Man*, regarded as complementary. Creation, fall, and redemption, and particularly the historical unfolding of the one covenant of grace, is clearly set within the framework of systematic theology, employing its conceptuality. Witsius's work was organized in terms of four topics: the Covenant of Works, the Covenant of Redemption, the Covenant of Grace, and the fourth on Covenant Ordinancies. Yet "he treats each topic analytically, and draws with evident happiness on the expository resources produced by systematicians during the previous 150 years."[3]

This is the theology of the history of redemption, or, as might be said currently, narrative theology within a systematic theological framework. In the body of this book I shall be arguing that a careful balance between theological narrative set within a systematic framework is exactly right. The mix of these two elements is obviously a matter of judgment; nevertheless each is indispensable, because central to the Christian faith are the actions and words of God, the eternally triune Lord and creator, in human history. One reason for writing this book is to show the perils and dangers of current attempts to "theologize" without that framework of systematic theology in place. So is it to be biblical theology at the expense of systematic theology,

---

3. Packer, "Introduction: On Covenant Theology," no pagination.

or the reverse? The unoriginal answer that I shall give and defend is "it is to be both," but with logical priority being given to systematic theological reasoning.

Intellectual Structure

So there will be gains and losses in any way of organizing a work of systematic theology. But this is not our chief concern, either in this chapter or in the book. Rather we are concerned in the first place not with the literary character but the *intellectual* structure of Christian systematic theology, with the appropriate manner in which Christian theological conclusions are to be drawn from both general and special revelation. Christian systematic theology builds on the work of exegetical theology, "biblical theology" in one sense of a phrase that has come to have other senses as well, as we shall see in due course. Exegetical theology informs the systematic theologian what a biblical passage means, or might plausibly mean, taking into account its scope and context, its situation in the canon, the genre of the work, and so on. The systematic theologian takes these results and links them to other biblical data concerned with the same or contrasting themes, employing them to contribute to the development or refining of the results, and then linking it with other themes.

It is important to note why this is done. It is not because the results of exegetical theology, the unfolding of the meaning of a biblical passage, are in any way imperfect or second-rate. It is to form an estimate of what a particular passage, in its particularity, contributes to the biblical revelation as a whole, and to the overall theme of that revelation under consideration, the doctrine of God, the work of Christ, the image of God in mankind, or whatever it may be. Parallel points arise about the relationship between systematic theology and historical theology. Doctrinal exactness has usually occurred when it has been possible to say what the doctrine implies, and also what it does *not* imply. It often takes the pressure of controversy to bring out the negative as well as the positive implications of a doctrine. That is why, once he has relied upon the exegetical theologian, the systematizer also has an eye to historical theology, for it is in discussion of some issue, even in historical controversy, that doctrines frequently receive their shape. For example, the controversies over Christology are in view in the Chalcedonian definition, and disputes over merit made possible the protest that justification is not by faith, but by faith *only*.

But what's the point of such systematic endeavors? There is a sense in which systematic theology provides its own justification. Our pragmatic age, in which what we do can only be justified by its immediate payoff, is likely to be irritated by such an answer. Systematic theology is an end in itself, attempting to display in an orderly and connected way the "whole counsel of God" as revealed in Scripture. It shows, when every allowance has been made for the historically situated and occasional character of the books of Scripture, what is the overall teaching of Scripture about the nature of God and man, of the person and work of Christ, and so on. It is foolish to suppose that such a program disdains the original literature of the Bible. Systematic theology is not an endeavor to improve on that literature, but to do something else, to set forth the overall teaching of Scripture on who God is and what he has done and said. This enables the church to set out the character of the faith in terms that contrast it at the most general level with non-Christian and sub-Christian theologies, as well as to form a corrective to the way in which the prevailing culture may distort or enhance its teaching.

But while systemic theology may be pursued as an end in itself, this does not mean that it is merely academic. The goal of *scientia* legitimately leads to that of *sapientia*. And *doctrine* leads to *application*. B. B. Warfield expresses the relation between systematics and its biblical foundations in the following terms:

> Systematic Theology is not founded on the direct and primary results of the exegetical process; it is founded on the final and complete results of exegesis as exhibited in Biblical Theology. Not exegesis itself, then, but Biblical Theology, provides the material for Systematics. Biblical Theology is not, then, a rival of Systematics; it is not even a parallel product of the same body of facts, provided by exegesis; it is the basis and source of Systematics. Systematic Theology is not a concatenation of the scattered theological data furnished by the exegetic process; it is the combination of the already concatenated data given to it by Biblical Theology. It uses the individual data furnished by exegesis, in a word, not crudely, not independently for itself, but only after these data have been worked up into Biblical Theology and have received from it their final coloring and subtlest shades of meaning—in other words, only in their true sense, and after Exegetics has said its last word upon them.[4]

This procedure is first exegetical, providing a "biblical theology," as Warfield calls it. By this he means the practice of exegesis, conveying the

---

4. Warfield, "The Idea of Systematic Theology," 66–67. Compare Bavinck, *Reformed Dogmatics*, I:617.

most exact sense of the original passages that it is possible currently to give. Since for Warfield these passages are God's word, the result is biblical theology. So his meaning is somewhat narrower in aim, and preparatory to biblical theology in its more recent meaning, which conveys in some sense the historical "story" or unfolding of God's acts. Then follows systematic theological construction, based upon inference from the biblical data.

So, intellectual structure, rather than mere organizational structure, is to be our chief concern. The elements of such a structure are drawn from general revelation, but especially from Scripture as the supreme theological authority for Christians, utilizing the fruits of exegetical theology. In this sequence the systematic theologian also takes into account the way in which these concepts have emerged from and have been shaped by and (because of their firm basis in Scripture) sharpened by the clashes of theological controversy.

System

What is systematic about systematic theology? Such theology is not a freestanding, merely speculative discipline, but depends both upon the fruits of exegetical theology, and of historical theology, in the ways just discussed. It seeks to exhibit two main features. One is establishing, or endeavoring to establish, a doctrine's faithfulness to Scripture, and the logical consistency of a doctrine, both internally and in its connection with other doctrines, and its place in the system of thought.

The second is to bring out the positive relationship between doctrines, the way in which they connect up with and enhance each other. This is a stronger requirement than mere logical consistency, important though such consistency is. These endeavors are warranted by the underlying conviction that Scripture is the one word of God. We may take each of these features in turn.

No doubt it is possible to offer a theological argument for the importance of logic, from the character of God whose word is necessarily veracious. But coming rather closer to home, logic is basic to all thought and speech. Take a simple example. If it's true that the apple is green, then it is false that the apple is red. If the apple is pear-shaped, then it is true that it is not round. And so on. What could be more basic to our thinking? So basic is it that in fact we largely take such matters for granted. It is obvious that when we assert something we are by implication not asserting some other thing (though perhaps not denying it either). When we ask someone to shut the door, they respond by shutting the door and not the window because

"The window is open" has a distinct meaning from "The door is open." A door is not a window, and so the requests to shut the door, and to shut the window, are distinct. In common with us all, the systematic theologian has this commitment to such basic logical implications of thought and speech, including of course God's thought as this is revealed to us in his speech. The incomprehensibility and mystery of God and his ways is no objection to this, provided such language is used univocally, for then it can be used consistently, even though the language may be metaphorical or analogical or hyperbolic.[5]

The Reformed systematicians, in common with many others, take the basic operations of logic for granted. For some reason there is currently a general suspicion of the place of logic in theology: it is said to be abstract, cold, and formal. Life is larger than logic. Maybe so. But logic is indispensable to life, especially to the life of theology.[6]

Something that is not quite as basic is the idea that thought and speech, both human and divine, have logical consequences. So it is that Christian systematic theologians think that not only the very words of Scripture have theological importance, but also that what can "by good and necessary consequence" be derived from them is also important. The meaning of Scripture is Scripture. So Herman Bavinck:

> If the knowledge of God has been revealed by himself in his Word, it cannot contain contradictory elements or be in conflict with what is known of God from nature and history. God's thoughts cannot be opposed to one another and thus necessarily from (sic) an organic unity.[7]

> But revelation is systematic disclosure of the words and deeds of God; it encompasses a world of thoughts and has its center in the incarnation of the Logos. And religion is not feeling and sensation alone but also belief, living for and serving of God with both heart and head. And that revelation of God can therefore be intellectually penetrated in order that it may all the better

---

5. The distinction between univocal and literal language needs to be borne on mind. To use language univocally is to use it consistently, whether its terms are understood literally or metaphorically. If every use of a metaphorical expression such as "our God is a consuming fire" is understood univocally, then the expression, so understood, can be used in arguments. Not otherwise. The same applies more obviously to terms used literally.

6. See the pertinent remarks of Turretin, *Institutes of Elenctic Theology*, I:18-34. (For ease of reference I shall refer to passages in Turretin's *Institutes* by volume and page of the English translation.)

7. Bavinck, *Reformed Dogmatics*, I:44.

enter into the human consciousness. In that connection one cannot even take ill of theology if it aims at clarity in thought, at making lucid distinctions and at precision in articulation. Such precision is pursued and valued in all the sciences; it is equally appropriate in theology.[8]

Obviously, for the theological tasks that Bavinck outlines, an understanding of the meaning of words, phrases, and sentences, and what they logically imply, is an indispensable tool.

Good and Necessary Consequences

We shall give a fuller treatment of logic and language in chapter 7. Note here, however, the phrase *"good* and necessary." Why not just "necessary"? Should not necessary consequences satisfy the logician? What are "good and necessary" consequences? They are consequences drawn from an informed induction of the relevant biblical data. So there is a balance to be struck at this point between induction and deduction. Here again the prior work of good exegesis shows its importance. Biblical doctrine should not be formed on the basis of one verse alone, nor on words and sentences taken out of context, but from a sound exegesis of all the relevant material. If God is spirit, then it is unwarranted to conclude from Psalm 18:6 that he has ears. Attention must be paid to the type of language in which thoughts are expressed in the particular passage of Scripture under discussion. So doctrinal formulations, which take us beyond the very words of Scripture, are validly made if they are based upon such good and necessary consequences. And that can only be decided by asking, for example, whether in the original text the language about God is literal or anthropomorphic in character. And genre. Is the Song of Solomon simply a love song, or something more? What does the parable of the sower teach us, how does it connect with other parables and with other teachings of Scripture? Such a procedure, that of establishing the "good" consequences of a text, implies a willingness to reconsider the exegetical foundations of a doctrine whenever there is a good, non-frivolous reason to do so.

So, for example, J. I. Packer has this to say about the use of the idea of imputation:

> Thus "Christ . . . is made unto us righteousness" (I Cor. I.30). This was the thought expressed in older protestant theology by the phrase "the imputation of Christ's righteousness." The

---

8. Bavinck, *Reformed Dogmatics*, I:605.

phrase is not in Paul, but its meaning is. The point that it makes is that believers are made righteous before God (Rom. V.19) through His admitting them to share Christ's status of acceptance. In other words, God treats them according to Christ's desert. There is nothing arbitrary or artificial in this, for God recognizes the existence of a real union of covenantal solidarity between them and Christ. For Paul, union with Christ is not fiction, but fact—the basic fact, indeed, of Christianity; and his doctrine of justification is simply his first step in analyzing its meaning.[9]

So, according to Packer here, the *thought* that Christ's righteousness is imputed to the believer is present in Paul. The *word* is not present, but the idea of imputation is expressed by Paul, for example, in the words "made unto us righteousness."

Calvin makes a parallel point in the following remarks on justification by faith alone:

> The reader now perceives with what fairness the sophists of the present day cavil at our doctrine, when we say that a man is justified by faith alone (Rom. 4.2). They dare not deny that he is justified by faith, seeing Scripture so often declares it; but as the word alone is nowhere expressly used, they will not tolerate its being added. Is it so? What answer, then will they give to the words of Paul, when he contends that righteousness is not of faith unless it be gratuitous? How can it be gratuitous, and yet by works? . . . Does he not plainly enough attribute everything to faith alone when he disconnects it with works?[10]

So how does the systematic theologian work systematically, using the fruits of the exegete, to form or re-form biblical doctrine and to situate one particular doctrine in relation to others? Such careful induction precedes the deduction of doctrinal consequences from the relevant texts, and in turn may lead to more general inductions. The systematic theologian first apprises himself of the data as comprehensively and thoroughly as he can, and then he endeavors to draws conclusions from them. Of course, he does not do this in a vacuum, but in his own particular situation, informed by the church's conciliar and confessional tradition, and pressed by the need to articulate the faith in his contemporary culture. So the exegetical fruits may be used to finesse or to articulate the tradition further, or to correct it—as in times of reformation. The tradition may provide him with a set of answers

---

9. Packer "Justification," 685.
10. Calvin, *Institutes*, III.11.19.

and raise a further set of questions. To endeavor to answer these questions the theologian must use both inductive and deductive inference.

The requirement that only "good and necessary consequences" may be drawn is a rather demanding one. It shows that theological deductions may legitimately be made from Scripture, but that the inferences must be "good," that is, as we have seen, they must not be drawn hastily, but from a full induction and with regard to the "analogy of faith." In practice the theologian may have to rest content with Scripture providing very good inductive support (as he believes) for some particular doctrine, but support that falls short of its deducibility from Scripture. The wise theologian proportions his belief to the evidence.

The Word and Our Words

So the fact that certain conclusions can be deduced from the language of Scripture when properly interpreted does not mean that all our conclusions must be deductions. While we may not deduce some doctrine from Scripture, drawing it as a necessary consequence, we may nevertheless have good reason to think that Scripture teaches such and such, reasons that fall short of a clear entailment. So we can think of a range of possibilities; perhaps on some matters Scripture gives us *some reason* to think that it teaches such and such, or a good reason, or a very good reason. We might, then, think of the strength of Christian beliefs arrayed like a web with a center and a periphery, each element supporting and being supported by the others, with greater or lesser degrees of strength.

The fact that scriptural expressions can be the basis for drawing conclusions expressed in language other than the very words of Scripture naturally raises the question of the consistency of one doctrine with another. Systematic theology is systematic partly because it has consistency as one of its aims. This is one simple reason, though not the only reason, why the various positions or doctrinal statements of systematic theology must be consistent, logically consistent. For consistency is a necessary condition of the truth of sets of statements. "This apple is red" must be consistent with "This apple is round" (same apple, of course) if the statement "The apple is both read and round" has any chance of being true. "Jesus is human" must be consistent with "Jesus is divine" if the theologian is validly to state "Jesus is human and divine." Of course such consistency is necessary but not sufficient for the truth of the sets, for a set of propositions may be consistent but false. By contrast, inconsistency is a tell-tale sign of lurking falsehood.

It is necessary that "This apple is both red and round" is *consistent*, but to be *true* that statement must not only be consistent but it must also be in accord with the facts, with how it is. It won't be true if the apple being referred to in our sentence is in fact red and pear-shaped. As this simple example shows, consistency is not enough for truth; to be true a set of statements must not only be consistent but must also be (putting the point roughly to begin with; we shall return to it) adequate to how things are, it must faithfully represent the facts, or correspond to those things, or however we may wish to express that relationship.

So the requirement of consistency is necessary, but not sufficient. It is necessary because consistency is necessary for truth. For example, the fact that (say) what the Apostle Peter says about God is different from what the Apostle Paul says about God does not mean that what Peter says is inconsistent with what Paul says. If you say "The apple is red" and I say "The apple is round" (when we are each referring to the same apple) then what each of us says is consistent with what the other says. There is reason to wonder if sometimes "different from" is clumsily regarded as equivalent to "inconsistent with" and the fact that there are in Scripture several different ways of depicting the work or atonement, or of the believer's relation to Christ, say, is used to call into question the theological unity of the New Testament. If what Peter says is *inconsistent* with what Paul says, then that unity is seriously imperilled, for we don't expect one Apostle of Christ to teach something that is inconsistent with the teaching of another Apostle. What this would mean is that what the Apostles together teach could not be true. For example, it would be possible for Paul's teaching about union with Christ to be inconsistent with what Peter teaches about the church being a royal priesthood.

Why does consistency, this basic requirement, matter in theology? One can think of a general answer to that question. Consistency in thought and speech is a virtue. But the primary reason is a theological one. God himself is truthful, veracious, faithful. The truth of God is one. And if special revelation is God's word, or if the gospel of grace it announces is one gospel, then there must be one consistent word, or one consistent teaching, which reflects the mind of God. The alternative, that God's word is not consistent, would carry the intolerable implication that the various teachings of Scripture cannot be *true together*. One Christian doctrine, such as the doctrine of justification by faith alone, must be consistent with all other Christian doctrines. Why? Because each doctrine considered separately, and the doctrines then considered together, are parts of the one divine revelation.

Later on we shall reflect on the claim of some theologians that utterances, whether they are human or divine utterances, are always made in a context and relate only to that context, that their meaning and their truth is established by the context in which they first occur. Here we simply note that such a basically relativistic view, were it true, would at one stroke undermine the entire project of Christian systematic theology. God's word is one word, uttered and augmented in distinct eras, and capable of being connected together in a way that may display its consistency, or at least ward off the claim that its inconsistency can be established. There are different contexts in which his word first arises, different genres of writing in which it is expressed, different historical and geographical and cultural situations, but these complement and qualify and interpret each other. As we saw earlier, it is the job of the exegete, the exegetical theologian, to determine in what ways the context and the genre and the syntax and the grammar of the language in which God's word is given bear upon its meaning. But it is an indispensable presupposition of Christian systematic theology that what the exegetical theologian then delivers is part of a consistent systematic theological "scheme."

As we have noted, this does not mean that there are not gaps, puzzles, lacunae, or mysteries. It does not mean that the theologian should force consistency upon the data in an unnatural way. The systematic theologian is not a know-all, knowing the mind of God as God himself does. Certainly not. Nor is the Bible an encyclopaedia. The systematic theologian must be prepared to say, in answer to some claim, that it is not known, or tentative, or pure speculation. (Incidentally, speculations have their place. For example, reflection on them may serve to reinforce our confidence in the meaning of what is non-speculatively revealed in Scripture). But as he ponders the overall biblical teaching on some particular matter, the theologian's underlying assumption is that the picture that he is attempting to draw of the revealed character and ways of God is one picture. And when it comes to the great and obvious mysteries of the faith, such as the Trinity and the incarnation, the theologian must assume the consistency of the teaching of Scripture even when he may not be able to demonstrate it. Perhaps the most that he can hope for in these areas is not to demonstrate that the threeness and oneness of God are consistent, but to show that the claim that they are inconsistent has not been proven.[11]

An interesting example of misunderstanding about the relation of logic to the mysteries of the faith is provided by Alister McGrath, who complains about those who claim that divine revelation is logically consistent. He reckons that such a claim is an example of too great a confidence in the capacity of reason to judge the truth of revelation, a case of the imprisoning

---

11. On this, see Anderson, *Paradox in Christian Theology*.

of revelation within the flawed limited of sinful human reason. McGrath illustrates the allegedly grave consequences of "talking loosely about the 'logical nature' of divine revelation"[12] by reference to the incarnation, "the definitive Christian teaching that Christ is both divine and human." "Even in the patristic period, such philosophers ['secular' philosophers] were quick to point out this alleged logical flaw in the doctrine. Those criticisms were intensified at the time of the Enlightenment."[13] Noting that the doctrine of the incarnation has regularly been criticized for being logically flawed, McGrath's response is not altogether clear, but he seems to argue that the orthodox doctrine of the incarnation cannot be claimed to be logical, or charged with being illogical because it is "above" or "beyond" logic.[14] What he fails to see, by his reference to being imprisoned by logic, is that there is a world of difference between a set of claims being proved to be self-contradictory, and that set being apparently self-contradictory, or not shown to be self-contradictory. And in addition, he fails to make the distinction made routinely by CRT between inductive and deductive reasoning, and reason in the sense of what seems to be reasonable to the philosopher, or to the man in the street. In the words of the Puritan theologian John Owen:

> So that though we will not admit of anything that is contrary to reason, yet the least intimation of a truth by divine revelation will make me embrace it, although it should be *contrary to the reason of all the Socinians in the world*. Reason in the abstract, or the just measure of the answering of one thing unto another, is of great moment; but reason—that is, what is pretended to be so, or appears to be so unto this or that man, especially in and about things of divine revelation—is of very small importance (or none at all) where it riseth up against the express testimonies of Scripture, and these multiplied, by their mutual confirmation and explanation.[15]

For Owen, all the Socinians in the world may regard the Trinity as contrary to reason, but this fact does not amount to a proof of its self-contradictoriness.

That the whole of Christian theology is consistent is not merely a working hypothesis that the Christian theologian may discard, a "model" that may be put it to one side. It is his non-negotiable presupposition. Nevertheless the work of the systematic theologian is never finished, as it is

12. McGrath, *A Passion for Truth*.
13. Ibid., 171.
14. Ibid.
15. Owen, *Works*, II:412. Emphasis in the original.

continually open to revision from refined interpretations of the biblical text on the one hand, and, on the other hand, the need for the re-statement and vindication of Christian theological claims in the light of questions raised about the faith, and challenges to it that may arise from the culture.

So the work of the theologian involves saying what a doctrine does not mean as well as what it does mean. The ability to do this may come as a result of self-conscious reflection on a doctrine and where it stands in relation to other doctrines and teachings within the Christian church. But as we noted earlier, in Christian theology this further aspect has usually arisen as a result of controversy over some doctrine. This discipline involves not only the use of language that is as clear as can be, but also saying what that language does not imply. By such endeavors the edges of a doctrine are sharpened; indeed, the understanding of the doctrine may itself be shaped through controversy. Such an approach is not a novel departure, for it is already to be found in the New Testament, particularly of course in Paul: justification is by faith, *not* of works; we are saved by grace, through faith, *not* of ourselves, it is the gift of God. There is to be a resurrection of the body, but the body in question will be a spiritual body, *not* a merely physical body. Shall we sin that grace may abound? *By no means.* In each of such cases Paul not only affirms, he denies. He tells us what God's revelation implies, and what it does not imply, and in this he sets the example that the Christian church, and especially the systematic theologian, follows, to distinguish one doctrine from another and by implication to connect up one doctrine with another.

Consistency is vital. Contradiction is fatal. However, we saw earlier, with one of our very simple examples, that consistency is also a very weak relationship. "My eyes are blue" is perfectly consistent with "The Moon is nearer to the Earth than to the Sun," but the two statements have precious little to do with each other.

Connectedness

What is connectedness? Sometimes consistency, which we have been discussing, is confused with a stronger requirement, and arising out of such confusion systematic theology may unfairly get a bad name. The stronger requirement is *logical entailment*. Logical entailment is another way of referring to deducibility. We have seen that CRT envisages the deduction of conclusions from Scripture. Let us suppose that there are many such deductions possible from various sets of statements in Scripture. It does not follow, however, that such deduced conclusions are in turn related to each other by entailment. From the fact that the rose is red, and that it has a scent, we can deduce that the rose is both red and scented. And from the fact that the violet is blue and has a scent it is possible to deduce that the violet is blue and scented. But it obviously does not follow that the rose is red and scented *entails that* the violet is blue and scented, or *vice versa*.

The idea that systematic theology is a deductive system consisting of one or more axioms, from which the entire remainder of the theology is deducible, and is in fact deduced, is a serious misunderstanding. For systematic theology to be systematic, it does not follow that there must be one theological axiom (or even several such axioms) from which all other true theological statement follow logically. Systematic theology does not have the shape of Euclidian geometry.

It's worth pausing a moment to see why this requirement of entailment is far too strong, and that requiring it would distort the entire fabric of Christian theology. Basically, it has to do with God's freedom. Or, putting the point a bit differently, it has to do with the fact that often there are alternative means to the same end. The Christian faith is intrinsically historical: it concerns God's action within his creation. God's plan of salvation is a free act. He did not have to decree it, he was not externally constrained to do what he did. In other words, it is impossible to deduce from the nature of God alone that there will be salvation, or that it must take the pattern that it in fact took. God freely chose to provide salvation, and this is incompatible with such deducibility.

But was he similarly free to choose the means of salvation? Perhaps he was. No less a figure that John Calvin claimed that God could have saved us by a word, and others, such as Augustine and Aquinas and Samuel Rutherford, held the same or a similar view. But let us suppose that all these notables are in fact wrong. Suppose the atonement by the God-man Jesus Christ was the only means available to God (given his justice and the nature of sin, and perhaps other factors), as John Owen, another notable, seems to have believed, at least in later life.[16] Then the theological page begins to get a bit complex. For granted the freely chosen end of salvation, it may be (for Owenians at this point) that there are elements of necessity to the means. Yet even so we are still far from the view that everything that occurs had to occur simply because of *who God is*. But the deductive view of theological connectedness requires us to believe that in principle if we knew enough about the nature of God we could have deduced what in fact has happened down to the last atom and molecule. What is more, such a view would have

---

16. There is a good general discussion of Owen's change of mind in Trueman, *The Claims of Truth*, 104–7.

us believe that it is the job of the systematic theologian to map out these necessities as best he can.

So there are three or four ideas (at least!) in play here: the matter of consistency or inconsistency of a doctrine or doctrines, the matter of entailment or non-entailment. And then there is reflection upon what has happened, as in the example of the atonement and controversies about it. Did what in fact happen have to happen?

How does this help us over the nature of connectedness in systematic theology? It indicates that the relationship between doctrines is not a sheer accident, nor is it mere consistency, nor (at the other extreme) is it a case of geometric proof. What is there left? Reformed theologians have often spoken of the organic connectedness of doctrines, and of theology as constituting a "body of divinity." What do they mean?

Suppose that we compare a Christian doctrine, say the doctrine of the atonement, to an organ of the human body, the liver, say. It is possible to study the composition of the liver, its various properties. But to fully understand the liver it is necessary to know how it connects up with other vital human organs, such as the pancreas, and the kidneys, and the heart. This connectedness has an operational or functional character. (There are non-organic analogues: think of what is involved in understanding a carburetor, or a water pump, in a car.) So it is with the atonement. One can study the atonement intrinsically, its internal features, the incarnation, death, and resurrection of Christ. But what makes that an atonement? An atonement for what? An atonement to whom? An atonement for whom? Why an atonement? To answer these questions we need to venture into other areas, or contexts, of Scripture, to the doctrine of God, to the nature of sin, and so on. The relation between atonement and these other doctrinal areas may be one of functional or operational interdependence. One doctrine makes other doctrines more intelligible, and necessary, albeit hypothetically or conditionally necessary, and we may come to appreciate this as we come to see the interdependence.

So systematic theology requires or works with different senses of connectedness, expressible in a form of sound words, not just consistency and logical or metaphysical necessity, but also functional interconnectedness. This is what B. B. Warfield identifies when he writes of the task of "discovering the inner relations of its [viz. theology's] several elements," setting it forth "as an organic whole, so that it may be grasped and held in its entirety, in the due relation of its parts to one another, and to the whole, and with a just distribution of emphasis among the several items of knowledge which combine to make up the totality of our knowledge of God." And later he writes of a "concatenated system of truth."[17] Can we be more precise than this?

By and large Scripture tells us what in fact has happened, not what must have happened, and when it does introduce the idea of necessity it often does so in a rather special and qualified way. This is what is sometimes referred to as hypothetical necessity, that is, the necessity of what occurs as a result of some prior divine prophecy or decree. It was impossible for death to hold Jesus, or for his bones to be broken, not because it was logically or metaphysically impossible for Jesus to remain in death (though that bears thinking about) but because his resurrection was prophesied, and so had to happen; his bones were unbreakable not because they were special, freakish bones, but because there was a divine prophecy that not one of his bones would be broken. Such necessity, hypothetical, decreed necessity, naturally enough applies to possible interconnections between events and how they are to be understood, not to the connection of one doctrine with another.

These cases of hypothetical necessity imply cases of strict necessity. It was impossible that Jesus' bones should be broken because it was impossible that the divine decree could be broken. Why was that? Because it is impossible that God should lie, or should fail in other ways. It is impossible for God to lie; God cannot be tempted with evil. These statements are expressions of God's essential character, his nature. More on this a little later on.

Due to the presence of this teleological and functional interdependence, parts of systematic theology may be very tightly connected. Take the prime instance of such connectedness, the doctrine of God. The seventeenth-century Dutch theologian Wilhelmus à Brakel, discussing the various attributes of God, states

> We understand these attributes to be one from *God's* perspective, however, such that they can neither be divorced from the divine Being nor essentially and properly from each other as they exist in God, but are the simple, absolute Being of God Himself.[18]

What is à Brakel saying? That God is an essence that comprises all divine perfections. It follows that all the perfections—perfections of oneness and of threeness, say—are held necessarily by God. They are as aspect of what God *is*. God does not simply happen to be truthful, or just, or gracious. He is *necessarily* truthful, just, and gracious. Moreover he has these perfections in an infinite, eternal, and unchangeable manner. Further, if we suppose that God does not have an essence, but that he *is* an essence, then

---

17. Warfield, "The Task and Method of Systematic Theology," 92–93.
18. Wilhelmus à Brakel, *The Christian's Reasonable Service*, I:89

the separate perfections of truthfulness, justice, and grace are distinctions within that essence (though not, of course, "parts" of it). These three attributes or perfections (among many others) must themselves be strongly united. They are warranted by the nature of the glorious essence that is God, but they are not separate aspects or features of that essence, and are certainly not features some or all of which God might have lacked. He could not have lacked justice, because his essence is pure justice; in the same way he could not have lacked truthfulness. Given his perfection, being truthful entails being just, and vice versa, and so with all his perfections.

More Examples

A similar point holds with regard to human nature, for necessity and impossibility do not pertain only to divine properties. It is not only God who has an essence. Following patristic and medieval theology, CRT saw how the use of modality is necessary in understanding the biblical account of human beings. Unlike the case of God, human beings, in common with trees and fish, are kinds of things. Part of this idea has to do with the capacity of human beings, and trees and fish, to reproduce. Unlike God, who is necessarily unique, kinds such as human persons, grizzly bears, and oak trees also have essential properties, we might call them general essential properties, properties capable of being had by more than one instance. When a grizzly bear produces offspring, they have the nature of grizzly bears, oak trees produce acorns, human persons produce human babies, and so on.

According to CRT, such an account of human beings, one in terms of kinds, is necessary to enable us to give a satisfactory account of what the fall has done to the human race. What is fallenness? Here we have the reverse procedure at work from that just discussed in the case of God's faithfulness, or so it would seem. In the case of God, he necessarily acts in accordance with his nature, and intrinsic to his nature is faithfulness and veracity. But here an action, the disobedience of taking the forbidden fruit, leads to a radical change, according to Scripture, to the loss of innocence, to rebellion, rupture, and the like. How are we to understand this? What we must say is that in the fall aspects of human nature were disordered, or lost, but that human nature itself remained. From a metaphysical point of view what was lost was accidental, or adventitious, for the fall did not literally dehumanize, changing mankind into a different kind of animal. So there are essential features of being a human being—whatever they are—and also accidental features, those lost in the fall, and those restored through Christ.

Let us consider another example. In his discussion of justification and sanctification in his *Systematic Theology* Charles Hodge offers a typical instance of the systematic theologian at work.[19] After his treatment of faith he considers what justification and sanctification are, first offering a characterization of justification. Justification is an act, a divine declaration, and not a continual and progressive work; it is an act of grace but one that does not produce a subjective change in the person justified. Its ground or basis is not faith, but the righteousness of Christ. Such righteousness is imputed to the believer; it is imputed as the believer (through grace) receives and rests on Christ alone for his salvation. In terms of the organization of the material, Hodge draws these statements from the Reformed symbols and the work of distinguished Reformed theologians such as Francis Turretin and Jonathan Edwards and only later considers the scriptural basis for the various positions he takes.[20]

So Hodge distinguishes justification and sanctification, though he does not separate them.[21] The divine declaration that the sinner is pardoned and reckoned righteous *is* his pardoning and *is* the change in his status to that of being righteous. It is a forensic act, with the authority *instantaneously* to change a person's moral and spiritual status. By contrast, sanctification is a *process* of renewal, wrought by divine power in the soul of the believer. Hodge disambiguates the word "righteous" and its equivalent in Greek, as between denoting a subjective character on the one hand, and a relation to justice on the other. He notes how the Bible connects the demand of the law, of the day of judgment, of the justice of God and its distinction from his benevolence, of the immutability of his law,[22] of the connection of justification with union with Christ, and of the effects of justification.

This is only a sketch, of course, but it is nonetheless revealing. What is Hodge doing? Three things: he is *defining, distinguishing,* and *connecting up* the data that he draws from Scripture. He provides definitions of justification and sanctification, he indicates some of the important respects in which they are distinct, and then in the case of justification, his main topic at this point, he proceeds further to connect up justification with the doctrine of God, his justice, his grace, his law, and then with other New

---

19. Hodge, *Systematic Theology*, III:17.

20. This procedure should lead us to question the idea of critics of Hodge that he is naively inductive in his theological method. Had they taken note as they read the work, it is likely that at points such as this they would offer the opposite criticism, not that Hodge was being "naively inductive" but that he imposes dogma on Scripture! We shall consider the role of induction in chapter 7.

21. Hodge, *Systematic Theology*, III:118f.

22. Ibid., III:125–27.

Testament depictions of the believer. In all this Hodge derives material not only from exegetical theology but also from historical theology (principally, in this case, the Reformation controversy with Rome), and reviews it in the light of relevant data of Scripture generally, but especially from Paul in Romans. Such connectedness, as we have seen, has an organic character. In an animal the heart is distinct from the lungs; they have different functions in maintaining life. But they are connected. No lungs, no life; no heart, no life. And both are related to other matters, such as the nervous system and the blood supply. So it is with justification and sanctification. There is a form of sound words. Systematic theology is a body of divinity.

One cannot have true connectedness unless the concepts and propositions of systematic theology being connected have a fairly clear meaning to begin with. That meaning was often secured by definitions of key terms. So it might be helpful to say a word or two here about the place of definitions in CRT.

Definitions

There are various kinds of definitions. For example, there are lexical definitions, defining one word in terms of another, and ostensive definitions, as when, pointing to the large beast with a trunk, someone says "That is what I mean by 'elephant,'" and there are stipulative definitions, as when a law says "A vehicle is . . ." Many legal definitions are of this kind. And there are persuasive definitions, as when a dictatorship defines itself as a "free democratic republic." It wants the connotations of freedom and democracy to rub off onto a state of affairs that is in fact neither free nor democratic.

Sometimes the very idea of formulating definitions is subject to a hilarious criticism, that to offer a definition of something is to make an attempt to "capture" that thing in words, and that this is an expression of fallen mankind's will to power, to domination. This proposal is hilarious because it confuses the idea and the thing. To "capture" something by a definition is not to capture the thing defined. The definition of what a pit bull terrier is does not (alas) lead to the capture of the animal itself. The elimination of all such terriers (devoutly to be wished, in my view) would not touch the definition. More worrying than this laughable misunderstanding is the anti-essentialist temper of the age expressed in the disdain of definitions by many contemporary theologians. This disdain is accompanied by a respectful attitude to context, to the idea of theology as a language game, and to meaning as use, and the like, and by a dislike of exactness of thought and expression in theology as something that is sacrilegious, an attempt to box God in, to bring him down to our size, or to dominate him.

Louis Berkhof's *Systematic Theology* is a standard textbook of CRT. "Berkhof," as people affectionately refer to it, comes in for more than its fair share of disparagement and misunderstanding nowadays. One of its features, though not one that is unique to the work, is that the author often offers definitions. Unlike Calvin in the *Institutes* he does not search for them, he finds them ready-made in the tradition of CRT inherited through Herman Bavinck and others. For instance, he offers a definition of divine omnipresence as *"that perfection of the Divine Being by which He transcends all spatial limitations, and yet is present in every point of space with His whole Being."*[23]

Some seem to think that a definition of something says it all. A definition of divine omnipresence tells us all that there is to know about that aspect of the divine nature. But producing a definition is not like the manufacture of a chemical essence or extract, which takes everything that is of value from a plant or a rock and discards the rest. A definition of omnipresence does not turn Psalm 139, for example, into waste, like ash or pith. The systematic theologian, with a string of such definitions at his disposal, is not smarter than Scripture. So what is going on? In defining omnipresence has Berkhof mastered the concept? In defining it, has he bottled it up, boxed it in? Or has he himself become omnipresent, or does he now know what it is like to be omnipresent, or is he able to explain it? These suggestions seem weird, especially in theology.

No, a definition is none of these things. It's especially important to underline the last of these suggestions. Defining is *not* explaining. A theologian brandishing definitions is not like a scientist or a detective, filling in the gaps in our knowledge, solving problems, developing a technology. Berkhof's definition of omnipresence does not solve the problem or the mystery of God's omnipresence, of how it can be that God is wholly and indivisibly present to all of space. It may even be said to accentuate the problem. At such a point CRT prefers to say that at the very least the definition protects that problem, and the biblical data that express it, and it provides us a way of talking about God's presence by distinguishing it from other kinds of diffuse presence, like the presence of a gas or of a radio signal or of an elephant.

Why is a problem such as the mystery of divine omnipresence worth protecting? Because the problem that is protected is less of a challenge than any alternative, positive proposal. Could God's omnipresence be understood in spatial terms? Is there more of God in an elephant than in a flea?

---

23. Berkhof, *Systematic Theology*, 60. Italics in the original.

No, obviously not. So his presence is non-spatial. Is his non-spatial presence local in character? Was part of God non-physically present partly in the church of Ephesus and partly in Corinth? No. The unity of God is such that he is indivisible. So God is wholly present here, and there, and at every point. Is this not very mysterious? To be sure it is. But the alternatives are also mysterious, and they have the added disadvantage of being manifestly at odds with God's infinity and perfection, which is also clearly taught in Scripture. We may be able to clarify the mystery further, but a Christian theologian is certainly not in the business of eliminating divine mysteries as a matter of principle.

At such points in their thinking the systematic theologians of the CRT are more like grammarians than like scientists or detectives. They attempt to show us (from Scripture, if they are being faithfully Christian) how to think, and how not to think, about God, and so how to talk about him. Or perhaps it is more faithful to the order of these things to say: taking our cue from Scripture we learn to talk in certain ways about God, and in learning to talk in these ways we learn to think reflectively in ways that our talk directs, and to avoid what it forbids (thinking of God as physically diffuse, or as merely local, say), and what it requires (thinking of all places as equally "open" to God), and what it allows (such as saying that God is "everywhere"). Definitions, drawn from Scripture and continually refined by the Scriptural data, tell us what to say and what not to say, in rather the way that grammarians codify a natural language, telling us what can and cannot make sense in that language, what is a mistake, which leads to the utterance of nonsense, and so on. Theological grammarians do not themselves control the things that we say: they attempt to indicate the rules of intelligible speech about revealed realities.

By drawing on scriptural data, a human definition of divine omnipresence (a fallible effort, of course) makes an attempt at saying what must be true if the assertions of Psalm 139 and other such assertions in Scripture are to be understood, or are not to be misunderstood. In a way that is surprising, we often take such definitions (or the intuitions that lie behind them) for granted. They undergird a lot of Scriptural exegesis and how we apply it. So, for example, the rhetorical force of "Where shall I go from your Spirit?" (with its implication, "absolutely nowhere") only indicates a truth about God's presence if it is true that God (who is spirit) is omnipresent in something like the Berkhofian fashion. Otherwise the question is no longer rhetorical. But Berkhof's definition is not an attempt to downgrade and replace the language of the Psalms or any other language, or to be cleverer than Scripture. His definition does not take us beyond Scripture, making Scripture second-rate. It is (at best) a skeleton, not the entire body. But it supports serious theological thought, like the skeleton supports the flesh and sinews of the body, and of course it has significant religious implications, as we can see, for example, from Psalm 139.

Insofar as Berkhof's or anyone's definition is faithful to the biblical data, it will uphold the biblical teaching on divine omnipresence and will in turn warrant us in concluding that Psalm 139 is a celebration of such omnipresence and so not something else. We might otherwise be quite attracted to the idea that the language of the psalmist is hyperbolic, or that it records an ecstatic experience of the writer, and does not express (through the repetitions of Hebrew poetry) the sober truth of divine omnipresence and its consequences. So awareness of the definition, or of what the definition defines, which is intended to be drawn from scriptural teaching as a whole, serves to integrate that psalm into the other, variously expressed, biblical teachings on divine omnipresence. If we are not approaching the Scriptures with the help of the skeleton of systematic theology that Scripture supplies, then our "body of divinity" will be flabby and misshapen. This does not mean, as already noted, that the assertions of the systematic theologian are incorrigible. Scripture must continue to bear down on them, to force reconsideration, reflection, and reconstruction. A skeleton is not a carapace. But at any one time the activity of Bible interpretation, if it is to have a hope of being theologically faithful, must have scaffolding in place to build from, making connections between one part of the scaffolding and others parts. So, at least, CRT maintains.

In CRT, as in classical Christian theology more generally, the definitions are, or aim at being, what we may call "real definitions," definitions of realities. Of course, the definitions are also lexical, for they are definitions of words in terms of other words. But the revealed words are not only words, merely what human beings have chosen to say, of merely conventional power. By what he says the biblical writer seeks to epitomize a reality: "Sin is the transgression of the law," "God is spirit," "God is love," "God is light"; "love is the fulfilling of the law," "faith is the assurance of things hoped for, the conviction of things not seen." But sometimes divine realities are not defined in Scripture, nor is the language easily appropriated as a definition. So it is, for example, with "union with Christ." Union with Christ is a reality, but it is a many-sided, rich reality typically picked out by Paul's phrase "in Christ." Because of this complexity, it is not easily captured in a definition. Nevertheless, we may attempt a definition in order to distinguish the biblical idea of union with Christ from false ideas of union, union as identity with God himself, for example, or union as mere *camaraderie*, such as membership of a club or society, or as a physical connection, like that of a bimetallic strip.

Such definitions, whether given in Scripture itself, or attempted by the theologian, suppose that there are divinely revealed realities to be defined. Definitions are particularly important where in the course of church history words used in theological discussion come to have multiple meanings, some of which are significantly at odds with others, even meanings that contradict each other. In sorting out such confusion, not only essentialism, but also metaphysical realism, or at the very least the objectivity of the world, is being assumed.

So the forming of definitions are not bids for power, a kind of linguistic imperialism, an invasion of territory, through which one captures the mind of another. In theology, different definitions—for example, differing and incompatible definitions of "justification"—stand side by side. This is recognized as a basic fact of theological discourse. The perennial question for the Reformed systematic theologian is which of the available definitions best captures the relevant biblical reality. And as with doctrines, so with definitions; they must be revisable as the theologian revisits the biblical data.

More than once in discussing and delivering various definitions in his *Institutes*, Calvin hints at this metaphysical outlook. Definitions are not merely verbal, defining one term or terms by another. They are not terms of convenience, arbitrarily given. It would be hard to develop a case for nominalism from Calvin's procedure. Although on one occasion he writes approvingly of us being "lords" of words, this is a remark about Christians, not one about the relation between words and reality.[24] The terms he defines are not merely Christian usage, how the Christian community happens to employ various terms, but they are intended to represent divine realities revealed or depicted in Scripture. They are intended as "real definitions," the specification of necessary and sufficient conditions for something's being, say, a case of original sin, or of omnipresence.

In Calvin's *Institutes* the discussion of a topic invariably starts with or includes a definition of it. His typical practice is to take a term used in the Christian theological tradition, such as original sin, or free will, and to provide his own definition of that term, or occasionally endorse another definition, and to justify this definition in terms of Scriptural teaching. Sometimes he thinks that a biblical writer himself offers a definition, and of course he uses or at least endorses that. So his practice is not stipulative but descriptive, to provide descriptive definitions drawn from Scripture. He has no interest at all in laying down his own meaning of a term. Among his definitions are: the image of God in man (I.15.4), the soul and its faculties (I.15.6), original sin (II.1.8), free will (II.2.4), faith (III.2), repentance

---

24. Calvin, *Institutes*, IV.19.1

(III.3.5), justification (III.11.4), and conscience (III.9.15). In an era of warm controversy he employs them to avoid misunderstanding: in effect, he says to the reader, "when I refer to justification I am not using it in the Roman sense, or in Osiander's sense, or in some vague or indeterminate sense, nor am I proposing my own idea, but I am carefully formulating what I believe is the biblical sense, a form of words that I believe captures the biblical view." For Calvin and the other Reformers, the Reformation was about the recovery of biblical realities, and one main way in which this recovering is achieved is in first carefully defining those realities and then incorporating them into their theology and the teaching and preaching ministry of the church.

So the definitions are meant to assist clear thinking, to set the agenda for teaching and discussion. Definitions are not imperialistic attempts to annex territory, but by exact and full investigation and thinking, to depict what God has revealed. We can depict the essence of regeneration but, in Herman Bavinck's words, we do not by the fact of possession of such a definition take away the mystery of God breathing new spiritual life into a dead soul.[25] To depict a reality accurately by means of a definition is not to explain it, much less is it to explain it away. So it is necessary to distinguish what is essential to, say, regeneration, and what is not essential and so a contingent or accidental feature.

The systematic theologian has to say what he means. And part of this task consists in the use of definitions. What is justification? Answer: *it is being reckoned righteous in the sight of God on account of the work of Christ*. No doubt that particular definition may be improved upon. But the definitions of the systematic theologian are not just made up. They are not just arbitrary stipulations on their part, acts of creativity, in effect saying, this is my idea of justification, or this is my "model" of the atonement. Theology is not about theologians. Nor are definitions merely statements about how words are in fact used, the meaning that as a matter of fact people attach to them. Some people define justification so as to include sanctification; the two are merged. This is a bad definition, Hodge says, bad because it confuses together what Scripture keeps separate, even though what is separate is none the less intimately connected.[26] By developing such definitions the systematic theologian does not intend to say anything new, but to report what is divine revealed reality.

---

25. For an interesting approach to a definition of regeneration, see Bavinck, "Regeneration: An Attempt at Definition," *Reformed Dogmatics*, IV:75f.

26. Hodge, *Systematic Theology*, III:17.

So the systematizing of systematic theology involves logical consistency, and connectedness of various kinds, and careful thought that involves definitions. But utilizing such resources does not ensure comprehensiveness in our understanding of God and his ways. Later on we shall meet theologians who think that the approach of CRT being sketched here claims that the result of such theology is a *comprehensive* understanding of revealed truth, and so aids and abets a kind of overturning of the creator-creature relationship. But this is far from being the case, partly because CRT respects the boundaries of the revelation. Not everything that could be known is revealed to us; obviously not. And just as obviously, much of what is revealed is mysterious, that we cannot fully grasp or comprehend: the Trinitarian being of God, the incarnation, creation, providence and human accountability, are among the central themes of Scripture about which theologians in the CRT tradition echo Paul's words in his doxology at the end of Romans 11.

Abstracting and Generalizing: Loss and Gain

So a good part of the work of the systematic theologian is endeavoring to draw out true and accurate statements of a general character from the particular statements of Scripture. For that is what Scripture largely is, sets of particular statements about particular events; these statements involve statements of fact (as in narratives), interpretations of these facts, arguments, objections, questions, commands, exclamations, promises, vows, and so on. However, to generalize from these particularities—to formulate Christian doctrine, the Christian view of the nature and the importance of the revealed events—is not to abstract from them some lowest common denominator, to draw out a series of vague generalizations. The bowl of fruit in front of me is just that, a bowl of fruit. It is certainly a matter of some significance to indicate what it is that makes an object a fruit and not a bowl, to say what the various fruit in the bowl have in common. I shall return to this point later on. But it is a matter of equal significance to identify and describe the variety of fruit, oranges and lemons, apples and pears, that the bowl contains.

It would be a poor systematic theology that contented itself with formulating a doctrine of God from what all statements about God in Scripture have in common. So when the systematic theologian generalizes from the Scriptural data about God, say, this does not mean reducing or leveling down. It means taking due note of the particularities of individual texts and ensuring that they make their contribution to the formulation of the doctrine. So that, to continue with the doctrine of God for a moment, due account has to taken of the oneness of God and also due account of his threeness. The data that are evidence for the oneness of God cannot be allowed to swamp or nullify the data that are evidence for the threeness of God, any more than the textual evidence for the justice of God can be allowed to swamp the evidence for his love. The system must be elastic-sided enough to make proper provision for the different facets of revelation, and this requires the theologian continually to revisit the particular texts of Scripture to correct and refresh his general doctrinal statements.

So the work of the Christian systematic theologian is not first to think up a system and then to impose it on the data like a grid. That would be to adopt an unfortunate, *a priori* attitude to Scripture, to take for granted what God must be saying to us, without actually looking to see. Nevertheless from a logical point of view it does not matter whether the theologian starts with the text, and draws general conclusions, doctrine, from it, or starts with a general idea or concept and tests and refines that by the biblical data, provided that some general idea is not imposed on the particularities of the text, making them say what they do not in fact say.

Perhaps each method, the top down and the bottom up, has its place. Take the following illustration. An archaeologist may come across a pile of broken pottery. In an endeavor to reconstruct the original object or objects suppose he prepares a frame of flexible wire around which he tries to place the pieces, taking note of their shape, their pattern, their fit, and so on. As he continues with his task he must be prepared to modify the frame in the light of the impact of the data, in this case the shards of pottery. Various hypotheses are tested—that it's round, that it's oval; that it's one vessel, that its two; that some pieces are missing, that all the pieces are present. Ideally, all but one of these hypotheses will be rejected in the course of the reassembly, though as a matter of fact the data may be incomplete, and the hypotheses correspondingly tentative. The wire, shaped according to an original, tentatively held hypothesis, may have to be altered in the light of the impact of the data. But as the task develops, so the present shape of the wire may give a good clue as to where the remaining pieces that are lying around, or the missing pieces, may fit or would have fitted.

So it is with the Christian systematic theologian. Systematic theology conveys the overall "shape" of the biblical revelation. But the revelation is not shaped by what the theologian brings to it, forced into a mold of the thinker's own making, or of something that he takes from the surrounding culture, or even from the history of the church. This is one reason why Warfield insists that systematic theology has a much closer relation with exegetical theology than it does with historical theology.[27] Obviously an individual theologian's particular interests, and also his personal idiosyncrasies, may show through. But whatever he brings to the data must be sufficiently flexible to bear its weight and variety. Unlike the archaeologist, who may finally succeed in reconstructing the bowl or vase, the systematic theologian never completes his task.

---

27. Warfield, "The Idea of Systematic Theology," 65.

2

Epistemology

In the opening chapter we noted some of the central logical and metaphysical features of CRT as this has developed from the time of the Reformation, features which in turn came from and build on the patristic, conciliar, and medieval outlook. On the principle of "one thing at a time" we have so far taken for granted that God has made himself known in nature and in Scripture in a way that is accessible to us, and that nature and Scripture are sources of reliable knowledge for us. As with Christian belief more generally, the systematic theologian not only endorses the faith of the church and how it is grounded in Scripture, he attempts to articulate and defend these beliefs in a more reflective way. Part of this way involves fashioning or adopting certain normative proposals. So we need to consider the character of such knowledge and belief. In this chapter, then, we look at the epistemological side of systematic theology. We shall necessarily be selective: this chapter will by no means cover or even touch on anything like a complete range of such issues. It is chiefly concerned with the account that CRT gives of the knowledge of God and of belief in him.

It might be helpful to think of such accounts as exercises in faith seeking understanding. That project has typically been concerned with metaphysical issues concerning Christian doctrine, such as the Trinity, the incarnation, the relation of God to the creation, and so on.[1] But Scripture, besides being concerned with the metaphysical dimensions of the faith, also involves epistemic claims. Indeed, it rests on one fundamental epistemic claim, that it is God's revelation. Further, embedded within it are a wide variety of epistemic claims and assumptions. To reflect on these is also an exercise in faith seeking understanding. Why that tradition should

1. Helm, *Faith and Understanding*.

have favored the discussion of the metaphysical over the epistemic is not altogether clear, but perhaps it has to do with the fact that in its dominant period, in the patristic and medieval eras, metaphysical issues were much more contentious than were epistemic issues. The same cannot be said of the period since the Enlightenment.

Modern Epistemology and CRT

For those who are familiar with modern epistemology an account of knowledge and belief offered by CRT will have some aspects that are obvious, and others that are strange. Whether one thinks of the operation of the *sensus divinitatis*, some awareness of God that everyone has, or the belief in the revealed word of God, both cognitive states have an evidentialist element. Faith for CRT is not fideistic. The heavens declare the glory of God; and we come to believe that there are promises of God and what those promises are from investigating the data of Holy Scripture in a way that is straightforward. Some of the features of such data will be explored shortly. The data are public and accessible, insofar as God and his ways can be. They can be assembled, assessed, and debated about. However, while these procedures are familiar, the matter of trusting what is understood is not so straightforward. For human beings are in a state of sin, and this creates antipathy to the revelation of God in Scripture. There are blocks to knowledge, and resistances. The human mind is a factory of idols, as Calvin put it. So that from the standpoint of CRT error may be due to a failure to investigate the data properly, or (more basically) to an antipathy to the data, or a more general failure to appreciate the significance or force of the revelation. Sin has multiple "noetic effects." Not just failures in memory and limitations of the senses and intellect, universal shortcomings, but moral and spiritual effects that are not universal, and so are liable to be contested

The knowledge of God and self-knowledge are intimately connected, as Calvin stressed. Because two equally well-endowed people have different self-understandings, they will react differently to the promises of God and the claims of Christ that they read and discuss together. To acquire the true knowledge and God and of ourselves, more is needed than the successful employment of the cognitive tools, God's grace must open the eyes of the mind, in rather the way that someone familiar with the colors and texture and subject matter of a painting may need the development of their aesthetic sense to discern the beauty of its form.

This needs to be borne in mind because it seems to be characteristic of post-conservative theologians with a generally Reformed outlook that we are to consider later, that in their critique of foundationalism and of much else in the epistemology of CRT they also ignore the connectedness of knowledge of God and knowledge of self that is characteristic of it. We shall return to this theme in chapter 9. We now turn to consider the more general epistemological features of CRT.

Truth

Something should be said about the nature of truth, and deviations from it. For the sort of systematizing that we discussed in chapter 1 is the systematizing of what is believed on good grounds to be true, particularly the divinely given truths of Holy Scripture. Some of these involve historical truths within the metaphysical framework of creation and redemption that encloses the biblical narratives and gives them significance. These include truths about the nature or essence of God, for example, and also contingent truths, what God has freely done and permitted: the entire creation, the entrance of sin, and then redemption in all its aspects.

For CRT, truth has its origin in the character of God, what God truly is and does.

> God is also the truth in a logical sense. This truth consists in correspondence between thought and reality, the conformity or adequation of the intellect to the [real] thing. Our concepts are true when they bear the exact imprint of reality. In this sense truth is opposed to error. Now God is the truth also in that he knows all things as they really are. His knowing is correct, unchangeable, fully adequate. Indeed, in his knowing he is the truth itself, just as in his being he is the ontological truth. God's knowledge is dynamic, absolute, fully correspondent truth.[2]

God is the true source of all other states of affairs than himself, and he knows in a clear and unconditional sense all that is true: himself, and all that he has brought to pass, and might have brought to pass and hasn't. Further, Bavinck appears to be saying that God is the exemplar and so the foundation of all that comes to pass. The language of Scripture, when it is taken to be true, is true because it faithfully represents certain facts, either necessary or contingent truths, or reliably reports what is in fact untrue. The representation in question must not be thought of an iconic or hieroglyphic "picturing" of the facts, as the "picture theory of meaning," popular in the early years of the twentieth century, maintained, but as a successful

---

2. Bavinck, *Reformed Dogmatics*, II:209

communication of truths about what is basically an objective reality, by successfully referring to an aspect of it and characterizing that aspect in such and such accurate ways. The truth that the apple is red in appearance (under normal conditions) depends upon its being red, and we communicate that fact by identifying or picking out this apple, and then describing its color. The assertion "God was in Christ reconciling the world unto himself" refers to God, and the rest of the expression tells us something about him. The statement is true if there is a God who did just that. So we might say, "God was in Christ reconciling the world unto himself" is true if and only if God was in Christ reconciling the world unto himself.

Such sentences, if true, do not tell us the whole truth about what they refer to and characterize, of course. Who Christ is, how he reconciled, what the reconciliation is, require many more sentences, and even then such a fuller account would not exhaustively describe or provide a fully comprehensive description of these matters. There's always more that could be said. But that's exactly how it is in non-theological contexts as well. The statement "The jug of milk on the table is sour" is true if and only if the jug of milk on the table is sour. The sentence picks out a subject, the jug of milk, and then asserts something about it, that the milk is sour. But from that sentence alone we do not know much about the milk, about what kind of milk, what its chemical composition is, its calorific value, how it comes to be sour, what chemical changes it underwent in becoming sour, and so on. In this sense this every day statement is very similar to the statements of the systematic theologian. But because we are not in possession of the whole truth it does not follow that we should systematically doubt the truth of what we do already know.

Later on we shall see that post-conservative revisionist theologians raise various difficulties about the account just sketched, and that these tend to rest on misunderstandings. The revisionists have a tendency to think that claims to knowledge by finite creatures are systematically suspect, and that because we express our beliefs, naturally enough, in our own particular situations, this fact means that the truths we express are nothing more than truths for me, in my situation, but not (perhaps) for you in yours, and as a consequence our beliefs are only relatively true. Of course we are finite and we err, but these facts about us do not imply that we have good reason to be agnostic about everything we claim to know, or that we should suspend our judgements in a systematic way.

Objective Knowledge

If one holds to the sort of realism that we have seen that CRT theologians such as Bavinck, Charles Hodge,[3] and CRT in general are committed to, and also holds (as they did) that despite the noetic effects of sin the human mind is a fairly reliable cognitive agent, then objectivism has followed. By objectivism here is meant the idea that much of what we refer to as reality is distinct from the human knower, and nevertheless reliably accessible to him. So that his beliefs do not construct reality, nor do they systematically distort it, but yield objective knowledge of it, though not infallibly so. Given these convictions, borne out in important segments of our everyday experience, there is the prospect of gaining objective knowledge about the world, including knowledge of truths about God, if he has been pleased to reveal such. Even the knowledge that a person has of himself, that he has a toothache, or feels depressed, are to be thought of as objective features of the world. But as we shall see such claims to have knowledge of God and his ways require careful statement. While such knowledge is related to our everyday knowledge such as the knowledge that I have five fingers on my right hand, that I am breathing, that today is Wednesday, that there is a piano against the wall opposite to me, and so on, it also has significantly different elements.

In their definitions of the biblical account of faith, CRT theologians discern three elements: knowledge, assent, and trust. The promises of God and their fulfilment, a pattern that epitomizes his revelation, are part of the objective world. The believer assents to these, that is, accepts their truth, and relies upon God, the one who has promised, for the good promised. He has knowledge of them based on the reliable testimony of God, not scientific or mathematical proof. In what follows, our discussion will focus on the first two elements of this account of faith, knowledge, and assent.

The knowledge in question is of an objective state of affairs, such as who God is and what he has promised, and it is public knowledge, available to more than one person, and in principle available to all. "The revelation of God is a system of words and deeds of God, which exist outside us and independently of us."[4] An important consequence of this, and a sign of divine objectivity, is that those who may disbelieve, who know what the revelation claims and who, for whatever reason, dissent from it, may dissent from the very same truth-claims, having the very same meaning, as those who rely upon them. That is, the revelation of God is objectively true, whether or

---

3. Hodge, *Systematic Theology*, I:22.
4. Bavinck, *Reformed Dogmatics*, I:565.

not men and women believe it. In this respect it is something like the truth that there is a piano in the room. That's a truth, whether men or women believe it. The revelation of God is not precisely the same. It does not necessarily lead to the very same truth claims, having the very same meanings, because different believers and disbelievers may have different degrees of understanding regarding the same claims.

Yet connected with our knowledge of God there are elements of implicit faith. Our human knowledge is partial. We may know what some of the revelation means, but be puzzled about other things that it says. More importantly, we are fallible in our knowledge. We make mistakes, even wilful mistakes, we may be tentative and unsure about some of our opinions. In this respect our cognitive map is rather like a personal web, with the center occupied by what we accept with full conviction, and the surrounding areas occupied with beliefs of varying degrees of strength.

In current discussion of Christian theological method, features of which we shall examine in the chapters to follow, the fact of human fallibility is treated as something of a novel discovery. It is emphasized in sharp contrast to the alleged infallibility of our beliefs as allegedly touted and claimed by the Enlightenment. It is even suggested that, influenced by the Enlightenment view of epistemology, CRT has itself become infallibilist in the claims that it makes about God and his ways. We shall look at this view of the Enlightenment later. In this charge of infallibilism there is serious anachronism and misunderstanding at work. One characteristic of the stance of the Reformation is the emphatic assertion, against the claims of the Church of Rome, that churches, councils, and individuals may err and have erred. No individual, no church, no council, is infallible. Only Scripture is infallible; interpreters of Scripture are fallible, partly due to their ignorance, but more significantly due to the workings of sinful biases, of which more shortly. The tradition makes this clear.

The confession of the church and in even greater measure the dogmatics of an individual person, is fallible, subject to Scripture, and never to be put on a level with it. It does not coincide with the truth but is a human, hence a fallible, transcript of the truth laid down in Scripture.[5]

> Doctrines have an absolute infallibility, but the human intellect has properly no infallibility (although it has its own certainty in working, which does not deceive). Nor is it necessary that what is fallible in its own nature, always actually deceives; otherwise there would be no certainty in knowledge (which nevertheless there is). There is no need, therefore, that the means which lead

---

5. Bavinck, *Reformed Dogmatics*, I:45.

us to the knowledge of an infallible doctrine should at once be infallible. It suffices that it be such as (rightly employed) does not deceive.[6]

Faced with the fallibility inherent in human enquiry, many think that once we recognize this fact we inexorably slide down the slippery slope to skepticism, to the denial that it is possible to know anything, or very little, which leads to a suspension of belief in theological matters, or at least to holding them very tentatively. For the argument is, if my judgements about Scripture are fallible, and I may be mistaken in what I believe about the central things that it teaches, then how can I be sure of anything that it teaches? Is it not wiser, more rational, in the face of my own and others' fallibility, to suspend judgement, or to be guarded, qualified, and suitably conditional in what I claim? For, being fallible, may I not be mistaken about my most fundamental and cherished beliefs? I believe that there is a piano against the opposite wall, but may I not be mistaken?

At this point we need to make a distinction. Of course I may be mistaken that I see the piano. It's logically possible that I have recurrent hallucinations whenever I look at the wall opposite. Maybe these are all the result of wishful thinking; I should dearly love to have a piano, and I am so disturbed by not having a piano, that my mind, by a curious kind of make-believe, makes an image of the piano appear, though in fact there is no piano. All that, and much more like it, is certainly logically possible. But while it is logically possible, and while there are myriads of other such logical possibilities, do I have the slightest reason to believe that any of these possibilities are true? The fact that a proposition is logically possibly true is not such a reason, or at least it is not a very good reason. It is logically possible that I am hallucinating a piano. But do I have a good reason that I am? No I do not. It is also logically possible that I am hallucinating not only the piano but the table and my laptop. When I read "God was in Christ reconciling the world unto himself" I take this to mean that God was in Christ reconciling the world unto himself. Of course I may be mistaken; it may mean something entirely different, say, that "once upon a time there were three bears . . ." But do I have the slightest reason to think it means that? No, I do not. And do I have a good reason to think that it means that God was in Christ reconciling the world unto himself? Yes, I do; from my knowledge of the English language, say, and of others' knowledge, and by consulting various different translations, and the original Greek, and so on. Could I still be mistaken? Yes, I could. Do I presently have the slightest reason to think that

---

6. Turretin, *Institutes of Elenctic Theology*, III:94.

I am mistaken? No, I do not. May there be such a reason in future? Yes, there may be. And so on.

Suppose that someone comes up with a good reason for me to doubt the meaning of that Pauline sentence. Perhaps further studies of Greek reveal different nuances to the word translated "reconciling." Words change their meaning: perhaps the discovery is that while the word was translated "reconciling" in Greek before Paul, or in Greek later than Paul, during Paul's time the word meant "presenting" and so should have been translated: God was in Christ presenting the world unto himself. That would be a good reason for taking stock of the standard translation, doing some further research, and at the end perhaps changing the understanding of this Pauline sentence. Or perhaps not. Undoubtedly there are circumstances in which I ought to suspend belief, namely if there is a good reason to do so. So fallibilism does not, or ought not, to lead all the way to skepticism.

But is fallibility a permanent affliction? Yes and no. We shall never cease to be fallible. But our tendency to make wrong judgments, and so display fallibility, can be controlled; we can approximate to the truth more and more closely by using various methods of checking and correcting. And in the *eschaton*, when our minds are clearer and better informed, there will be a kind of eschatological verification and falsification of our current beliefs. There are features that the objective truths of our everyday world have in common with the objective truths of the revelation, given our fallibility and tendency to self-deception. But there is one important, crucial dissimilarity. There are areas of the faith that are accessible (in principle) to rational and empirical testing. But there are other areas whose is truth is borne into the mind and spirit by the testimony of the Holy Spirit. There is word and spirit; there is nature and grace; there is natural epistemology and there is "supernatural" epistemology. The way these pairs intertwine will be an important theme of the remainder of the chapter.

Relativism

We have been dealing with our fallibility. But there is another possible source of uncertainty: relativism. Modern relativism stems from the constructivist legacy of Kant, the idea that reality is shaped by our minds, notably by the categories of space and time. From these beliefs (which Kant himself most certainly did not understand in a relativistic way) there is an easy step to the idea that reality is strongly influenced by, or even constructed by our minds. Creative anti-realism, such as that propounded by Richard Rorty and some who take their inspiration from the later Ludwig Wittgenstein, as well as from "Continental philosophy" in some of its various varieties, propound the idea that our minds are not seriously constrained by the nature of the reality that we occupy, the way the world is, but that we are able to impose our own perspective on what it is that is "out there" or that such an imposition is inevitable. John R. Franke endorses such constructivism in the sociology of knowledge in *The Character of Theology*,[7] so that what is true for me and my cultural circle is precisely that—it is true *for me* (and my circle), but it is not, or may not be, true for you (and your circle) or, say, for Augustine of Hippo and his friends. It could be false or fundamentally puzzling for you. Or, what is even more drastic, it could be meaningless for you, and your utterances meaningless for me. Why? Because what your mind brings to the raw data may be so different from what my mind brings to them that we may not only not believe ourselves to occupy a common world, but we may not even be able to understand what others, occupying other cultural circles, mean by what they say.

Once we have that thought, the thought of the relativism of truth and of belief, we can quickly see that it can come in various hues. It can be individualistic: my mind creates "truths" for me, and for me alone. It can be social or cultural relativism, the idea that, say, the world of the Kikuyu is a different world from that of modern Western culture. There is a kind of temporal version of relativism; our world, the contemporary world, is different from the world of Augustine, the world of fifth-century North Africa, say. What is true for the Kikuyu is false for us; what is true for us was false for Augustine, and so on. There are even deeper forms of such relativism. For (as we have noted) one cannot rule out semantic variants of these mere epistemic forms. Not only may what is false for me be true for you, but what has meaning for you may have no meaning for me. Not only can we not know the same propositions to be true as Augustine knew, but we cannot be sure, perhaps we can have no inkling, about what Augustine *meant* by what he wrote. So that the most developed form of conversational exchange it may be possible for us to achieve is:

Person A: "I don't understand what you are saying."
Person B: "And I don't understand what *you're* saying."

But, as Alvin Plantinga and others have pointed out, there is a deep incoherence about such a philosophy. For if I am a relativist, then I cannot argue with anyone who does not happen to share my "form of life." Not only can I not argue with such a person, I cannot disagree with him, since to disagree is to be on the way to contradicting. For if you speak as a consistent relativist, your relativism is the truth for you, just as what I believe is the

---

7. Chapter 3. We shall consider his views in chapter 8.

truth for me. For a relativist, all views are equally valid for those who hold them.[8]

Relativism goes deeper than its obvious undercutting of systematic theology; it goes to the heart of the Christian faith in its simplest, most naive and unsystematic expression. For at this level also Christians express and confess what they take to be true, objectively true, as we have seen. But if the relativists are correct, then what they confess could not be true, only true for them, or true for the Christian community; *a fortiori* Christian systematic theology could only be theology that is true for Christians. Theology then degenerates into a form of sociology, the study of nothing more than the various belief patterns of the Christian communities of the past and of the present. Such constructs may be public, but they are human creations, and so not objective in the sense discussed.

Realism

By and large, CRT, building on its catholic heritage, has accepted some form of epistemic realism. Even if there have been doubts about whether empirical states of affairs, for example, are the proper objects of knowledge, we are nevertheless capable of forming reliable beliefs about them, beliefs that we have good reason to trust, and which have stood the test of time. This reliability of our beliefs in an external world has been taken to be an inescapable, intuitive belief of human beings. Objections may be made to realism, to the mind-independent reality of the external world, but such a view is too fundamental and immediate to be proved *ab initio* by independent argumentation. What we know exists prior to our knowing it, if we do know it. But the very idea of mistaken beliefs is parasitic on cases of reliable belief. It seems to be possible to judge that a belief is mistaken only if we know what would count as a true belief.

Besides recognizing human fallibility, the Christian attitude to the nature and scope of our knowledge reckons that our powers of understanding and knowledge are skewed. Through the influence of sin the mind is capable of hiding itself from the truth, of being subject to forms of self-deception, and of believing what is false, particularly about ourselves and our relation to God. Besides this, as we saw, we are all subject to bias and partiality, including the moral and cultural biases formed by the circumstances in which we grow up, and the self-deceptions that may arise when our own interests are at stake. Nevertheless, there remains an important sense in which as knowers we receive information provided by a world that is independent

---

8. Plantinga, "Augustinian Christian Philosophy."

of us, and that would exist even if we did not, and that we form true beliefs about it. There once were dinosaurs.

In affirming such realism as the correlate of the objectivism we were discussing earlier, mainstream Christian and Reformed theology has generally been uncomfortable with certain forms of idealism. In the eighteenth century, the age of deism, philosophers such as George Berkeley repudiated the idea of matter as something that exists independently of the mind of God. Berkeley thought the idea of such independently existing matter is an atheistic doctrine. As a consequence he defended a form of idealism, subjective idealism as it is called. The world we perceive is the world of ideas provided for us by a benevolent God, the stability and coherence of the data being testimony to his wisdom and power. We may call this "receptive idealism." For Berkeley, to exist is to perceive or to be perceived by some mind; by finite minds, but pre-eminently by the divine mind who by his wisdom sustains an immaterial world of order by willing it for us. Jonathan Edwards was very close to this outlook. Such idealism does not deny a world distinct from the human mind. For on such a view the external world is first and foremost a set of ideas in the mind of God that our finite minds may in turn finitely and fallibly experience. Human minds receive information about this distinct world by their senses and intellect, and respond to it in thought, feeling, and will. Such a world, for such idealists, does not have independent existence in virtue of being material or physical, but simply because it consists of ideas in the mind of God that are "projected" by him to form our environment, our external world. Such idealism has certainly not been a mainstream Christian view, which is that the external world is independent of our minds, both human and divine, but sustained by the immediate power of God. However, little that Christian theology claims is straightforwardly called into question by such receptive idealism.[9]

Though some theologians, such as Berkeley and Edwards (a thinker who falls more or less within the mainstream of Reformed theology), were each attracted by a form of receptive idealism, neither they nor the realist core of CRT has been attracted by the idea, stemming from the philosophical "Copernican Revolution" initiated by Immanuel Kant, another Enlightenment philosopher, that the human mind itself provides categories of understanding and sensibility without which what is independent of us would be totally unintelligible. Such a view has given rise to various varieties of what we might call "constructive idealism," the idealist tradition of continental Europe and of Anglophone writers such as Bradley, Bosanquet,

---

9. An excellent current example of receptive idealism is described and defended by Robert M. Adams "Idealism Vindicated."

Josiah Royce, and so on. The post-Kantian Protestant theological tradition, exemplified in Schleiermacher, Ritschl, and others, was strongly influenced by this constructivist view of the mind, particularly in the nineteenth century and now, more recently, through postmodernism. Valuable and interesting though the work of Schleiermacher is, CRT has not accepted his assumption that theology must be constructed from the religious human consciousness, nor the basic agnosticism about God that such a view entailed. CRT has much more in common with the realism of the patristic and medieval eras, in which the main spine of Christian theology was developed.

Such realism is seen, for example, in the position of Charles Hodge who claims that the mind has a constitution, that the theologian comes to his task assuming the trustworthiness of his senses and his mental operations, and the certainty of truths such as "every effect must have a cause" and that in the same circumstances like effects will produce like causes. The possession of such a constitution enables us not to *construct* an external world, but to *receive* reliable information about it. Further, the theologian has the role of a student whose task it is to perceive, gather, and combine the facts. "These he does not pretend to manufacture, nor presume to modify. He must take them as they are. He is only careful to be sure that they are real, and that he has them all, or, at least all that are necessary to justify any inference which he may draw from them, or any theory which he may build upon them."[10] "It is to be observed that these laws or general principles are not derived from the mind, and attributed to external objects, but derived and deduced from the objects and impressed upon the mind."[11] These are, he goes on to say, "the laws of belief which God has impressed upon our nature" and there are others too, having to do with morality and God's relation to it. It is sometimes said that Hodge here relies upon Scottish Common Sense Philosophy, and perhaps he does. But it is also worth noting that he goes on to say,

> Lest we should err in our inferences from the works of God, we have a clearer revelation of all that nature reveals, in his word; and lest we should misinterpret our own consciousness and the laws of our nature, everything that can be legitimately learned from that source will be found recognized and authenticated in the Scriptures; and lest we should attribute to the teaching of the Spirit the operations of our own natural affections, we

---

10. Hodge, *Systematic Theology*, I:9.
11. Ibid., I:10.

find in the Bible the norm and standard of all genuine religious experience.[12]

In his discussion of theology as a science Bavinck adopts a very similar approach to Hodge, though one that is arrived at independently. He says:

> Tertullian rightly says: First there was man, then the philosopher or the poet.... Natural certainty is the indispensable foundation of science. Scientific knowledge is not a destruction but a purification, expansion and completion of ordinary knowledge. Every being, after all, accepts the reliability of the senses and the existence of the external world, not by a logical inference from the effect, in this case the representation in his consciousness, to the cause outside of himself, nor by reasoning from the resistance his will encounters to an objective reality that generates this resistance. Prior to all reflection and reasoning, everyone is in fact fully assured of the real existence of the world.[13]

Later we shall come to consider the issue of foundationalism and whether CRT is foundationalistic. The question is probably anachronistic when asked of theologians before the eighteenth century. But there is no doubt that there is a foundationalistic "shape" to their thinking.

According to CRT the mind we bring to the Bible is not a complete *tabula rasa*, as in the case of empiricism, but its powers of sensing, discerning, ordering, judging, and knowing are a part of human nature. The mind is receptive, but not passive, like blotting paper or a photographic plate. And, Hodge claims, even had the philosophers not argued for it, the Bible itself teaches that such capacities are essential to the human mind and that the mind is distinct from external reality, the features of which it seeks faithfully to depict. From a strictly philosophical point of view it would no doubt have been more satisfactory had Hodge himself devoted time and effort to offering philosophical clarification of this outlook, but here we are concerned not so much with how such realism may be given a philosophical defense as with noting that, as a matter of fact, such realism is the shared outlook of the bulk of the tradition of CRT and of the Christian theological tradition more generally. In chapter 8 we shall consider the cogency of the reasons currently offered by "postfoundationalist" theologians who are themselves in the Reformed tradition for departing from this realist, receptivist outlook.

With these preliminary discussions in mind, let us turn to theological epistemology, and the balance between nature and grace.

---

12. Ibid., I:11.
13. Bavinck, *Reformed Dogmatics*, I:223.

Theological Foundationalism

Let us say that foundationalism is the view that beliefs are warranted by beliefs that are more basic than themselves and that there are sets of beliefs that are ultimately basic, or foundational. As we shall see later on, in contemporary discussion of theological method by theologians such as Vanhoozer and Franke, disquiet over epistemic foundationalism in general is used to cast doubt on the idea of *theological* foundationalism in particular. The claims are, roughly, that a belief that is warranted foundationalistically must express some form of rationalism, and that Enlightenment foundationalism, an intrinsic part of the "Enlightenment project," has in any case been shown to fail. Therefore, Christian theology cannot have foundations. Foundationalism of any kind must in every instance be judged to be a failure. It follows that anything that smacks of foundationalism in Christian theology must be eliminated in favor of some form of "post-foundationalism."

In these next sections we shall approach this nest of claims by beginning with theology. For CRT, theology has a foundational character. We shall explore this, and then return to the broader and more basic question of whether in the case of CRT such an edifice is supported by an even broader foundationalism, what we might call general epistemic foundationalism. First, then, theological foundationalism.

For CRT the principled dismissal of theological foundationalism strikes at the heart of the distinctiveness of Christianity. For does it not seem obvious that anyone who subscribes to a canon, such as the canon of Scripture, attaches theological priority to what that canon contains and teaches? This is so, even if they the canon were to be regarded as no more than a unique *source* of Christian teaching and not as containing in so many words a set of privileged theological claims. In addition, the Protestant and Reformed emphasis upon the necessity and sufficiency of Scripture seems obviously "foundationalistic" in character. Scripture is the "rule of faith and life."[14] Besides, the proposal to abandon the very idea of the foundational character of Christian theology seems ironic in view of the fact that the writers of the New Testament refer to the testimony of the prophets and apostles, using explicitly foundational language. Their faith is built upon the foundations of prophets and apostles. Jesus Christ is the chief corner-stone. There is no other foundation than Christ, and so on.

To a man, CRT theologians offer a theology erected on the epistemic foundations of Holy Scripture. So, for example, Herman Bavinck distinguishes between the external basis or principle of theology (*Principium*

---

14 *Westminster Confession* III/I.

Externum), which centers upon the authority of Scripture, its necessity and sufficiency, and the internal basis or principle (*Principium Internum*), faith. He expresses the authority of Scripture using very strong language.

> The authority of Scripture extends to the whole person and over all humankind. It is above the intellect and the will, the heart and the conscience, and cannot be compared with any other authority. Its authority, being divine, is absolute. It is entitled to be believed and obeyed by everyone at all times. In majesty it far transcends all other powers. But, in order to gain recognition and dominion, it asks for no one's assistance. It does not need the strong arm of the government. It does not need the support of the church and does not conscript anyone's sword and inquisition. It does not desire to rule by coercion and violence but seeks free and willing recognition. For that reason it brings about its own recognition by the work of the Holy Spirit.[15]

Clearly Bavinck is here referring to Scripture as the epistemic foundation of Christian theology.

Intrinsic to what Bavinck states here, and to what CRT generally holds about the necessity and sufficiency of Scripture, is the idea of reliable testimony, and the further idea that what we know about the past may exert decisive epistemic authority over the present. Such an idea, that of the past being authoritative for the present, an idea which is intrinsic to CRT, and to creedal and conciliar Christian theology more generally, is clean contrary to the epistemology (and the hermeneutics) of the Enlightenment. For according to the Enlightenment temper, the direction is the other way. For we are living in an unprecedented time, the modern era. Although we recognize the importance of testimony, and its general reliability, its usefulness is simply that it is convenient. There is nothing about the human condition that logically requires that we depend upon testimony for our knowledge. We stand on the shoulders of giants, but we ourselves are capable in principle of being one of those giants, except for the contingent impediments of not having enough time and energy. Further, and because of this, as the favored occupants of the "enlightened ages" (David Hume's phrase), we judge the past, reinterpreting it in terms of the intellectual mores of modernity. For example, our present experience shows that miracles do not occur, and so those in the past who testified that they did occur must have been either deceived or deceiving.

---

15. Bavinck, *Reformed Dogmatics*, I:465 and IV:14.

Referential Success

We are engaged in reflecting on theological method, with how sets of ideas are to be organized and given coherent shape and form. The tendency of such enquiries is to focus the attention of the enquirer upon the relations between these ideas and to sideline this question: how do we know that these ideas of God, who he is and what he is like, actually succeed in referring to God? Let's call this the issue of *referential success*. It is an issue that the New Testament itself raises, as when Peter says that Christians have not followed cunningly devised myths. "We did not follow cleverly devised myths when we made known to you the power and coming of our Lord Jesus Christ, but we were eyewitnesses of his majesty. For when he received honour and glory from God the Father, and the voice was borne to him by the Majestic Glory, 'This is my beloved Son, with whom I am well pleased,' we ourselves heard the very voice borne from heaven" (2 Pet 1:16–18a). Peter appeals to the public, objective (though not universal) voice of the Father and of the transfigured Son. And the Apostle Paul seems to have taken the question seriously when he claimed that the God whom he declared was in fact the unknown God whom the Athenian philosophers worshipped in ignorance. The use of the phrase "the unknown god" may succeed in referring to the true and living God (Acts 17:23).

Here I am for the moment bracketing from consideration the epistemic failures that may be due to wilfulness or blindness or self-deception. Such factors, in the eyes of CRT, are undoubtedly sources of referential failure. But we shall postpone consideration of them until later. That does not mean that there won't be areas where we need to take care. And religion may well be one of these, involving as it does transcultural and trans-temporal comparisons, and dealing with issues of great moment, where the possibility of self-deception is a very real one.

What is interesting about much modern theology is that there is a deafening silence regarding the issue of referential success or failure in religion, especially of course in the Christian religion. Anyone who has any experience of the character of theological discussion that prevails in academic departments of religion and theology will be familiar with the sociological phenomenon of *theological autonomy*. The business of theology is conducted exclusively between theologians with rules that exclude or forbid raising questions of truth and falsity, or at least questions regarding objective truth and falsity. That mindset also forbids the raising of such questions from outside the charmed circle of theological discussants. For theological debate is a game, as its practitioners will often concede. Basil Mitchell has an amusing essay "How to Play Theological Ping-Pong."[16] Such theology is just words about words about words. It is theologians' words about theologians' words about theologians' God-talk. It is this fact, the fact of theological cultural insulation and an unconcern about truth, that develops in the minds of non-theologians the thought that theology is "not a subject," and which is slowly but surely contributing to the demise of university departments of theology. Why should tax-payers' money be spent on word games?

To take a recent example, academic theology has been at the center of the flourishing of "Trinitarian studies." Which model of the Trinity is to preferred? Eastern or Western? A model that tends to tritheism or the opposite, which tends to modalism? Is the Trinity in turn a model for human community? Such questions have spawned learned books and articles galore, and without doubt, these are good, interesting, and important questions. But they are surely only worthwhile questions if there is first a satisfactory answer to the question, have we reason to think that there is a God who is triune? But this question, which is a logically prior question to a discussion of God's triune nature, is scarcely raised. Imagine a discussion about the biology of unicorns. Where exactly is the heart of a unicorn to be found? What is its diet? What are its habits of procreation? Imagine books and monographs on these and other similar issues to the student of unicorns. Imagine a *Journal of Unicorn Studies*. Ought we not first to establish whether or not there are unicorns?

It is true there may be reticence to declare or deny a personal belief, or to bring issues of personal belief into academic enquiry. The neglecting of the question of truth may also arise because it is thought that the discussions have reached degrees of sophistication that makes checking well-nigh impossible. But nevertheless, academic discussion proceeds under its own steam, with the prospect of checking for truth never being raised; the dominant questions raised are whether theologian A has correctly understood theologian B's ideas and their implications. Words about words.

In keeping with this, those seeking an answer to the question, "do words such as "God" and "Lord" actually succeed in referring to anything?" will find no satisfactory response from the more recent proposals of post-conservative theologians such as Vanhoozer and Franke, whose views we shall later examine in detail. For they more or less follow the academic temper of the times, making their own proposals as contributions to the in-house language of the church. In Vanhoozer's case this shows itself in linguistic terms, the language of speech acts and language games and theo-drama,

---

16. In Mitchell, *How to Play Theological Ping Pong: Collected Essays on Faith and Reason*.

the fine tuning of the language of faith, and in a total disinterest in the need for the language of theology to be grounded in something outside itself. Though he dissents from George Lindbeck's communitarianism, Vanhoozer is attracted to Lindbeckian themes that stress the importance of interpersonal and social agreement and downplay issues of reference and truth. In Franke's case the terms of the debate are explicitly sociological, the local church and its language, first-order language, with the theologians' job being to fine tune that language, paying considerable attention in doing so to the "context" in which church and theologians are each situated. Christians talk to each other, confessing their faith, participating in the drama. But is there really a drama? Is anyone out there? Is there a God who occupies reality beyond the limits of the Christian village, beyond the moat and the drawbridge, and all similar enclosures? Franke assumes, it seems, that there is or must be a positive answer to that question, though he does not hint at its shape, and simply ignores questions of objectivity and reality because he thinks that they are figments of the Enlightenment.[17]

Nature and Grace

At this point, the contrast with CRT is sharp. In CRT's formative period it emphasized the *duplex cognitio dei*, the two-fold knowledge of God, a marked distinction from the *monoplex cognitio* that is currently prevalent in the church and its academies. *Duplex cognitio dei* is a significant theme in Calvin, and one that placed its stamp on subsequent theological discussions in early Reformed orthodoxy.[18] For, according to Calvin, "[s]ince then, the Lord first appears, as well in the creation of the world as in the general doctrine of Scripture, simply as a creator, and afterwards as a redeemer in Christ, a twofold knowledge of him hence arises."[19] The two-fold knowledge of God is the knowledge of God the creator, and then, as a distinct though related matter, the knowledge of God the redeemer in Christ. That distinction impressed itself on the structure of the *Institutes*, for example. The first five chapters of Book I have to do with the following matters:

> Chapter 1: The knowledge of God and of ourselves mutually connected; the nature of the connection.
>
> Chapter 2: What it is to know God; the tendency of this knowledge.

---

17. Franke, *The Character of Theology*, 15.
18. Muller, "'Duplex Cognitio Dei,'" 51–61.
19. Calvin, *Institutes* I.2.1.

Chapter 3: The knowledge of God naturally implanted in the human mind.

Chapter 4: The knowledge of God stifled or corrupted, ignorantly or maliciously.

Chapter 5: The knowledge of God conspicuous in the creation and continual government of the world.

It is not until chapter 13, after Calvin has discussed the nature of Scripture as the revelation of God in chapters 6 to 9, that the biblical doctrine of God, and especially its Trinitarian character, is introduced. It is impossible not to notice how different such a view is from the one that prevails in our post-Barthian theological world.

So what does the *duplex cognitio* imply for the knowledge of God and of ourselves? To answer that question, we shall consider the contribution of Francis Turretin. In his account of theological method he emphasizes the importance of human resources or tools. Christian theology, particularly CRT, does not ignore the issue of referential success, but nor does it rely for an answer upon the exclusive operation of a superhuman sixth-sense, or a special mystical *afflatus* in order to gain true, saving knowledge of God. Further, our knowledge of God is not the result of what we feel or imagine. Rather, in a way that Turretin no doubt thought that it was vital to grasp, but which it is easy to skip over, at the very outset of his enquiry he unfolds the place of reason in faith. Before this he had dismissed outright rationalism, the idea that human reason is the principle and rule by which the doctrines of the Christian religion and theology ought to be measured. Nonetheless in his view reason still has a crucial role, as we shall see.

Reason and the Senses

So to the questions "does any judgment belong to reason in matters of faith?" or "is there no use at all for it?"[20] Turretin proceeds to discriminate carefully between those who give reason too great a role in religion, and those who give it too little. (At the time when Turretin wrote the issue raised tensions because of the then-current prominence and influence of Socinianism.) The issue is whether reason has a part to play in the "judgment of private discretion by which truth is distinguished from falsehood." He is concerned with reason in understanding and discriminating. He holds that it plays a role in judging the truth of conclusions in all propositions, whatever their source, whether from general or special revelation. But in the case of propositions

20. Turretin, *Institutes of Elenctic Theology*, I:28.

that are from general revelation only, it is used both to establish the truth of such propositions and then what follows from them. So natural reason may judge of the truth of natural matters, in physics or history or traffic control, say, but it plays a subordinate though real role in determining the truth of supernatural matters. So in the case of revealed truth, the knowledge of God the redeemer,

> Although the human understanding is very dark, yet there still remains in it some rays of natural light and certain first principles, the truth of which is unquestionable, such as, the whole is greater than its part, an effect supposes a cause, to be and not to be at the same time is incompatible, etc. If this were not the case, there could be no science, nor art, nor certainty in the nature of things. These first principles are not only true in nature, but also in grace and the mysteries of faith.[21]

But even then Turretin observes several cautions. These are in order to underline the fact that reason is not the source of Christian theology but is useful for illustrating it, for comparing one thing with another, for drawing inferences, and for establishing proofs. First, he deals with logic, but as we have looked at this in the first chapter we may ignore it here. More interestingly for us, Turretin next asks, is there any use of the testimony of the senses in the mysteries of faith, or ought such testimony be entirely rejected? To this he says "We affirm the former and deny the latter." Reliance on the senses ought not to be rejected. The senses are needed.

> Although the orthodox are unwilling that the testimony of the senses should be heard in all mysteries, they nevertheless maintain that a proper regard should be paid to their testimony when the discussion concerns sensible and corporeal things which come within the sphere of their activity.[22]

That is, we may rely on them. If we could not, how would we know that we were opening the Bible and not *Gulliver's Travels*? And how could we identify the marks on its pages so that we can read them? So according to Turretin, both human reason and the senses have a distinct role to play in Christian systematic theology. (He has a nice proof text: "Touch me and see" [Luke 24:39].)

What is the point of stressing such basic matters? Turretin is making the point that gifts and powers that are essentially human play a role in theology. Theology is a humane discipline. These gifts are, as we might

21. Ibid., I:29–30.
22. Ibid., I:35.

put it, natural in the sense that they are universally distributed. They are the resources that we rely on in making observations, and drawing inferences, and making calculations about all matters of fact, including those matters of fact that are presupposed by or embedded in the Christian faith. But he makes a qualification. Besides stressing human finiteness, and the consequent mysteriousness to us of the doctrines of our faith, Turretin also maintains that these gifts of God are universally corrupted by sin, and that for a true, spiritual understanding of the teaching of Holy Scripture, and the appropriate responses of faith and obedience, the regenerating and illuminating work of the Holy Spirit are necessary, indispensable. He is, when all is said and done, a Reformed theologian.

So there is, besides the resources of unaided senses and intellect, which are natural epistemic powers, the need for the resources of supernatural epistemic powers. These involve the illuminating and testifying activity of the Holy Spirit who gives us confidence in the authority of Scripture. He does this not by providing us with new cognitive powers, but by enhancing those we have already. In particular, the Spirit makes evident to us, as we consider the data of Scripture, that it has God-given reliability. So these supernatural epistemic powers operate as part of a form of evidentialism.

Turretin is not so emphatic upon asserting the need for special revelation and supernatural grace that its operation overrides or bypasses natural powers in favor of some direct, mystical, inner light. Rather he attempts to hold a fine balance between nature, human nature, even of fallen human nature, and grace, the supernaturally acquired knowledge of God our creator and redeemer through his revelation. But, he is implying, in theological work, human nature, the intellect, the senses, and the will, are all indispensably involved.

Alongside this, Turretin argues in true Calvinian fashion for the twofold knowledge of God, God our creator and God our redeemer. However it must be stressed that there is not for him (any more than for Calvin himself) a one-to-one correspondence between nature and the knowledge of the creator on the one hand, and special grace and the knowledge of the redeemer on the other. To know of the true God the creator, special revelation and divine grace are every bit as much needed as they are in order to know God the redeemer in Christ. Nevertheless, there is some rudimentary and rather inchoate knowledge of God the creator that is possessed by everyone. It is this God, the creator and sustainer, of nature, who is our redeemer in Christ. In such ways grace builds upon nature, it does not destroy it.

In addition to this, and in a rather more formal way than Calvin, Turretin argues for what he calls "natural theology," a term that he does not use only to refer to arguments for God's existence.[23] He uses it interchangeably with "knowledge" as in the phrase "natural theology or [natural] knowledge of God." There are, in fact, two parts to such natural knowledge, one "partly innate (derived from the book of conscience by means of common notions)," the other "partly acquired (drawn from the book of creatures discursively)."[24] The first kind of knowledge is derived from the natural law written upon each person's conscience, which necessarily implies some innate knowledge of God the lawgiver. So the acquired knowledge of God (and the scope of the term "natural theology") is not confined by Turretin to cosmological proofs for the existence of God, for example, but includes those matters referred to in passages of Scripture such as Psalm 19:1, Acts 14:15-17, and Romans 1:19. Obviously enough, such natural knowledge of God cannot be derived from Scripture, and Turretin goes on to claim that it is a matter of universal experience, referring to Cicero as well as to the reports of contemporary explorers,[25] to provide evidence for this universality. "The special knowledge of true faith (by which believers please God and have access to him, of which Paul speaks) does not exclude but supposes [i.e., presupposes] the general knowledge from nature."[26]

It is at such points that the Magisterial Reformers, as well as clearly referring to such biblical data, also draw upon Augustine, especially from his anti-Pelagian work *On Nature and Grace*. In the short chapter 3 (and also chapter 22) Augustine makes a series of distinctions that became very important. The first is between two senses of "nature": nature as unfallen and as fallen. "Man's nature, indeed, was created at first faultless and without any sin; but that nature of man in which every one is born from Adam, now wants the Physician, because it is not sound." Second, he draws a distinction between the good qualities that remain in human nature despite the fall and the evil qualities acquired as a result of the fall. "All good qualities, no doubt, which it still possesses in its make, life, senses, intellect, it has of the Most High God, its Creator and Maker."[27] Here we see a possible antecedent of the later emphases upon natural law and common grace. But we also note that these distinctions are fundamental to the idea that human nature is fallen but not thereby obliterated. It is this nature on which grace builds.

The coming of sin led to loss, since sin is itself a loss, infecting us with defects, disabilities, and infirmities, as Augustine calls them. This is

23. Turretin, *Institutes of Elenctic Theology*, I:7-9
24. Ibid., I:6
25. Ibid., I:7-8
26. Ibid., I:8
27. Augustine, *On Nature and Grace*.

a forceful expression both of Augustine's view of evil as basically privative and also of the organic character of human nature; our fallenness, like a pathogen, infects human nature without immediately annihilating it.

All this is in sharp contrast to the modern theological outlook, both conservative and liberal, which has less and less time for the biblical doctrine of the fall. One characteristic of modern narrative theology is that all too frequently the narrative begins not with the creation and fall but with the Abrahamic covenant, though Vanhoozer's version is a welcome exception to this. Similarly, the biblical account of the Noahic covenant is downplayed. In it the Lord appears to covenant with himself on behalf of mankind, giving the rainbow as a covenant sign that is common both to himself and to the human race, to preserve and regulate nature for the benefit of mankind, notwithstanding his sin. Just as *Torah* excludes natural law, so Abraham displaces Adam and Noah. Disregard for such features may partly be due to perplexity over the doctrine of evolution by natural selection, which tends to shut theologians' mouths at this point. But it is also due to a more widespread departure from the very idea of nature as a theological resource.

According to CRT, then, grace builds upon human nature. Human nature is fallen and perverted, but it remains functioning human nature nonetheless. As we earlier noted from Turretin. "If this were not the case, there could be no science, nor art, nor certainty in the nature of things." Of course, more than nature is needed, but not less.

Part of modern resistance to the idea of natural law, or to the natural knowledge of God, or to the idea that the conscience is natural (besides the weird objection that the use of the term "natural law" belongs exclusively to the Roman Catholic Church), is impatience over the multiple ambiguity of the adjective "natural." As an example, take an apple tree—the apples it bears are natural; they are the product of the processes intrinsic to an apple tree's being an apple tree and not a cherry tree. If someone attaches wax apples to the apple tree, then these are not natural apples, for they are not true apples. But now suppose that the apple tree is diseased and what it produces are scabby, gnarled specimens of apple-hood, hardly edible. These are natural in the sense that they are the true product of the tree, but in another sense they are not natural. The fruit have been contaminated by disease of some kind, and so they are not natural in the (further) sense in which honey without any additives is "natural honey," that is pure, unmodified honey. So there's "natural" in the sense of being natural as opposed to artificial, or conventional, or "introduced," and "natural" in the sense of true and pure as against contaminated or added to. Two other senses of "natural" are relevant here: "natural" in the sense of universal, and in the sense of original—it's natural for the sun to rise, because the sun rises every day, or for apple trees to bear apples; it is natural, in the sense of being part of its original nature for a viper to bite, or for a ferret to run through pipes.

What of the natural knowledge of God, or natural law? How is "natural" being used here? In the thought of people such as Calvin and Turretin, this is "natural" in the sense of being both universal and original; the presence of such law, and its recognition as such by men and women, are part of mankind's primitive endowment. But it's not natural in the sense that its operation in human life is normal or pure; rather it is presently diseased and contaminated by fallen nature. In the case of the operation of the natural law or the natural knowledge of God, the fall has intervened.

As a result of the fall, mankind's supernatural gifts comprising the *imago dei* are vitiated. To be shorn of supernatural gifts entails the disordering of the various natural powers and abilities that remain. The consequence is "total depravity," where the adjective is understood in an extensive rather than an intensive sense. Writing of fallen mankind Calvin says:

> True! he has a mind capable of understanding, though incapable of attaining to heavenly and spiritual wisdom; he has some discernment of what is honourable; he has some sense of the divinity, though he cannot reach the true knowledge of God. But to what does these amount? They certainly do not refute the doctrine of Augustine—a doctrine confirmed by the common suffrages even of the Schoolmen, that after the fall, the free gifts on which salvation depends were withdrawn, and natural gifts corrupted and defiled.[28]

So natural law and the natural knowledge of God show us something else: the "natural" as it was created is not equivalent to the "secular," a set of powers that are at best neutral as between the claims of theism and atheism, or between rival religions and no religion at all. Also the fall does not mean that the contrast between "natural" and "supernatural" is obliterated, but that (in the sense in which we are using it) the "natural" is equivalent to the originally God-given, a created endowment. So that natural law has a supernatural origin, being universally distributed, innate, and so forth, in the senses that I have been trying to set out.

"Natural" also has a sense that testifies to the fact that man's nature is intrinsically religious, intrinsically orientated to the knowledge of God; nature that was ordered in un-fallen mankind, but became perverted (not extinguished) in fallen mankind. What Calvin calls the *sensus divinitatis* is part of the essence of human nature, as is shown by the fact that it remains, albeit in a perverted form, after the fall. An apple tree produces apple leaves

---

28. Calvin, *Institutes*, II.5.19

even though its blossom and fruit-producing powers may have been extinguished by the blight. And similarly with the other aspects of mankind's original powers. The "ordering" of nature is not therefore a religious icing on a secular cake, it is the ordering of a nature which is, for such as Calvin and Turretin, and for CRT more generally, essentially religious.

Some Implications

What follows for theological method from all this? In coming to understand the faith, our minds and our senses are to be used in a quite natural way. Because of this the Christian message is not at all discontinuous from "the natural," even though our natural powers are fallen. We take this for granted, I suspect, and only notice the fact when it is drawn to our attention. Our senses are fallen but not obliterated. Christianity is not Gnosticism, which requires its disciples to be initiated into a special "language of heaven," one that is discontinuous from the natural languages we all speak. Nor does Christianity require special non-natural or supernatural access to the basic factual claims of the faith, even though, because of our fallenness, the enlightening and reviving work of the Spirit is needed to enable us to understand the significance of what we learn, and to apply it to our lives.

The Apostles themselves "saw with their eyes" they "looked upon and touched with their hands," concerning the Word of Life, the life which was "made manifest and [which] we have seen and heard." They saw, they heard, and they touched the incarnate Son of God, and these facts provided John with an argument against Gnosticism. That which their senses informed them of "we proclaim also to you" (1 John 1:1–3). What John and the others had seen and heard formed the basis of his declaration of the gospel and of the fellowship all believers have with the Father and his Son. Earlier we noted that the exercise of senses and intellect provided the Apostle Peter with some reason, a good reason, for thinking that he and the other apostles have not followed "cleverly devised myths . . ." Why? Because "we were eye witnesses of his majesty, for when he received honor and glory from God the Father, and the voice was borne to him in the Majestic Glory, 'This is my beloved Son, with whom I am well pleased,' we ourselves heard this very voice, for we were with him on the holy mountain" (2 Pet 1:16). When Paul met with the risen Christ on the road to Damascus he saw a light from heaven, and heard a voice, and was then deprived of his sight. The men who were with him also heard the voice (Acts 9; cf. John 12:29). Similarly, the Savior said to doubting Thomas, "Put your finger here, and see my hands, and put out your hand, and place it in my side. Do not disbelieve. But believe" (John 21:27). In a similar way Paul drew attention to the physical evidence of Christ's resurrection (1 Cor 15:3–7). Seeing, hearing, touching —these were all involved in learning of Christ, confirming the character of God's revelation, and it seems that the apostles went out of their way to stress the importance of the senses.

What did exercising their senses in such ways tell them? First, that their faith was not a case of private or collective hallucination or delusion. They were not following myths, magical events in which the senses are tricked and deceived. The Savior, being God made flesh, had that sort of objectivity that our senses routinely convey to us. The absence of such objectivity, as with "cleverly devised myths," is something that the senses are also able to detect. We are tricked and puzzled by the cleverness of a magician for some time, but not for all the time. We do not actually believe that the woman has been sawn in half, or that the rabbits were all in the hat. The Savior did not *seem* to be magically "present" on the Mount of Transfiguration; he *was* present—physically, palpably present—for the one transfigured had a physical body, and the glory that surrounded him was visible to the human eye. Even the voice from heaven was not a purely interior voice of the sort we refer to when we talk of, say, the voice of conscience, but "we ourselves heard this very voice," not a sound physically produced by means of human lungs and larynx, but nevertheless a voice identifiable through hearing.

This account of identification by means of the senses is not the whole story, of course, but it is part of the story, and an essential part. Grace builds upon nature. Peter himself goes on to refer to a "more sure" word of prophecy (2 Pet 1:19). The disciples' experience on the holy mountain provided some degree of certainty, God's word, the product of the inspiring activity of the Holy Spirit, afforded a surer ground of belief and hope than what they witnessed, when this is considered merely as a series of events. Peter speaks of these data as if they were on a sliding scale, with the significance of the matters eye-witnessed (considered in isolation) being less sure than the word of prophecy revealed to them, which is, by comparison, like "a lamp shining in a dark place."

There is no other recourse at this point than to recognize the working of learning processes that function successfully prior to meeting Christ (in the case of the disciples) or to reading Scripture (in our case). There must therefore be sources of information that are distinct from and successful prior to Scripture, though operating consistently with what it teaches us about our condition as a fallen race. It is at this point that (for some theologians) the panic seems to set in. By and large CRT has taken the view that any epistemology that—consistently with what Scripture teaches generally about fallen human nature—warrants uses of our senses and intellect, and any account of such a warrant that is not at odds with reliance upon the senses and intellect, will do.

That is, though we may rely proximately on some philosophy, such as Scottish Common Sense Realism, the epistemology of the Stoics, or of Aristotle, or of modern externalism, for the articulating and expressing of the doctrine of epistemological realism presupposed in Scripture, ultimately our reason for endorsing it (apart from its indispensability in life) is that though there is no revealed epistemology, some account is presupposed or implied by Scripture itself, in its testimony to the objectivity of the created order, including human writings, and their success in being able to gather reliable information from such sources.[29]

So for the apostles at least, and for CRT, the apostolic teaching was not words about words about words, but words that identified and described realities that they learned of with their eyes and ears and fingers, a necessary condition for referential success. To be sure, there is more to the revelation of God's mercy and grace in Jesus Christ than this, but there is not less. Grace builds upon nature, it does not ignore it or supplant it. This places the gospel in the realm of objective realities. It not a purely subjective teaching or a scripturalism that has a kind of Platonic, non-sensory character, any more than it is communitarianism and nothing more.

The knowledge of God and of ourselves in which, as John Calvin said, true wisdom chiefly consists, is not a gnostic, secret knowledge, available only to a few initiates. The doctrines of the Christian faith are public, available to anyone who wishes to study them. They are, in that sense, universally accessible. But the use to which God the Holy Spirit may put these doctrines, his intended use, so to speak, is particular. It is God the Spirit who grants the ability to be convinced that these doctrines are true. The overall "message" come to people as they attend to it, and as the Spirit breaks down their resistance, enlightens their minds, and renews their wills, and in these ways convinces them that this is the saving truth of God. "Word and Spirit" is one great watchword of the Reformation. Through the agency of the Christian ministry (considered in its widest sense) the prospect of enjoying such knowledge is made available to as many as it is humanly possible to reach, but the knowledge itself comes to those who, receiving the word of God, are also imbued with this renewing power of the Holy Spirit, and so inwardly convinced of the truth of what they read and hear.

---

29. It might be though that an epistemology such as W. V. O. Quine's "naturalized epistemology," which is intentionally non-theistic, could not be a candidate for a usable epistemology. Perhaps not. But Plantinga's externalism as deployed in *Warranted Christian Belief* and elsewhere, could be. After all, since nature is God's gift, a naturalistic epistemology (*sans* reductionism) would seem to be an eminently fitting option.

Are there not ways of seeking to establish the truth and trustworthiness of Holy Scripture, apart from reliance upon the internal testimony of the Spirit? Surely, it may be said, there are proofs of God's existence that are the work of human reason, and that in turn appeal to natural human reason. And, surely, mankind is naturally religious, imbued with a religious sensibility. And, surely, there are arguments for the reliability of Holy Scripture that are accessible to all. Do these play no part in Christian epistemology? As for the religious sensibility, this is not denied, but the point is made that this sensibility is fallen and so cannot be completely relied on. As for the viability and importance of natural theology, this is one area of Reformed theology in which there have been different views, and a policy of live and let live. There have been different views of the viability of natural theology and its place not only in apologetics but in developing a systematic theology. It is well known that Calvin has little or nothing to say about the proofs in the *Institutes*. Charles Hodge provides a serious discussion of various arguments for God's existence,[30] while Herman Bavinck may at first appear less sanguine:

> The so-called proofs may introduce greater distinctness and lucidity but they are by no means the final grounds on which our certainty regarding God' existence is ultimately based. This certainty is solely determined by faith, that is, the spontaneity with which our consciousness bears witness to the existence of God that urges itself upon us from all directions. The proofs as proofs, are not the grounds but rather the products of faith.[31]

But note that he does not deny value to the proofs, but asserts that they are subordinate to faith and its certainty. And certainly general proofs of the reliability of Holy Scripture have been offered, and some have given them a more prominent place than others. For instance, Calvin places greater emphasis upon the internal testimony of the Holy Spirit than does, for example, B. B. Warfield.[32] But all have been united in the conviction that even if natural theology and proofs of the reliability of Holy Scripture have a place, these do not supplant the "supernatural evidentialism" that we have been sketching.

---

30. Hodge, *Systematic Theology*, I:191f.

31. Bavinck, *Reformed Dogmatics*, II:90; compare II:59: "The arguments for the existence of God may be weak, but in any case they are stronger than those advanced for its denial." For further discussion of the Reformed attitude to natural theology, see Sudduth, *The Reformed Objection to Natural Theology*.

32. For discussion of this issue see Helm, *John Calvin's Ideas*, 278f.

It is important to understand that in the case of such evidentialism the articulation and defense of it has followed the conviction that men and women have had that the Christian gospel is indeed the truth of God. It is not that an epistemology, a theory, has first been devised, and then "supernatural evidentialism" has been defended in the light of it. It has been the other way around. Christian epistemology has been "particularist" rather than "methodist," from the time of the apostles and their immediate disciples, and ever since. Men and women have become convinced of the truth of the gospel, and their lives have been significantly altered.[33] As a result they have come to be convinced that there is knowledge of God and of his disclosure of himself in Christ that is as objective as our everyday knowledge of the external world, our belief that there has been a past, and so forth. But (as it turns out) such knowledge is not knowledge that is available to all in the way that the knowledge that there is a piano in front of me is available to anyone who may enter the room whose faculties are not seriously impaired.

In the Christian church this point was quickly appreciated and reflected on. So Paul distinguishes between the wisdom of this world and the wisdom that is from God, and words taught to us as children and words the Holy Ghost teaches, just as Jesus tells his disciples that they know things that are hidden from others. The doctrine of Christian knowledge, as we might put it, was formulated after the *experience* of such knowledge and the onset of convictions about it. Not theory first, but facts about faith and its impact, and then the theory, or better the doctrine, which expresses and articulates these convictions.

There is another important and obvious difference between the foundations of classical modern Western philosophy, of rationalism and empiricism, and the foundations of what I have called Christian supernaturalism. The foundations of modern epistemology, arising from the Enlightenment, are modest and minimalist, though ambitious claims are made for them. After all, "I have a green sensation" and "I know that I am conscious even when I am in a state of systematic doubt" do not seem to amount to much. By contrast the epistemic foundations of Christian theology embrace both our judgement about the reliability of our own sensory and intellectual capacities, and further, the sixty-six canonical books, or good slices thereof (i.e., those parts that reproduce in written form the central shape, claims, and glories of the Christian gospel).

---

33. For the use of the distinction between "methodism" and "particularism" in epistemology, see Chisholm, *Theory of Knowledge*, chapter 4.

SOME NEW PROPOSALS CONSIDERED

3

Nature and Narrative

In the opening chapters we have reviewed some important structural principles about the intellectual character of CRT, and some basic epistemological principles about the knowledge of God and ourselves. Nothing has so far been said about the application of doctrine to the Christian life and the life of the church, but this will emerge incidentally as part of the remainder of the book. We now turn our attention to some trends in current thinking about doctrine and systematic theology, some of them made, surprisingly enough, by evangelical thinkers in the Reformed tradition. In this chapter we shall begin our examination of Kevin Vanhoozer's use of "theo-drama." Any theo-drama is a narrative, or has the form of a narrative, and it forms part of a contemporary trend of understanding theology in narrative terms. Here God is both the author of the "plot" of the drama and its director.

In the course of this chapter I wish to show what are the theological consequences of a switch to narrative, by looking at the logical structure of a narrative and its bearing on what the narrative means.

Theo-drama

Early in *The Drama of Doctrine* Vanhoozer stresses that "The Christian faith [is] . . . a five act theo-drama in which God's speech and action plays the decisive parts. Many of the climactic scenes—passion, Easter, Pentecost—have already taken place."[1] So by now much of the drama is past, and we wait while its last act takes place. As is frequently said, we live "between the times." A related point is that the normative account of that drama, of the elements of it that have already taken place, have a fixed form given to them

---

1. Vanhoozer, *The Drama of Doctrine*, 57.

in the canonical accounts of doctrine and of theology, accounts that will occupy us a good deal in what follows.

Towards the end of the book, writing of the character of creeds and confessions, two sections are headed, "Masterpiece Theater: Creedal Theology" and "Regional Theater: Confessional Theology,"[2] which strongly suggest that creeds and confessions themselves have (or have had) a dramatic character, being instances of "theater." But anyone hoping that the author will expand on that theme will be disappointed. Creeds are summarizings of the biblical witness and the preaching and teaching of the universal church.[3]

The critique of CRT implied here emphasizes that it is defective in being a de-dramatization of Scripture. Vanhoozer suggests that Scripture presents an account of God's mighty acts that is a drama in the fullest, most theatrical sense. But the chief actors in this drama don't learn their lines, or try on costumes, or apply face-paint, or rehearse a part which is not a portrayal of their true selves. The apostles and the Gospel of Mark, for example, teach that God is the director of the whole, but that cannot easily be gleaned from the main action, so to speak. The agony and the ecstasy is unrehearsed and "real-time," the tears and the wounds are real tears and wounds, and so on. So, not a drama in the strict sense, but undoubtedly one having real-life drama as an ingredient. So there are some analogies between theater and theo-drama, but some serious dis-analogies as well.

This needs to be borne in mind when later on, we shall consider Vanhoozer's view that Scripture is "de-dramatized" by theologians of the likes of Thomas Aquinas and Charles Hodge. For it may be that judged by the character of the original actions, Vanhoozer's call for their true dramatic character to be restored is in fact a bid for the opposite—for their "re-dramatization," in the full theatrical sense. This has an important bearing on the wisdom of his stress on our "participation" in the drama—situated as we are long after the first four acts are completed, and occupying as we do part of a long intermission before the fifth and final act in which, willy-nilly, we shall all have parts, but not be play-acting.

The problem is that Vanhoozer is faced with a dilemma of exposition. If Scripture has canonical force then as he sees it theology is a play with canonical participants. But if the "drama" encompasses extra-canonical readers and recipients, then what is their role? How does their participation relate to that of the main players? In other words Vanhoozer's theo-dramatical language encompasses both what takes place on the stage and

---

2. Ibid., 449, 451.
3. Ibid., 449.

those "participants" who, on our understanding of theatre in the literal sense, form the audience.

A Critical Turn

Vanhoozer distinguishes between Performance I and Performance II. The first is what he calls faithful performance,[4] which endeavors to respect the authorial intent of the script, and to replicate the author's illocutionary intent, that is, the *force* that he intends arising from the words that he uses. Performance I is acknowledging this intent and responding appropriately. Performance II by contrast "is not interested in finding out what the authors did with their words."[5] Vanhoozer explains that theo-drama ought to carry out the intent of the author, and not simply use the author's words as a springboard.[6] This is obviously an important distinction in which Vanhoozer seeks to respect the canonical authority of Scripture.

Performance is thus center-stage. Yet granted the importance of Performance I, even more important than this is his understanding of another relation between the Christian's (or church's) performance and the theo-drama, what Vanhoozer says about performance itself. So a crucial question is, is what the book deals with *the drama that is Christian doctrine*, or *the drama that Christian doctrine presents in a de-dramatized form, though in a form that contains a narrative*? Trying to get clear on this question will occupy us a good deal in the coming chapters.

There are literally dozens of occasions in which Vanhoozer refers our to participation in the drama. Here are some: "doctrine poses a spiritual challenge, a challenge to become a Christian and to perform one's faith" (93); it enables us to participate in the drama competently (80, 102); "Scripture . . . calls for appropriation on the part of the believing community—in a word, *performance*" (101); "Scripture aims to draw people into the action" (101); doctrine is "direction for fitting participation in the drama of redemption" (102); "the church is indeed an embodiment, enactment and performance of the biblical text" (170); "performing theo-drama" (180); "one is either in God's play or in a drama of one's own making" (183); "the church's fitting participation in the drama of redemption as transmitted by canonical practices" (239); "to participate faithfully in the drama of redemption" (240); "the theologian as an advocate both of the script and of the performing

---

4. Ibid., 180.
5. Ibid.
6. Ibid., 180f.

company" (247); "rightly to get i*nvolved* in the action, to speak, think and live out the theo-drama" (307); and so on.

It seems from this that intrinsic to Vanhoozer's understanding is overlapping continuity between the theo-drama portrayed in Scripture and the Christian's and the church's participation in that drama. Sometimes he uses language that conflates redemption and its accomplishment with the enjoyment of redemption and its benefits, its application. There is redemption in its "archetypal" form and an "ectypal" understanding and response to it, and I shall try to show that in his continual use of the language of "participation" for each Vanhoozer slurs accomplishment and application. I shall then argue that this stress on participation is not persuasive, not required, since the arguments that Vanhoozer presents, especially the philosophical ones, on language, foundationalism, and so on are not sufficiently strong to make the theo-dramatic language a compelling or an attractive option, even without its intrinsic difficulties. It cannot be other than a metaphor, which some might find helpful and others not. It does not have any compelling force, and some drawbacks.

We need to bear in mind that participation comes in a variety of strengths. For example, in a democratic society, voters, Members of Parliament, the Civil Service, street-protestors, ministers of the government, journalists, all "participate" in the political process. But the strength of that participation ascends from the humble voter through to the (sometimes) not-so-humble member of the ruling elite. In a theatrical production the audience, the director and producer, the designers and technicians, the cast, the audience, reviewers in the press, all participate in the drama. But obviously the cast participate by enacting the play, the audience participate by watching and enjoying it, or by protesting against it.

Sometimes it is not clear whether the narrative is to be structured in terms of the interaction of characters referred to in the third person, or whether one (or more) of them refers to the narrator who is himself the director, and may also be a participant in the narrative or drama. But such niceties need not trouble us here. We shall be concerned with the basic logical, metaphysical, and epistemological character of this general outlook and so we shall focus upon the theo-dramatic *approach*.

Narrative Theology

The term "narrative theology" in its modern usage arose some years ago through the work of Hans Frei. But here I shall use it as an umbrella term to cover otherwise disparate proposals and procedures, for example, the biblical theology approach stemming from the pioneering work of Geerhardus Vos, and the "theo-dramatic" proposals of Kevin Vanhoozer, and of Michael Horton, as well as aspects of the theology of N. T. Wright, who occasionally refers to Christian theology as having a theo-dramatic character.[7] John R. Franke also favors a narrative approach, though that fact does not figure centrally in his account of the character of theology.[8]

Vanhoozer sees his idea of theo-drama as a development of narrative theology combining narrative and speech act elements.[9] "While it is true that much of the Bible is written in the form of a story, narratives and dramas represent stories differently. Narratives require narrators and recount their tales in the first or third person. Dramas, by contrast, *show* rather than tell."[10] They unfold in the real time of the performance. Intrinsic to this approach is the idea of a theology that records temporal sequences in which God acts and human beings respond, and a commentary to this interaction. We are not provided with a description of a participant's character in so many words, instead the drama manifests that character in action, "showing" rather than describing it. Such an approach is said to be more biblical because it keeps the style of the historical sequences that the Bible itself recounts, and so provides the opportunity of developing a theology that is not affected, or not so much affected, by the categories of systematic theology of the CRT, which are alleged to be "timeless," abstract, and purely cerebral.

So this "dynamic" or "theo-dramatic" approach to the understanding of Christian doctrine is motivated by a strong desire to move away from the allegedly "static" categories of traditional systematic theology. But I shall argue that such a separation of the two is doomed to inconsistency, and that a "theo-dramatic" approach to doctrine, if the result is to be remotely intelligible as Christian doctrine, must invariably borrow from these de-dramatized and allegedly "timeless" theological statements that it is bent on supplanting. It must live off the systematic theological and dogmatic heritage of the church even as it seeks to take its place. Narrators wish to break the mold of traditional systematic theology but find themselves unable to do so consistently because, despite themselves, the narratives need to borrow the results of the older systematic theology, and expressed in its language—in presupposing the Trinity, or the doctrine of creation, for example. Further, I shall argue that the language of narrative is necessarily set within a non-narratival theological framework and so the narrative can

---

7. Wright, *The Last Word*, 121.
8. Franke, *The Character of Theology*, 175–78.
9. Vanhoozer, *The Drama of Doctrine*, 49, fn 48.
10. Ibid., 48.

only be a subordinate part of the overall theological picture that the canon of Scripture has bequeathed to us.

This is not to say that the indispensable presence of systematic theological categories eliminates the narrative and dramatic aspects of Scripture. As we saw in our brief allusion to covenant theology, that theology successfully combines both ways of thinking. Each has their place, their indispensable place. The claim is not, then, that narrative is unimportant. Obviously not. Narrative has a vital role. Narratives convey knowledge of the events that are at the heart of the Christian faith, the mighty acts of God.[11] Much of the Bible is in the form of histories and stories, and so on. But the question is, can Christian doctrine itself take on a dominantly narrative form, or are the narratives of Scripture to be understood within a wider, non-narrative framework that Christian theology is concerned to understand?

Narrative Sequences

As we have stressed, and as is obvious, Christian systematic theology depends upon the accounts given of Scripture by exegetical theologians, and so it inevitably has to do justice to temporal sequences, to the entire unfolding of redemption. It has also to do with sequences within the grand sequence of God's redemptive acts, such as the call of Abraham, the exodus, the exile, the ministry of Jesus, the nature of Christian conversion, and of the stages of the Christian life. But it does not treat these sequences simply or chiefly *as* sequences, as theatrical performances to be performed time and again, but as attempts to integrate their permanent, abiding features with other aspects of God's revelation that are not temporally sequential, aspects that have to do (in the older language that makes some people shudder) with essences and natures, such as the existence and nature of Almighty God, Father, Son, and Holy Spirit; and with human nature: pre-lapsarian, lapsed, redeemed, and glorified; with the nature of faith, and the nature of sin, and so on.

Geerhardus Vos

Geerhardus Vos, an early influential proponent of biblical theology, seems to have been fully at ease with the validity of the distinction between systematic theology and biblical theology, and with the legitimacy of each. (He

---

11. For an interesting discussion of the epistemology of narrative see the discussion of Eleonore Stump, "The Problem of Evil: Analytic Philosophy and Narrative."

was himself the author of a multi-volume systematic theology in Dutch.) His view of the relation between the two is worth noting.

> There is no difference in that one would be more closely bound to the Scriptures than the other. In this they are wholly alike. Nor does the difference lie in this, that the one transforms the Biblical material, whereas the other would leave it unmodified. Both equally make the truth deposited in the Bible undergo a transformation: but the difference arises from the fact that the principles by which the transformation is effected differ. In Biblical Theology the principle is one of historical, in Systematic Theology it is one of logical construction. Biblical Theology draws a *line* of development. Systematic Theology draws a *circle*.[12]

The problem for purely narrative or theo-dramatic theology, when it is adopted as *the* theological style of the Christian church, is that lines and circles can't be integrated. Those who seek to supplant the one with the other face an insoluble problem. They overlook the following fundamental point: that logical and metaphysical distinctions that it are necessary to make in articulating the doctrine of the church do not necessarily correspond with temporal sequences, and that temporal sequences may have non-temporal aspects, or gain their intelligibility and their importance from what is non-temporal. To make any sense, the line must be enclosed by the circle.

Those who readily talk of systematic *or* biblical theology do not remind us that in making the comparison there is necessarily an equivocation of the term "theology." It is not as if there is a genus, theology, with two species, biblical and systematic theology, and perhaps more. Biblical or narrative theology is developmental, and ideas are deployed in a given sequence.

To take an example from Vos's *Biblical Theology*, he provides a succession of discussions of the developing revelation of God in the Old Testament. So he notes that God's name is the chief character of the divine self-revelation in the Mosaic period, the various names of God having various titles and connotations.[13] In the patriarchal period the most characteristic form of revelation is through the "Angel of Jehovah" and in the characteristic name of "El-Shaddai."[14] In the Mosaic period emphasis was placed on the "face" and presence of God,[15] who displayed his power and grace in the exodus.[16]

---

12. Vos, *Biblical Theology*, 15–16.
13. Ibid., 64, 115.
14. Ibid., 72–73, 81.
15. Ibid., 108.
16. Ibid., 112–13.

An aspect of the character God only partly brought out to the patriarchs is his holiness, which is more fully disclosed by the prophets, for example, in Isaiah 6.[17] Not only the infinite majesty of God, but also the need to surrender to his divine glory, is characteristic of the ministry of the prophets. And so on. These successive descriptions are no doubt complementary, but the fact that this complexity is revealed step by step means that in the Old Testament we have a succession of temporally indexed theologies, each of which is partial by comparison with the fully integrated account of God and his ways that systematic theology aims to display. So the biblical theologian is talking about theology in a different sense, and with a different focus, than is the systematic theologian. For the biblical theologian it is perfectly appropriate to refer to *theologies* in the plural. To change Vos's figure a little, biblical theologies form a line that steadily thickens, providing a trajectory displayed in an ever-thickening line or a wedge.[18]

Even when Jesus says that he who has seen him has seen the Father, this cannot be understood in an unqualified sense, since the persons of each are distinct and the Father is never said to be incarnate. The significant epistemological point is often buried in a conflation between the *identity* of God and the *identifying* of God. In Christian theism, God may reveal himself by contingent matters of fact that are expressive of his nature, but that are made at his discretion. The phenomena tell us something about what God is like, and provide identification of God, and so begin to convey his identity, what he is essentially. And if theology is exclusively narrative in form, then the series of God's revealings, however long, never move from successive identifications of God to a full account of who God is, his identity.

---

17. Ibid., 150.

18. There is reason to think that at one stage at least Vos experienced a tension between his idea of biblical theology being *revelational*, and it being *covenantal* in character. Writing to Herman Bavinck he states, "I have reflected long on the question of how to deal with the subject, so that justice will be done to both the theoretical and practical character of revelation, while at the same time deducing the principle of how to deal with the subject from the Scriptures. I have come to the conclusion that the covenant idea fulfills the requirements the best of all and so I think I will start with that. At the same time I remain grounded on Reformed theology. When Dr Kuyper says that Coccieus, by bringing the covenant idea itself into prominence, already inflicted losses on the claims of Reformed principles, I cannot go along with that view" (Vos to Bavinck, July 3, 1893. In *The Letters of Geerhardus Vos*, 175–76). He also states, "It was not my intention to take the covenant idea as a guiding principle in Biblical Theology to the exclusion of Revelation. But beneath that I place the covenant concept, because God has revealed himself in the covenant" (Vos to Bavinck, Nov. 21, 1893. In ibid., 80).

Logical and Temporal Distinctions

We need not only narrative sequences but also logical distinctions. Here's an example from CRT. The *ordo salutis* as it is expressed, for example, in Romans 8 is in the form of a sequence, one sequence that occurs innumerable times within the grand narrative of redemption, in the conversion of Zacchaeus, the conversion of Paul, and so on. But the concepts introduced into our understanding of that sequence, and the distinctions within them, as it has been developed on the warrant of Romans 8, the differences between conviction of sin, penitence, regeneration, faith, assured faith, the external call, effectual calling, justification, and sanctification, etc., are first and foremost logical distinctions. But do they not all also record temporal distinctions as well?

In some cases they do, and in other cases they don't. Is justification an event? And is sanctification another event, coupled to the carriage of justification and pulled along by it? Is the carriage of justification in turn pulled along by the carriage of faith? Where does adoption fit in? Have they to be squeezed in somewhere between regeneration and faith? Or between faith and justification? Or is adoption simply another description of one or more of these elements? And what about union with Christ: is this also part of the temporal sequence of separately identifiable occurrences? If so, can we find a gap for it, a spare carriage for it to occupy? Or is it an umbrella term, with justification, sanctification, etc., as aspects of it? Logical and chronological sequences do not necessarily coincide.

Systematic theology in the propositionalist sense habitually has its eye on distinctions and discriminations in an effort to carefully appraise the implications of the assertions of Scripture that bear upon a given topic, and to link one area of biblical revelation consistently with all the others, making discriminations and connections in order to do so, so as to integrate the whole in one consistent and interconnected framework. Hence Vos's figure of a circle. Some of these distinctions are temporal, one thing following in time after another, some are not only temporal but causal, one thing both preceding and bringing about the other, while others are purely logical, one thing being distinct from another in thought but inseparable from that other in fact. Some are in time, some are apart from time. But biblical theology in the Vosian sense, and narrative theology more generally, has its eye simply on the temporal unfolding of the one redemptive-historical sequence. It is a line.

Effectual Calling

Distinctions between merely logical and temporal and causal sequences are inherent in Christian systematic theology, and though we may be inclined to dismiss such distinctions as "academic," they are vital for the business of clearly articulating the place and value of the concepts that enter into theological accounts. If for the moment we remain in the area of the *ordo salutis*, we need to be able to think clearly about what goes on, and the significance of what goes on, when men and women are called by grace.

But the goings-on may be distorted through an over concentration on divine human interaction, understood as a participation in a personal conversation. Here's an illustration of this tendency. In his later work *Remythologizing Theology*, Vanhoozer develops the findings of *The Drama of Doctrine* in a more theological way, in terms of his fundamental idea of God as an essentially communicative agent, who communicates and interacts with his creatures in ways that are personal. He illustrates this by showing how this works out in the case of the characteristically Reformed doctrine of effectual calling.

Vanhoozer's project at this point is to replace theologies of causal agency with a theology of divine convincing presence, a matter of God's and humankind's interpersonal interaction.[19] To replace generalities about causation with specifics about divine personal action was Karl Barth's "stroke of genius" and Vanhoozer willingly takes his cue from it.[20] In this he follows the "personalist" turn in modern theology, which he outlines and critically assesses in Part II of *Remythologizing Theology*. God's call of people by grace serves Vanhoozer's expository and exploratory purposes well, for it is a clear case of God speaking and acting. He takes as one example of such acting the opening of the heart of Lydia of Thyatira (Acts 16:14).

He is unconvinced by Calvin's (and, more generally, by the Reformed tradition's) view that in effectual calling it is the Spirit that causes the preached word to dwell in human hearts. "And lest the flesh should glory, in at least responding to him, when he calls and spontaneously offers himself, he affirms that there would be no ears to hear, no eyes to see, did not he give them."[21] Rather, he thinks that God's relation with Lydia has to be understood as an exclusively person-to-person relation. That is, it has to involve both divine and human persons at the level of conscious belief and intention, and responding, *and only at that level*. At any deeper level, personal relations

---

19. Vanhoozer, *Remythologizing Theology*, 367–68.
20. Ibid., 370.
21. *Calvin, Institutes*, III.24.2.

degenerate into the impersonal. "Is the grace that changes human hearts thus a matter of energy or information? It is both."[22] What kind of energy? The effectual call is a divine speech act that has both illocutionary and perlocutionary force.[23] It has both *force* and *effect*. It is the Spirit's energy, a kind of personal magnetism, presumably, which imparts force to speech acts. But Calvin and the Reformed tradition extend that energy to the "opening of the heart," which then ensures an appreciation of the force of the apostolic language. Vanhoozer cannot go as far as this. Like Augustine and Calvin, he recognizes this calling to be effectual, that is, it successfully brings about the divinely intended changes, because of the self-communicative power of the Triune God. "The effectual call is a sovereign summons to participate in the light and life of the triune God."[24] So the effectual call represents a distinct communicative causality, "one that moreover lies at the core of the theo-dramatic action, where infinite and finite freedom meet."[25] So it is causal, as Calvin makes clear, but not mechanically causal, which is the only other alternative that Vanhoozer envisages. For Calvin the Spirit has the power to bring it about that the speech of God is received *both* with its intended significance, *and* appropriately responded to. So the theological alternatives (for Vanhoozer, as far as providence is concerned) are: a response that is free and willing, or one that is brought about coercively or mechanically. Naturally, faced with such a choice, Vanhoozer opts for freedom and willingness.

So far, he may be wise to do so. Who can deny that a free and willing response may be part of the effectual call? But if a free and willing response is the whole story, then why do some receive the perlocutionary force of the story of Jesus and others not? Here I do not wish to go where Vanhoozer himself does not venture. That apart, what he has given us may be part of the effectual call, but can it be the whole of it? For on the Vanhoozerian interpretation Luke's account is back to front. According to re-mythologized theology Luke's account should have read that Lydia "attended to things spoken of by Paul, and so the Lord opened her heart." But Luke in fact says "whose heart the Lord opened, that she attended to the things . . ." This looks to mean: being opened by the Lord, her heart then attended to the apostolic message about Jesus the Savior. Not so much a free response as a freed response.

Whatever the phenomenology of conversion, it is essential to the Augustinian and Reformed view of divine grace that in regeneration the soul is

22. Vanhoozer, *Remythologizing Theology,* 373.
23. This terminology will be explained in greater detail later on.
24. Ibid.
25. Ibid.

passive. This is because the soul is spiritually dead until it receives new life from God, regeneration. So there has to be a way of thinking about this in which the choices are more than "either communicative or manipulative."[26] At least, the communication must include the granting of new life. However described, there is a moment in which the soul, being helpless to produce its own life, is acted upon, and as a result comes to life. As Calvin puts it elsewhere, "there is a special call which, for the most part, God bestows on believers only, when by the internal illumination of the Spirit he causes the word preached to take deep root in their hearts."[27] And as the *Westminster Confession* expresses it:

> This effectual call is of God's free and special grace alone, not from any thing at all foreseen in man, *who is altogether passive therein*, until, being quickened and renewed by the Holy Spirit, he is thereby enabled to answer this call, and to embrace the grace offered and conveyed to it.[28]

This suggests that the grid of Vanhoozer's theo-dramatic, communicatively active, remythologized theology is not sufficiently fine and discriminating. Sir Arthur Eddington famously quipped "What my net cannot catch isn't fish," and that's what is seriously adrift with Vanhoozer's new proposal. His net misses important fish. The data of Scripture regarding the effectual call include not only narratives such as that of Lydia's conversion, but also a commentary on it, such assertions as that the Lord will give a new heart to people who are dead in trespasses and in sins, shining in hearts to give them the light of the knowledge of God in the face of Jesus Christ, sprinkling them with clean water, opening their eyes—expressions which strongly imply a divine agency unilaterally granting the ability to receive the true force of apostolic verbal communications.

These expressions are not mere metaphors, or biblical raw data in need of manipulation by the theological modeler, but they are already theologically-loaded, carrying unavoidable theological implications. Besides, the dichotomy: "either personal and so not manipulable" or "coercive and so not personal," looks like a failure in imagination. The slapping of a newborn baby ensuring a first sharp intake of breath: is that a personal or a mechanical action? Dragging a person from the freezing lake and giving him the kiss of life. Personal or mechanistic? Considered narrowly, no doubt mechanical, but if we think in terms of the true interests of the recipient of

---

26. Ibid., 494.
27. Calvin, *Institutes*, III.24.8.
28. *Westminster Confession of Faith* X.II, emphasis added.

the action, then personal. We may think of some other cases of conversion besides Lydia's. Was Saul's conversion "free and voluntary"? Being thrown to the floor and blinded by light seems coercive. And we must also bear in mind some of the complications and nuances over the words "free" and "voluntary."[29]

These data are missed because Vanhoozer's net is of a shape and size only to pick up instances of causation that are to be found in consciously interpersonal dialogue, and so monergic data slip through it and so cannot be regarded as relevant data for formulating a biblical doctrine of the effectual call. To refer to an intellectual procedure that I think that Vanhoozer does not much like when used as a theological tool, his new proposal is based upon an incomplete *induction* of the biblical data relevant for outlining an effectual call by grace.

A systematic theological understanding of conversion integrates the various elements disclosed in Scripture that we have noted, both the personal and the "impersonal," the conscious and the unconscious, the merely logically separable and the temporally separable. These accounts will include, of course, reports of conversion, such as those of Lydia and of Saul, which are part of its narrative. But these various data are to be combined together with the teaching of other areas of revelation. For example, about the effect of sin in the darkening and deadening of the human mind and will, and the work of the Holy Spirit in applying the fruits of Christ's redemption. Or perhaps it is more accurate to say that the systematic theologian must make the various discriminations of the elements within effectual calling with an eye that is fixed at the same time on the biblical teaching on, for example, the work of the Holy Spirit.

One clear moral of this is that one cannot formulate an adequate doctrine of conversion simply by studying conversions in their respective narrative settings. The differences between the narrated cases are fascinating and important, but they are accidental as far as understanding the nature of regeneration itself is concerned.

How, then, is a theology of conversion to be established? The answer is, by taking the biblical narratives of (real or apparent) conversion as one datum, the biblical teaching on human sin as another datum, its teaching on the work of the Holy Spirit as another, and so on. To be sure, aspects of each of these data are revealed in narratives, but as often as not they are disclosed as non-narratival teaching—expressed say, in the teaching of Christ (about the new birth, say, and the seed and the sower) and Paul (about slavery to sin and divine illumination)—which, though that teaching was given

---

29. Vanhoozer, *Remythologizing Theology*, 373, fn. 104

at particular times, and so forms part of its own narrative sequence—the ministry of Jesus and the apostolic career of Paul—it applies to all times. The original setting has a rationale and contains details that are unique to it, but the teaching itself can be carefully lifted out of that setting, combined with other data, and "reissued" in new settings. But how are these various data to be brought together? That's work for the systematic theologian, a work that a purely narrative approach must miss because it does not possess the necessary categories to handle all the relevant biblical information and put it in a form that ensures that it can be applied to new situations.

Further Issues: The Doctrine of God

If the Bible is to be thought of as one overarching drama, an account of God's dealings in "redemptive-historical" terms, and nothing more than that, where can a doctrine of God, delineating his nature and purposes, itself come from? Who is the God who deals with us, who in succeeding eras communicates his redemptive grace? As a matter of logic, an answer to these questions for the consistent narrative theologian can only arise as the result of a generalization from all the actions of "God" or "the Lord" that it is possible to identify in the narrative. Attempting to answer these questions requires us first to attend to something that has until now has only been in the background of our discussion: the logic of narrative sequence.

From

> God (i.e., some agent in the sequence who is referred to by this or a similar title and by personal pronouns) brings about A and then B, followed by C, and all these are faithful (or righteous, or loving, or wise) actions.

It cannot follow that

> Necessarily, this God (the true and living God) is faithful (or righteous, or loving, or wise).

The inference fails because "God has in fact been faithful" is understood in a similar way to the way that you and I may have been faithful. From the fact that I have been faithful on a number of occasions it does not follow that I will be faithful on the next occasion, and similarly with God himself, understood narratively. But if the term "God," as occurring in the narrative, refers to an agent who is more than he does, and that "more" concerns his nature or essence, what he essentially is, and with the fact that what he does is necessarily an expression of that essence, then God's righteousness cannot be *equivalent to* or *exhausted by* any sequence of actions recorded in Scripture or elsewhere, to his covenant faithfulness, for example, though covenant faithfulness follows from it. If God is not essentially faithful, or if we do not know that he is, then God might swear an oath, and he might confirm this with another oath. But what is this worth? And what about next time?

It is frustrating that Vanhoozer, for example, partly sees this, but cannot go all the way. In *Remythologizing Theology* he argues against what he calls the "new relational ontology," claiming that God is more than sets of relationships. He does not consist of relationships all the way down, as he expresses it.[30] He rightly makes the point that for there to be relationships there must be *relata*, subjects in relation. So God must be a *relatum*, a subject. So what is the nature of the divine subject? It's a pity that he does not thoroughly follow up such a question. His answer is simply that "theology begins with and is governed by God's speaking and acting." This is but a hairsbreadth from saying that God is nothing other than his speaking and acting, that he *is* a "bundle" of actions.[31] God asserts what his nature is, but the presence of such assertions in Scripture need not be, and sometimes are not, an intrinsic part of any narrative.

Theo-dramatic Difficulties

I wish now to make clear some of the difficulties that lie in the way of the theo-dramatic project as they arise concretely in Vanhoozer's earlier book, *The Drama of Doctrine*, as well as in his later *Remythologizing Theology*. He himself sees strong continuity from the dramatic analogy to the concept of God developed in the later book, that of God understood as "being-in-act."[32]

The Drama of Doctrine is self-evidently a modern work, not of course by being an immediate product of the Enlightenment, but one which is nevertheless conducted in the spirit of the Enlightenment. For it does not seek to build on the past, but to propose a novel approach to the theological task. Vanhoozer makes space for developing his own proposals—clears the stage, so to say—by distancing his ideas from those of "cognitivists" (in the shape of the likes of Charles Hodge) and "expressivists" (for example, George Lindbeck).[33] He tell us that he sits somewhere in the middle, borrowing

---

30. Vanhoozer, *Remythologizing Theology*, 143.
31. Ibid., 217.
32. Ibid. Chapter 4 is entitled "God's being is in communicating."
33. Vanhoozer, *The Drama of Doctrine*, 88–89. Vanhoozer is referring to George Lindbeck, *The Nature of Doctrine*.

from each. From Hodge he takes the emphasis that doctrine is somewhat cognitive, having propositional content, while from Lindbeck he borrows the idea of a performance, not as an interpretation of something prior to the performance, but as that which itself creates meaning. But Lindbeck, with his emphasis upon community, tends to think of theology in cultural and anthropological terms, and tends to non-realism.[34] It is to avoid these tendencies Vanhoozer appropriates theological cognitivism from Charles Hodge, but at the same time rejects Hodge's view (as he sees it) that propositions are the exclusive bearers of knowledge.[35]

The idea of such a division, or polarity, between expressivism and cognitivism is itself a recent phenomenon, to be dated no earlier than from the various reactions to the logical positivism of the mid-twentieth century. Hodge is the farthest Vanhoozer goes back in appropriating views for this reworking of the idea of Christian doctrine. Hodge is placed (rather anachronistically) at one extreme of this much more recent polarity in a way that would have utterly bemused the Princeton theologian.

It is true that Vanhoozer does not altogether reject the creeds and confessions of the church. He may even claim that in terms of his own outlook he gives them pride of place, but only because he treats them as dramatic forms. The creeds, and creedal theology, he says, are instances of "masterpiece theatre." The history of dogma is the history of "great performances," and in a similar way, confessional theology is "regional theatre."[36] But this will hardly do, and certainly not from a theologian who is sensitive to genre. What is remotely theatrical about the Nicene Creed, or the *Westminster Confession of Faith*?[37] Vanhoozer is closer to the truth when he asserts, quoting from Philip Turner, that a creed "is a guide to correct reading of Scripture and an adequate expression of belief and identity."[38] But then, Turner's language is that of "propositionalism," of propositional belief and of the permanent theological deposit of the church's faith. But he cannot have things both ways. Either this deposit is of permanent theological importance, or confessions and creeds are simply the record of past theo-dramatic performances, as transitory as are our present performances.

So in taking up this novel stance, by developing the idea of theo-drama as a mid position between the extremes of cognitivism and expressivism

---

34. See for example, Vanhoozer, *The Drama of Doctrine*, 171–75.

35. Ibid., 83f.

36. Ibid., 445f.

37. Though creeds may have dramatic effect when set to music, as (for example) Bach's B Minor Mass testifies.

38. Vanhoozer, *The Drama of Doctrine*, 449.

(though borrowing from each) Vanhoozer does not offer any consistent advice as to what we are now to make of the creedal and confessional documents of Christian theology. We may press the point: where do the great doctrinal works of Christian genius stand? What of Athanasius's *On the Incarnation of the Word*, or Augustine's *De Trinitate*, or Anselm's *Cur Deus Homo?* or the *Summae* of Thomas Aquinas, or Luther's *Bondage of the Will*, or Calvin's *Institutes*, or Edwards's *Religious Affections*? Are these works to be dismissed with the wave of the hand, or treated as curiosities from the past? Vanhoozer never seriously takes up such an issue. For he does not see himself as standing on the shoulders of giants, but instead as being a participant in the latest theo-dramatic performances. Apart from the appeal to Scripture itself, the past does not exert much, if any, authority over his present. For the past is simply the history of past performances. This too, is indicative of the modernist temper of *The Drama of Doctrine*.

However, none of these considerations, interesting and disturbing though they are, take us to the heart of the matter. The central difficulty is the failure to answer the question: how does one actually get to doctrine (the book is offered, it must be remembered, as a novel approach to Christian *doctrine*) from theo-drama? It would have been a help to his readers if he had offered some case studies. It is frustrating too that the reader is given no inkling as to how theo-dramatic doctrines *look*. The question can be asked of *The Drama of Doctrine* in different ways.

For example, take Vanhoozer's first references to God in the work. Among the opening sentences of the work are these: "The human discourse in the Bible is so caught up in God's triune communicative action that it participates in what we may call the economy of the gospel, mediating both revelation and redemption."[39] "Theology would know nothing of God if God had not taken the initiative to 'unveil' himself and raise the curtain on the theo-drama."[40]

These are, of course, second-order sentences—sentences about certain theological sentences. Among these sentences are:

(a) God's Triune communicative action participates in the economy of the gospel, and

(b) God takes the initiative to "unveil" himself.

These are two statements about God that look to be of a permanently true theological kind. God is Triune; apart from the drama he is Triune. God reveals himself in and through the drama on his own initiative. How do we know this? How are we to understand these statements? What warrants

39. Ibid., 35.
40. Ibid., 38.

them? How do we know that they are true, or at least that it is reasonable to believe them? One answer might be, "we know who God is by what he does, by studying the theo-drama in which he acts communicatively." So are such statements simply a summation drawn from the project of *The Drama of Doctrine*? But we have already seen that such an answer is not very satisfactory.

We must not lose sight of how radical Vanhoozer's basic thesis is. The book is not an argument for the conclusion that the idea of theo-drama is a *picture* or *analogy* or *model* or *illustration* of the nature of doctrine, one helpful way of thinking about it. The proposal has to do with the very character of Christian theology, what it essentially is (though Vanhoozer may not be attracted to such essentialist language), and with showing how cognitivism and expressivism are, in turn, serious theological deformations. To suppose something weaker, that drama is an apt *illustration* of Christian doctrine, would merely be to propose a new addition to a list of such illustrations that can be found in the history of doctrine: Christian doctrine as medicine, the medicine of the soul; as armor to enable us to fight the good fight of faith; as food, to fortify the spirit; and so on. To which we might add: as a drama, to fire the imagination and to energize the will. One pretty good reason for thinking that Vanhoozer is not intent only on providing an extended theological illustration is that he has followed *The Drama of Doctrine* with *Remythologizing Theology*, which sets forth how a theo-dramatic theology should *look*.

However, when later on Vanhoozer wishes to speak of God as a personal being who stands over and apart from the "storied practices" that comprise the believing community,[41] the theo-dramatic proposal begins to unravel. Because if God is a communicative agent, then we need to ask, "Who is God?" "What is he like?" "What does he say?" From time to time in *The Drama of Doctrine* Vanhoozer makes what appear to be timeless propositional statements about God. For example, he states that God is not a being who can be encompassed by space and time.[42] But how could he know this? Which theo-dramatic actions tell us that? Can he, by reference to other acts and scenes of the theo-drama, tell us anything more about God? It is possible that he does not intend these as statements about God in himself, but simply as the language in which we "model" God. But if so, then at this point the pendulum is swinging back in the direction of George Lindbeck's *The Nature of Doctrine*.

---

41. Ibid., 99f.
42. Ibid., 100.

The book is written as if the author and the reader already know who God is, what his nature is, and so on. But of course, taken on its own terms—that Christian doctrine is (essentially) theo-dramatic—we *do not* and *cannot* know who God is before the drama begins. Further, there is no place for systematic theology as in CRT, based upon the permanently true propositions of special revelation, to inform us about the nature and perfections of God. In order to claim to know who God is before we know to interpret Scripture in theo-dramatic fashion, anticipating that theo-drama for ourselves, we must be in possession of a concept of God. If the doctrine of God is gained solely from studying the drama, then such a God will himself be nothing other than a player in the drama, albeit one with the leading role. His "nature" will consist of a "bundle" of properties, the awareness of which is the result of our induction of the unfolding role that he plays in the drama. The result will inevitably be a highly anthropomorphic deity. More on this in the next chapter.

At one point in the book, in a footnote, Vanhoozer alludes to the presence of "creedal" language within Scripture, that is, within the drama. But he fails to see what explosive consequences such a recognition has for his proposal. For the footnote makes clear that it is impossible to be faithful to Scripture without referring to such "inner-biblical" direction to display it. In the note he cites an article by Terence E. Fretheim, entitled "The God Who Acts." In it Fretheim shows with great clarity the limitations of the "God who acts" paradigm, and by the same token the limitations of narrative or theo-dramatic theology. After listing various of the inadequacies of narrative theology, Fretheim then turns to "The Issue of Genre" and reminds us that there is more to the OT than narrative. He refers to these creedal interpolations as "gathering genres."

> Two types of gathering genres might be noticed here, both of which may be designated as "creedal." One type of creedal statement gathers claims about God that focus on divine acts (for example, Deut 26:5–9; Josh 24:2–13). . . . Another type of creedal statement articulates those claims about God in more abstract ways: God is compassionate (Exod 22:27); gracious, merciful, slow to anger, and abounding in steadfast love (Exod 34:6–7; Num 14:18); holy (Lev 19:2); great, mighty, awesome, is not partial and takes no bribe, executes justice for the orphan and the widow and loves the stranger (Deut 10:10, 17–18).[43]

That footnote seriously compromises Vanhoozer's thesis taken as a way of providing an account of God. How does theology or, more pointedly,

---

43. Fretheim, "The God Who Acts," 17. See Vanhoozer, *The Drama of Doctrine*, 95.

how does God himself get into theo-drama? Not chiefly because he enters it as one of the players, for were he to do so we would need to know from somewhere, other than from the drama, who this strange actor is. He gets into the drama (or more exactly, the narrative) only through what is told us about God at points where the drama is suspended. At such a point the players receive a "creedal" statement from their creator or author. The occurrence of those passages cited by Fretheim, and of course of hosts more that could be cited, are not part of the action of the biblical narrative, nor are they a direct commentary on it. They interrupt it, but at the same time they must control it. They are statements, assertions, which physically intrude into the narrative telling us who the God of the narrative is. This is, of course, supremely true of the account of the incarnation. Vanhoozer briefly recognizes the need for such interpretations in *Remythologizing Theology*, citing Exodus 34:5–7, the occasion on which the Lord descended and proclaimed his name. He notes a number of other occurrences of this formula in Scripture.[44] But by and large their consequences for theo-drama or remything are missed.

It is ironic that CRT relied on this very data to articulate the doctrine of God. For example, on Exodus 34:6–7 Calvin says

> Here we may observe, first, that his eternity and self-existence are declared by his magnificent name twice repeated; and, secondly, that in the enumeration of his perfections, he is described not as he is in himself, but in relation to us, in order that our acknowledgement of him may be more a vivid actual impression than empty visionary speculation. Moreover, the perfections that are enumerated are just those we saw shining in the heavens, and on the earth—compassion, goodness, mercy, justice, judgment, and truth. For power and energy are comprehended under the name Jehovah.[45]

To CRT it matters crucially that such general disclosures by God of his names and perfections have logical priority over his actions. To give priority to the actions would mean that the general statements are nothing other than generalizations drawn from the actions of one whose divinity is drawn exclusively from them.

---

44. Vanhoozer, *Remythologizing Theology*, 45–46.

45. John Calvin, *Institutes* I.10.2 The exegetical foundations of the doctrine of God typical of CRT are set out at length in Muller, *Post-Reformation Reformed Dogmatics*, Vol. 3.

The Utterance Fallacy

What do these creedal, non-dramatic statements look like? They look like all the things that Vanhoozer thinks is the matter with CRT. Are these statements propositions? Yes, they are propositions. Are they abstract propositions? Indeed they are. Are they propositions with a permanent truth value? Certainly. For it's not a good idea to suppose that as these statements intrude into the drama on one particular occasion they are only about that occasion. Of course, creedal statements have an occasion when they are first uttered, but they are not about that occasion, or not primarily or specially about that occasion. Not at all. To imagine that the significance of such expressions is strongly, if not exclusively, tied to their occasions of utterance is to commit what we might call the *Utterance Fallacy*. Rather, they state the same truth when uttered time and time again; their truth is indifferent to time, to any occasion when they may be restated. In that sense they are "timeless," "time-indifferent." We shall consider this issue of the timelessness of propositions more fully in chapter 6.

These statements, as they occur, for example, in Exodus 34:5–7, are about the eternal God who is not only merciful and gracious on Monday, and who could change on Tuesday. They disclose aspects of part of his "name," his character, an aspect of which is to be merciful and gracious. Where do the necessities and impossibilities about God, about what he can and cannot be and do, which are central features of his essence or nature, such as are found in, for example Hebrews 6:8, 2 Timothy 2:1–3, come from? They are "creedal" insertions into the text of the narrative, and other similar occurrences in Scripture, together with their good and necessary consequences. Who is the God that leads Israel? He is the incorruptible God whom he declares himself to be, the creator of the heavens and the earth, the judge of all the earth for whom it is impossible to act wrongly, whose word is utterly trustworthy. Fretheim's remarks, even though presented as remarks on "genre," are in fact nothing new. He's noticing what any attentive Bible-reader sees—the presence of brief statements in Scripture about God's nature or character that together form the central datum of Christian theology, its doctrine of God. More than this, he is reminding us of the importance of texts such as Exodus 34:6 in the history of Christian dogma.

One Liners

Here is a sample of twenty-one of these one-liners about God himself, taken at random from the scores that are to be found in Scripture.

- Deut 32:40 "As I live forever . . ."
- Rev 1:8 "I am the Alpha and Omega . . . who is and who was and who is to come the Almighty."
- Phil 4:7 "And the peace of God, which surpasses all understanding . . ."
- Job 11: 7 "Can you find out the limit of the Almighty?"
- Isa 40:13 "Who has measured the Spirit of the Lord, or what man shows him his counsel?"
- Eph 3:10 "the manifold wisdom of God."
- Job 28: 24 "He looks to the ends of the earth and sees everything under the heavens."
- Acts 15:17 "The Lord makes these things known of old."
- 1 Sam 16:7 "The Lord looks on the heart."
- Ps 94:10–11 "He who teaches man knowledge—the Lord—knows the thoughts of man, that they are a breath."
- Rom 3:30 "God is one."
- Heb 1:8 "Jesus Christ is the same yesterday and today and forever."
- Ps 16:2 "You are my Lord; I have no good apart from you."
- Matt 5:48 "Your heavenly Father is perfect."
- 2 Pet 3:8 "With the Lord one day is as a thousand years, and a thousand years as one day."
- Rom 16:27 "the only wise God."
- 1 Sam 2:2 "there is none holy like the Lord."
- 1 Thess 1:9 "the living and true God."
- 1 John 5:20 "that we may know him who is true, and we are in him who is true."
- John 5:26 "The Father has life in himself."
- John 4:24 "God is spirit."

Only twenty-one, out of many hundreds. These have to do mainly with the life, and power, and steadfastness, and energy, and uniqueness of God. They are by no means generalizations drawn from the mighty acts of God, but record what God is in himself. They are logically prior to any narrative-statements about the actions of God in time. It is *this* God, the God of the one liners, who has in these last days spoken to us by his Son

(Heb 1:2). Of course, other statements could be added, having to do with his Trinitarian nature, and his moral and spiritual character. All such one liners, creedal statements, or statements that have immediate creedal implications, although they first occur in one part of the *mythos*, may be abstracted from that particular context and re-issued, time and again, in other contexts. For they are permanently true statements about God, as God himself is permanent. They help to provide us with the biblical doctrine of God, and so to provide the permanent theological context in which a Christian theologian must work, which he must emphasize, and which he must not infringe.

Not only that, the one-liners also provide the theological scaffolding of the mighty acts of God, reminding us, by their frequent and often seemingly incidental occurrence in Scripture, of the character of the so-called "director" of the drama.

The Pastoral Epistles

We may look at this point in a different way, by considering the Pastoral Epistles. One might think, on Vanhoozer's schema, that coming towards the end of the NT canon they would provide guidance for all those ministers whose function it is, according to Vanhoozer, to portray the drama of redemption and to initiate new players into how to be participants in it. But what we find is something rather different: a stress on teaching, in which any theo-dramatic note is noticeably absent. (1 Tim 1:3-8; 3:9; 4:2, 10, 13, 16; 5:17; 6:3; 2 Tim 1:13; 2:2, 14, 23; 3:10, 14; 4:2-3; Titus 1:9; 2:1, 7, 15; 3:8.)

Second, the Pastoral letters also contain their own share of one liners:

1 Timothy

- "Christ Jesus came into the world to save sinners" (1:15)
- "To the King of ages, immortal, invisible, the only God, be honor and glory for ever and ever" (1:17)
- ". . . God our Savior, who desires all people to be saved . . ." (2:3-4)
- "For there is one God, and there is one mediator between God and men, the man Christ Jesus" (2:5)
- "For everything created by God is good, and nothing is to be rejected if it is received with thanksgiving . . ." (4:4)
- ". . . the living God, who is the Savior of all people, especially of those who believe" (4:10)

- "... God, who gives life to all things ..." (6:13)
- "... the blessed and only Sovereign, the King of kings and Lord of lords, who alone has immortality, who dwells in unapproachable light, whom no one has ever seen or can see" (6:15–16)

2 Timothy

- "... the power of God, who saved us and called us to a holy calling, not because of our works but because of his own purpose and grace ..." (1:8–9)
- "But God's firm foundation stands ..." (2:19)
- "All Scripture is breathed out by God ..." (3:16)
- "... of God and of Christ Jesus, who is to judge the living and the dead ..." (4:1)
- "... the Lord stood by me and strengthened me ..." (4:17)

Titus

- "... God, who never lies, promised before the ages began" (1:2)

And in addition there is this epitome of the gospel so admired by the hymn-writer John Newton:

> For the grace of God has appeared, bringing salvation for all people, training us to renounce ungodliness and worldly passions, and to live self-controlled, upright, and godly lives in the present age, waiting for our blessed hope, the appearing of the glory of our great God and Savior Jesus Christ, who gave himself for us to redeem us from all lawlessness and to purify for himself a people for his own possession who are zealous for good works. (Titus 2:11–12)

What role do such pivotal texts play? We might say that a relevant datum (a "proof text," in older language) for constructing a doctrine (such as the doctrine of God) is a text that, although it occurs, or first occurs, in one particular context (naturally enough), does not depend upon that context for its truth. This is because what is stated in the text is a general, permanently true statement about the character of God, holding for all times. In other words, this language is seriously non-dramatic in that who God is not reducible to an event or events in a narrative.

So far I have argued that the biblical narrative is what it is because God reveals himself in Scripture by means of representative statements about his nature or essence, and then narrates what he has freely initiated and endured for our sakes and for our salvation. So at once we see that the Christian doctrine of God cannot be nothing but theo-dramatic since it rests upon a bedrock of a pre-narrative or narrative-indifferent assertions. As we noted earlier, theology and the overall character of Scripture might be *illustrated* by means of the idea of a drama, or be said to embody a drama, but that's a different matter, and a much weaker proposal than the one Kevin Vanhoozer makes.

History and Dogma

Old theological conflicts frequently reappear dressed in a new outfit. So it is with narrative theologies and their theological output. Currently, in the guise of narrative theologies of one sort and another, we are presented with a version of the nineteenth-century conflict between history and dogma in new dress. Not the denial by history of the necessity of dogma, but its subtle and sometimes not-so-subtle attenuation. This attenuation may not be intentional but it is real for all that. It's a result of the constraints of history upon doctrine.

History is concerned with what is the case, with what we have good evidence to believe has in fact happened, and history ought not to stray beyond that. All else is historical speculation that takes us beyond the facts. History attends to this world, to the episodes and narratives of what, in the best judgment of the historians, based on the best available evidence, has in fact taken place. But a record of what was in fact, or what is in fact, is not strong enough for the purposes of constructing Christian dogma.

Treating the Gospel narratives in a primarily theo-dramatic way may lead us to the reasonable conclusion that Jesus did not sin. From this we may conclude that it is true that "Jesus is sinless." Is that piece of reasoning, from "Jesus did not sin" to "Jesus is sinless" satisfactory for dogmatic purposes? No, it is not. It crucially is not. For there was a time when it was true that "Adam is sinless," but then he sinned, bringing death into the world and all our woe. If as a result of an investigation of what Jesus said and did we come to the conclusion that Jesus is sinless, this is indeed a striking conclusion, but dogmatically speaking it is as weak as water. It is still weak, even if we are able to conclude, on historical grounds that, unlike Adam, Jesus never sinned.

To say that Jesus was in fact sinless, that he never sinned, is to make a statement about the actual world, the world of the historian. But that affirmation does not answer the question, *could* Jesus have sinned? To use Oliver Crisp's terminology, was Christ sinless, or was he *impeccable*?[46] An account of what actually happened cannot by itself answer that question, for the question enquires about not only what is in fact the case, but also what could be the case. It is quite consistent with the actual sinlessness of Jesus that he could have become sinful. Although he did not in fact sin, yet perhaps if he had been subject to more temptation, or have been less on his guard, or . . . then he would have sinned.

In the particular case of the dogma of the sinlessness of Jesus, of the impossibility of him committing sin, dogma arises from data of two sorts. One might think, the dogma of Jesus sinlessness comes simply from explicit biblical statements of Jesus that state this fact. "For our sake he made him to be sin who knew no sin" (2 Cor 5:21); "Which one of you convicts me of sin?" (John 8:46); "Yet without sin" (Heb 4:15); "without blemish" (Heb 9:14); "in him there is no sin" (1 John 3:5); "Great is the mystery of godliness" (1 Tim 3:6). These data certainly take us in the right direction. Yet even these are statements only about what is the case, about what (from a logical or metaphysical point of view) happens in fact to be the case.

So it is necessary to consider other data of Scripture, to link Jesus's sinlessness with his true deity, to connect this up with other statements about Jesus that, together with statements about God, imply his *necessary* sinlessness. We need to be able to employ arguments of the form:

Jesus is God having taken on human nature.

God is sinless.

therefore, Jesus is sinless.

The premises of that argument come from Scripture, but they don't come from explicit statements about Jesus' sinless words and deeds, but in a rather more roundabout way. And so, as regards his deity, there is the abundant data from the Gospel of John (John 1:1–3; 2:24–25; 3:16–18; 5:18–20), from Paul (Rom 1:7; 9:5; 1 Cor 1:1–3; 2 Cor 5:10), and from the author of Hebrews (Heb 1:1–3; 4:14; 5:8). And if Jesus is God made flesh, then the character of God's sinlessness becomes relevant to assessing the peccability or impeccability of Jesus. "Majestic in holiness" (Exod 15:11); "There is none holy like the Lord" (1 Sam 2.2); "The holy one" (Job 6:10; Isa. 17:7); "The Holy One of Israel" (Isa 41:20); "Of purer eyes than to behold evil"

---

46. Crisp, "Was Christ Sinless or Impeccable?" In *God Incarnate*.

(Hab 1:13); "Holy is his name" (Luke 1:49); "I am holy" (2 Pet 3:11). And from the fact that Jesus is worthy of worship (Phil 2:10; Acts 9:14; 1 Cor: 1:2; Rev 5:13). These and more such texts are evidence for original and essential divine holiness. Holiness is not a virtue that God acquires, nor does he simply happen to be holy. If Christ is divine, then he has such necessary holiness. But such conclusions cannot be provided by the biblical narrative alone.

Is this proof texting? Of course it is. But it is what might be called "open-eyed" proof texting. The texts are assembled in the light of their contexts and their theological value, with an eye to what used to be called (rather opaquely, it seems to me) "the analogy of the faith."

It is possible to treat even these normative utterances, the interpretative statements of apostles (especially John), as merely historical, as statements of what, at a time, Jesus or Paul or Peter or John believed. There is some purpose to noting this. The original interpretative statements are historical occurrences, of course. Paul wrote to Rome, to Corinth, to Timothy and Titus, etc. at roughly around the times that we think that he did, and so on. He asserted what he is recorded as having said in these letters. All this is history, recounting what is the case, or what was the case in the life of a Jewish Rabbi, Saul of Tarsus, a Pharisee of the Pharisees, two millennia ago.

But these utterances of Paul are not simply historical, as (say) the utterances of Cicero or Seneca, writing in roughly the same period, are historical. They are (for the Christian, and the Christian church) assertions. They are not simply events, or opinions, they are God-given judgments, including God-given judgments about God himself. As such they are elevated beyond mere narrative, and beyond their status as the opinions of Paul about what must be the case in respect of Jesus of Nazareth, to what (without qualification) must be the case in respect of Jesus of Nazareth. What's the difference?

We may look at it in this way. We may naturally think of narratives as enclosed within sets of speech marks. As speech marks indicate occasions of speaking, so narratives are made up of sets of such occasions shaped into a story. So it is with the Gospel narratives: this is Matthew's story written in the 50s or 60s AD, this is John's story, written about 85 AD, and so on. Similarly we can treat the letters of Paul or the reported discourses of Jesus as contained within speech marks, and thus as occasional utterances. We may even think of Paul's apostolic life as part of his presentation of the gospel.[47] It was that, as well as his teaching. But his teaching, "my gospel" as he called it, was reproducible in a way that his life was not. But so long as we keep the speech marks in the forefront of our minds then the normative

---

47. Vanhoozer, *The Drama of Doctrine*, 100–101.

status of what Jesus or Paul say is, to put it mildly, endangered. For so long as the speech marks remain, the question of truth and hence the question of authority may be suspended. We may say: it is true that Paul said that God justifies the ungodly, but we may go on to ask: but does God in fact justify the ungodly? For the church, Paul's statements (or at least most of them) take on a normative status in which the speech marks drop away. Paul the Apostle said "Jesus Christ came into the world to save sinners." The occasions on which he wrote this is a matter of history. But that in fact Jesus Christ came into the world to save sinners (and all that this presupposes and entails) is true well after, even endlessly after, the occurrence of the first inscription of the words and is, or becomes, revealed truth about the incarnate Logos, and so material for Christian dogma.

The narratives also contain statements of what is impossible and necessary for God: he cannot lie, or deny himself, or mutate. But are not all things possible with God? Such statements are very important, for they are part of the scaffolding of dogmatic theology. But even these must have a certain sense. The sense in which God cannot lie is rather different from the sense in which George Washington could not. George Washington could not lie because of his resolve not to lie. But God cannot lie for a deeper reason, that his nature is such that he is impeccable. Dogma comes to us through history, but it is more than history.

So Christian dogma often requires us to say more than what has happened. This is the consequence of using the language of essence and nature and person. We need to be able to say what could and could not be the case. And the Christian dogma of the person of Christ states that it is impossible for Christ to have sinned because he is a divine person, and so could not sin. Hence the need to talk not only of Jesus's being without sin or even of his sinlessness, but of his *necessary* sinlessness. In other words, we need to be able to talk about *natures*. Jesus's divine nature, the nature of his person, was such that he could not sin. Of course "Christ did not in fact sin" (as a statement about this world) is perfectly compatible or consistent with the dogma of Christ's necessary sinlessness, but it does not require it. It falls far short of it.

Perfect Being Theology

An objection to the course of this discussion may be that this is nothing other than perfect being theology, a classic case of biblical theology being corrupted by the *a priori* application of pagan categories. In order to consider this, let us briefly examine another biblical example, the discussion of the immutability of God in Hebrews 6:13-14. This is an interesting and significant argument. It goes something like this

- Necessarily, anyone who swears an oath, swears by someone greater than themselves.
- Necessarily, had there been a greater than God, then God would have sworn by that greater.
- He swore by himself.
- Therefore, there is none greater than God.

Therefore, God is the greatest being. Here is (apparently) a statement of perfect being theology, not from pagan thought, but from the scriptural witness.

But that may be thought to be a little too quick. Perhaps we ought only to conclude that God is the greatest in respect of veracity, or faithfulness, leaving it an open question as to whether he is the greatest in love, or mercy, or some other attribute. So perhaps we ought to conclude the argument:

- There is none greater than God in respect of veracity, or faithfulness.
- Therefore, God is the greatest being in respect of faithfulness.

It is interesting, however, that regarding the greatness of God, the writer makes his point in an unqualified way, referring to *the one* besides whom there is no greater, and not simply to some attribute of that being. It seems a valid inference from what he is saying to conclude that he is talking about the being of God, and therefore saying, or implying, that he is a being which none greater can be conceived.

A Moral

One important moral may be drawn from this discussion. If one's theological resources are exclusively narrative or historical accounts of what happened, then as a matter of simple logic the theological results will be dogmatically impoverished or substandard. They will at best tell us what happened, including what was said on some occasion, and so what was in fact the case, not what must have been the case and must now be the case. From what is the case it is logically impossible to conclude what must be the case. And Christian dogma, having its logical beginning, naturally enough, with the doctrine of God, embodies statements about what must be the case;

statements about natures and essences, about necessities and impossibilities, *modal* statements.

Of course the language of the CRT dogmatician may be dismissed, as it has been from time to time, as hyperbole, as mere rhetoric, as when a person might, licking his lips, say "I couldn't have a better ice-cream!" Or maybe, it is thought of as the "hardening" of the language of praise and prayer. On such an account, to say that Jesus is impeccable is not to speak the truth, but to honor his success in not sinning by exaggerating the fact. Or alternatively, and notoriously, the dogma about the person and the natures of Christ has emerged from the simple narratives of Jesus the teacher due to the intrusion of Greek thought that overlays the pure biblical narrative with alien philosophical categories.

So where does dogma come from? Answering that question in the most general way, it comes from interpretation. And where (for the CRT dogmatician) does the interpretation come from? Answer: interpretations are provided by the non-narrative parts of Scripture, which are introduced into the narrative and tell us what God must be like, and what he can and cannot do.

Kevin Vanhoozer's theo-dramatic proposal for re-casting our understanding of Christian doctrine cannot be the *whole* story, or even the *main* story. But can it be an account of Christian doctrine at all? Can it be *any* of the story? Can it turn out to be anything other than an extended rhetorical embellishment of the idea of Christian theology? I shall bring this discussion to a close by trying to answer that question, by briefly considering another feature of the Scriptural pattern that Vanhoozer's net fails to catch.

Participating in the Narrative? Doctrine and Application

At least since the time when the Apostle Paul wrote his letter to the Romans, an important structural distinction has been recognized between Christian doctrine, on the one hand, and its application to the lives of individual Christians and families, and to the church, on the other. In his letter Paul teaches us about sin and righteousness and grace and atonement in (roughly) the first eleven chapters, and then (roughly again) from chapter 12 onwards applies these truths practically. It's similar in Galatians and Ephesians and Colossians and is foreshadowed by Jesus' teaching on bearing fruit, the danger of looking back, on not only being hearers of the word but doers of it also, and so on. In addition there is his emphasis, especially in the Gospel of John, on love as the basis of true discipleship; an emphasis followed by

James's teaching on faith and works, and John's teaching in his first letter on the "tests of life."

So from these first Christian times the distinction, though not the separation, between doctrine, the teaching about God and salvation we are to believe and to rely on, and application, the consequences of that belief in the doctrine of our salvation should have for our human life in the widest sense, has become deep-seated in Christian thought. The one is to lead to the other, but each is nevertheless distinct from the other, and the one may not in fact lead to the other; at best it will do so only imperfectly. A person may be a hearer of the word, but not a doer of it. The seed may not bear fruit. Or it may bear only a little fruit. The profession of faith may not even be skin-deep.

Vanhoozer's proposal that Christian doctrine is a theo-drama in which Christians are participants, and is thus a continuation of the theo-drama, were it to be taken seriously, would blur if not require us entirely to abandon this formative, time-honored distinction and connection, one that is embedded in CRT. It is therefore one thing to speak of "doctrinal direction,"[48] a phrase easily assimilated into the age-old "doctrine and application" approach to Christian theology; it is another thing to talk of "engaging in a theater of martyrdom,"[49] which (I suggest) takes us well beyond the parameters of the New Testament. Here we need to emphasize the point that Vanhoozer himself makes but does not see the significance it has for his project, that the theo-drama, acted out in real time, is now in suspense. This is also a theological datum *about* the drama rather than an element of it. As he notes, the Christian church lives "between the times," between what the drama accomplished, and its consummation in the full deployment and enjoyment of its fruits. But in the present in-between state the church cannot participate in the drama, except in the sense that it lives by appropriating and having applied to it the fruit of what Jesus did and suffered.

When the NT refers to the relation of Christians to the work of redemption it uses a sense or senses of "participate" that does not at all justify the attempt to recast Christian doctrine in the wholesale way that Vanhoozer proposes. Ironically, it is when, in Part IV of the book, "The Performance," he comes to work out the role of doctrine in the drama, that Vanhoozer himself is content to recognize a weaker sense of "performance," the sense that hardly justifies his theo-dramatic framework and language. So he says, in the place already noted, that doctrine prepares us for fitting participation in

---

48. Vanhoozer, *The Drama of Doctrine*, 362.
49. Ibid.

the drama of redemption.[50] He seems forced to explain or gloss the language of theo-drama using non-dramatic terms that are already richly displayed on the surface of the New Testament—calling, union, sanctification, and so on, the staple of standard CRT. "Those who participate in the theo-dramatic missions do so through union with Christ, a union that is wrought by the Spirit yet worked out in history by us."[51] "It is the Spirit who creates a new 'role' (character, 'spirit') in us through the process of sanctification."[52] Here he employs the rhetoric of drama to do nothing more than to adorn the time-honored understanding of the relation between doctrine and practice. Once more we note that the rhetoric of theo-drama depends for its force on the solid, permanent dogmatic framework of the Christian faith. But Vanhoozer does not seem to see this.

---

50. Ibid., 363.
51. Ibid., 366.
52. Ibid., 373.

4

Being and Doing

In the last chapter a contrast was drawn between the narrative and what may transcend it, even though the evidence for this contrast may be physically present within them. The *penchant* for narrative and historical sequence that presently tends to dominate some theology either excludes what transcends narrative, or what transcends the narrative is tacitly and is perhaps unconsciously smuggled in. Considered by itself narrative does not have the resources to express the natures of the actors who live in the various sequences of history, or of God who transcends and directs history. What are these actors like, and what are their powers? What can they do, and what are their limits? For a narrative stresses development, change, historical progress, process, and drama—what in fact happens. It pays little or no attention to the character of its creator and director, or the natures of the actors whose parts in the drama reveal something of who they are. Finally, it does not recognize what the exclusion of what transcends the narrative does to the project of CRT. This expression is typical of these failures.

> The way forward, beyond relational theism or panentheism and back to something more like classical theism, is to think through God's love, and being, in terms of neither impersonal causality nor personal mutuality alone but rather in terms of communicative and self-communicative action. The love of God is the triune God in self-communicative action, God's sharing his own life with what is other than himself.[1]

So Vanhoozer indicates his intention to move away from much modern theology in which what God is in himself is conflated with what God does. He favors moving from such panentheism towards classical theism. Nevertheless, while such a move is in principle welcome from the point of view of CRT, he goes on to show that in fact he has not shaken himself free from the clutches of panentheistic thinking. For a fundamental feature

---

1. Vanhoozer, *Remythologizing Theology*, 176–77.

of the nature of God, his love, is regarded as nothing over and above his self-communicative action, and so God is (nothing more than) his self-communicative action.

We shall now explore these claims about the Triune God that is "something like classical theism" by first considering two questions that have already been foreshadowed in the last chapter.

How to Think of God?

We saw in chapter 1 that CRT has an essentialist approach to the doctrine of God. Stephen Charnock's (1628–28) statement is typical.

> The essence of God, with all the perfections of his nature, are pronounced the same, without any variation from eternity to eternity; so that the text [Ps 102: 26–27] doth not only assert the eternal duration of God, but his immutability in that duration. His eternity is signified in that expression, "Thou shalt endure"; his immutability in this, "Thou art the same." To endure, argues indeed his immutability as well as eternity; for what endures, is not changed, and what is changed, doth not endure....
>
> "Thou art the same," that is, the same God; the same in essence and nature; the same in will and purpose. Thou doest change all other things as thou pleases, but thou art immutable in every respect.[2]

Can a narrative approach to doctrine provide us with a doctrine of God of this type? When "God" or "the Lord" is the subject of statements or assertions within the narrative, in what way are we to think of him? Surprisingly, perhaps, there are in principle very few possible answers to that question. How must a narrative approach answer it? If not with the type of statement given by Charnock, then how?

As we have seen, one possibility is that the logic of narrative drives us in the direction of thinking that the term "God," whenever it appears, refers to one who on one occasion expresses this particular power or virtue, and then who, on another occasion, expresses some other particular power and virtue, as he manifests himself in the narrative through redemptive history and as the director of the theo-drama. Consistently understood in this fashion, "God" can refer to no more than a "bundle" of particular instances of properties, a larger and larger bundle as the narrative proceeds, the sum of God's actions to date. The individual properties, of being faithful on one

---

2. Charnock, *Discourse Upon the Existence and Attributes of God*, 198.

occasion, of judging on another, or being gracious on another, and so on, accumulate.

Let us suppose, to keep the discussion within reasonable limits, that we know that there is not more than one God. What is this one God's relation to these properties, the accumulating set? The most obvious answer is: *he is nothing other than the bundle, he is the bundle.* In this view the properties have a mere accidental relationship to each other, and God is the merely the sum of them. If God lost or gained such properties, his godhood would not be imperiled. It is certainly consistent with the bundle view that such a God could be capricious, or whimsical, or unstable in other ways. Who can tell what God might do next? What would a covenant promise from such a God be worth? Further, what is the relation of "God" to the bundle of these properties? Is it just a short-hand for them all? It would seem that Vanhoozer is not likely to be favorably disposed to this type of answer, since (as we have noted) in *Remythologizing Theology* he objects to God being nothing but sets of relations on the ground that a relation implies *relata*, those subjects that are in relation.[3] So there cannot be a God who is nothing but relations. In the same way there cannot be a God who is nothing but a bundle of properties, each of them the property of "God," certainly not the God of Scripture, who has an essence. But then in the case of a "bundle" the term "God" cannot fail to function in a purely nominal way. There is nothing that is God but simply the same word used to name each of a varying set of properties. Hardly a satisfactory result for a Christian understanding of who God is.

Another possible answer to our question, what is God's relation to the bundle, the sum of actions attributed to him in the narrative? is that "God" is the name of what or who merely holds the bundle together. In such a view, what gives the bundle its permanence is that these are all the actions of one God, a God who is necessarily a "hidden" God. Take the mug in front of me. It is made of clay, it is glazed, it has a blue handle, it does not wobble. This is the beginning of the bundle of *its* properties. Some of these are relatively permanent, others, like its property of presently being full of hot coffee, are less permanent. What are these properties the properties of? Answer: they are *its* properties, the properties of the mug!

But then what is the mug? Suppose we continue to reel off the mug's properties, past, present, and future. If we are not going to reinstate the bundle theory, we must say something like, "the mug" is the name that refers to something that plays a unique role, that of being a property holder, what is sometimes referred to as a *substratum* or "bare particular," bare

---

3. Vanhoozer, *Remythologizing Theology*, 141–44.

because it itself has no further properties. In fact, it is completely propertyless, a completely unknowable "substance," some unknown "thing" that supports and unifies the bundle, and nothing more. Well, many who have thought about such matters have held that to be a true account of things like mugs, but (whatever its merits in accounting for how we talk about mugs) it hardly delivers a satisfactory account of God. God may have a substance, or he may be a substance, but on the view being discussed he is necessarily unknowable, apart from what his actions tell us. Is he necessarily faithful? Is he necessarily wise and just? We cannot tell. Inspecting the bundle does not tell us, for God himself is at best a black hole.

So "God" cannot be the name for a bundle of properties occurring in a particular sequence, nor is it promising to think of him as an unknown or unknowable something or other that transcends the bundle and holds it in place. Neither of these suggestions seems to be plausible or palatable. There is only one other type of alternative. We must think (as CRT, along with the Catholic tradition, thinks) of God as having a nature or essence, or even of God as *being* an essence, something that is both knowable, though not exhaustively known by us, his creatures, and something in virtue of which he is God.[4] To support this suggestion we now look at two recent discussions, the first in which the need for such a God becomes apparent, the other in which the concept of God is unclear.

John Piper and Tom Wright

In his discussion of the place of righteousness in justification John Piper claims that Tom Wright's "definition of righteousness does not go deep enough."[5] What this means is that Wright's account of divine righteousness in terms of God's covenant faithfulness starts and stops with his account of divine actions.[6] For Wright understands God's righteousness wholly in terms of what God does. That is, Wright's theology, his doctrine of God, is controlled by the recounting of divine action. Wright believes that God's covenant faithfulness *is* his righteousness. Piper asks a question about this.

> *What is it about God's righteousness that inclines him to act in these ways?* Behind each of those actions is the assumption that there is something about God's righteousness that explains why

---

4. For an insightful discussion of God's nature, whether it is to be considered as an essence, ("constitutive") or as a being with a set of properties ("relational"), see Wolterstorff, "Divine Simplicity."

5. Piper, *The Future of Justification*, 62.

6. Ibid., 62–64.

he acts as he does. What is that? That is the question, so far as I can see, that Wright does not ask.[7]

> God's righteousness, before there was a covenant, determined that punishment for sin would be part of what happens in the covenant (and outside it!) . . . limiting the "righteousness of God" in this context [i.e., that of Rom 3:25, etc.] to covenantal categories is too narrow.[8]

Note Piper's references to what goes "before" and "behind" the divine action. Of course, he does not mean "before" and "behind" in time or space, as where the piano is behind the door, or the leaders in the race are two minutes before the laggards. Rather, what is God's righteousness like *before* he acts, where this is considered as a logical distinction? What is the nature in terms of which he acts? What is God's righteousness before there was a covenant?

In developing and discussing Christian doctrine, as Piper and Wright are doing, is it possible to ask such questions, questions about the nature of God, about his righteousness and others of his features, and expect to gain answers? In particular, to gain answers from Scripture? As was argued in the previous chapter, if history is all that we have, then it is hard to see how such questions can be answered. Take the illustration of a series of camera shots, either stills or clips of video. Of each phase of this sequence, however we measure the phases, we can ask who appears in them, who are the players, the agents. Is the figure in phase one, which is in continuity with the figure in some later phase or phases, actually the same? Clearly, the figure has changed, he looks different, he says and does different things, he is related to others in different ways, and so on. Who is the person who brings about or undergoes these changes? What sort of being is he?

Thinking further of Piper and Wright, the issue between them, at least as Piper construes it, is not a question of one definition of God's righteousness not being adequate, of rival accounts of the righteousness of God, what that righteousness is like, and how we are to understand it. The issue is about the coherence of an account of divine righteousness (however understood) that does not begin with who God *is* but with what God *does*. Although he does not quite put things in these terms, Piper is arguing that being, the being of God, must come first; acting is a consequence of being. Being is logically prior to doing. This is true generally; glass is not fragile because it easily smashes, it easily smashes because it is fragile. Henry is not

---

7. Ibid., 63, Piper's emphasis.
8. Ibid., 68.

vain because he is always preening himself in front of the mirror, but his preening is an expression of his vain disposition. The tree is not an apple tree because it bears apples, but it bears apples because it is an apple tree. In God's case, *doing* righteously follows from *being* righteous. *Acting* faithfully is a logical consequence of *being* faithful, of having a faithful character, or a character apt for being faithful. Wright's account is not deep enough, in Piper's estimate, because it does not start with the nature or character of God, but with the actions of God.

This is how Tom Wright replies:

> Piper's attempt to show that there must be a "righteousness" *behind* God's covenant faithfulness is simply unconvincing. . . . Again, it seems that Piper has read it, but he never engages with the basic proposal I make, which is that—fully in line with Daniel 9 and the multitude of Isaiah and Psalms that talk in the same way—God's righteousness here is his faithfulness to the covenant, *specifically to the covenant with Abraham in Genesis 15*, and that it is because of this covenant that God deals with sins through the faithful, obedient death of Jesus the messiah (Rom 3:22–24).[9]

This is a good example of the regular way in which "narrative" approaches to the text of Scripture reduce God's nature from who he is to what he does. In Wright's approach, "God is righteous" means "God is faithful to the covenant," and it means nothing more than this, though even Wright cannot hold consistently to this theological partiality.

Such an approach excludes any reference to the *need* for a covenant (a unilaterally established way of salvation from sin). It starts the theology too late. Does God's righteousness have nothing to do with covenant making? As Wright himself puts it, "*Dealing with sin, saving humans from it, giving them grace, forgiveness, justification, glorification—all this was the purpose of the single covenant from the beginning, now revealed in Jesus Christ.*"[10] But this, as I see it, is Piper's main point. All this—God's attitude to sin, his grace, the provision of forgiveness, vindication by Christ—is no doubt part of God's single covenant, but it cannot exhaust God's righteousness. Without doubt such activity as covenant-establishing expresses the character of God's righteousness. God is gracious in establishing the covenant and faithful to it and to the redemption from sin that he has established. So far

---

9. Wright, *Justification*, 46, 48. It is interesting that the Daniel 9 passage Wright cites (43) begins with the words "Ah, Lord, great and awesome God," and at this point Wright himself recognizes the need to talk of the "sort of God he is" (53).

10. Ibid., 74. Wright's italics.

is Piper from reducing the character of God, "belittling" Paul's meaning, as Wright puts it,[11] he is intent on filling it out.

Mercifully, narrative theologians such as Tom Wright are not completely consistent with their own outlook at such points. So Wright writes of "the apostle's [Paul's] understanding of the story of Israel, and of the whole world, as a single continuous narrative which, having reached its climax in Jesus the Messiah, was now developed in fresh ways which God the Creator, the Lord of history, had always intended."[12] Here we have not merely the God who creates, but God the creator, and not merely the Lord who acts in history, but the Lord of history. But where does the narrative provide us with such information? Considered simply as a narrative, it doesn't and can't. What is starkly absent from Vanhoozer's account of doctrine as drama, namely the creator-creature distinction, here makes a welcome, if brief, appearance.

There is another, deeper and more abstract reason why we must go behind and before God's covenant making activity, not to consider activity at a more basic level, such as God's work as creator, but to consider God himself. How do we know, or did Abraham know, that in establishing his covenant, God could be relied upon? How do we know that God is not an arbitrary tyrant, the God of absolute power, pure will? Might not God command at one time what he forbids at some other time? Occasionally one reads something like the following: that by establishing his covenant God binds himself to a people, to Abraham and the seed of promise, to be their faithful God. But how could such a promise be relied upon unless somehow we are assured that God cannot be a tyrant? Does someone who rules by arbitrary fiat recognize obligations?

In focussing upon this narrative, this history, and constructing a doctrine of God from it, the impression is conveyed that this narrative is the only one there could be. This is one consequence of the panentheizing tendency of modern theology that Vanhoozer also draws attention to in *Remythologizing Theology*, but which (I believe) he does not altogether extricate himself from.[13] Could not God freely have chosen to actualize other possibilities than this, the actual world? Nevertheless any alternative world creatable by God must surely be consistent with God's nature whatever character that nature has.

---

11. Ibid., 74.

12. Ibid., 17.

13. Vanhoozer, *Remythologizing Theology*, ch. 2. For an excellent account of modern panentheism see Cooper, *Panentheism*.

The systematic theologian does not need narrative theology or any of its friends. What he does need, as CRT made clear, is *exegetical* theology. What John Piper says is entirely in line with this. "Behind each of those actions is the assumption that there is something about God's righteousness that explains why he acts as he does. What is that? I do not ask it for speculative reasons but exegetical ones."[14] Exegesis shows (Piper believes) that "What we find therefore in the Old Testament and in Paul is that God defines 'right' in terms of *himself*. There is no other standard to consult than his own infinitely worthy being."[15] God acts consistently with who he is.

Vanhoozer on God

The theological constructions that occupy Parts II and III of Vanhoozer's most recent book, *Remythologizing Theology*, illustrate the method of theology set forth in Part I. In *The Drama of Doctrine* the author had the aim of offering an understanding of Christian doctrine as being essentially theo-dramatic. In the later book he seeks to construe (or to construct) Christian theology as the "metaphysics of the theo-drama," a way of understanding, a conceptual analysis, that will intellectually sustain the theo-dramatic narrative, making it more than a mere story. The doctrine of God that the author offers vividly illustrates the tension between being and doing that we are exploring.

What's the difference between doctrine and theology, as Vanhoozer sees things? Something like this, perhaps: a biblical doctrine is a teaching of Scripture on a particular topic. For Vanhoozer the earlier concern was, how are we to understand such doctrines? Answer: they are intrinsic parts of a theo-drama, they are what it means to understand and participate in God's dramatic work in Christ, to appreciate how we ourselves are to be caught up in that drama, participants in it. Doctrine is God in interaction, in dialogue, through the polyphonic character of Scripture, entering the drama himself in the Incarnate Logos. So doctrine is not monologic, nor merely cognitive, or cerebral, mere teaching (à la Charles Hodge, as Vanhoozer believes), but dialogic interaction displayed differently through the varied genres of Scripture, engaging (in one sweep) not only our minds, but our imaginations, affections, and wills.

So what is theology, on this view? Theology is a second-order activity, taking the theo-drama, and its various elements as just described, and reflecting upon it by connecting them up. What does such theo-drama

---

14. Piper, *The Future of Justification*, 63.
15. Ibid., 64, Piper's italics

imply? To answer this question is to become engaged in the remythologizing of theology. The term, "remythologizing," is potentially confusing, and it seems a pity that Vanhoozer has to spend a couple of dozen pages offering an *apologia* for the use of a word on the title page. But this nevertheless gives the author the opportunity to say that remythologizing has nothing to do with Bultmann, but with understanding the Bible not as myth in the sense of a set of ancient fables, but as *mythos*, as a dramatic plot, a plot of this-wordly events, of ordinary as well as heroic stories. That's theo-drama again, of course. And remythologized theology is theology that does not proceed from the bottom up, from a merely human set of ideas, such as Hegel or (allegedly) Anselm offer, or the "five speculative 'ways' of Aquinas," but in terms of Scripture's own theo-drama, God's ways.

So remythologized theology must be systematic, metaphysical reflection on Scripture from Scripture's own point of view, from the point of view of the depiction of God as a Triune communicative agent, the author and director of the drama. It is more than reflection, then; it is a metaphysical endeavor. To start with, and as the key to the whole, we need to ask what sort of a God must the God be who creates and redeems in such theo-dramatic ways? The answer to this question provides us with a "system of projection" that will depict onto the theological screen a portrayal of a certain type and shape, the contours of remythologized theology.

The term "projection" calls to mind Ludwig Feuerbach, the idea of religion and its associated theologies as a mechanism of compensation, as nothing but the expression and projection of human ideals, the screening of a supposedly objectively real account of the divine that is (and must be, according to Feuerbach) only the stylizing of a person's deepest needs, his spiritual aches and pains, as well as his aims, which compensate for these. But that's Bultmann's trajectory, not mine, Vanhoozer says. Theo-dramatic projection, unlike Bultmann's project of demythologizing, starts not from the anthropocentric but from the theocentric, from the point of view of the God of the theo-drama, from the author's study and the director's chair, so to speak. So it is not the objectifying of the merely subjective, but reflection on who the director is and what he can and cannot do, reflection that arises from what we know that he has in fact done and not done in enacting the theo-drama.

The remythologizer must ask the question: What must God be like if he is actually the speaking and acting agent depicted in the Bible? For "[t]he Bible is the means whereby God projects his own voice onto the stage of world history." And "both the transcendence and immanence of God are best viewed in terms of communicative agency rather than motional causality."[16] As noted earlier, it is crucial to such theology that it uses only personal rather than causal and mechanical categories, the two being regarded as exclusive of each other. The coherence of theology is not to be sought in logical consistency or inter-relatedness, but in a personal plan as the plot uncovers this. So Christian theology remains as much a metaphysical endeavor as it was for Hodge or for Anselm.

But a metaphysics of the Christian theo-drama will therefore give pride of place to the speech and action of the divine *dramatis persona*. For an account of the Triune God in communicative action is the touchstone of the reality of this theo-dramatic vision of the whole. But that does not mean that there is no place for metaphysics. Rather metaphysics becomes the attempt to reflect on subjects, human and divine, who are "actively engaged, through dialogue, in the process of mutual self-communication."[17]

Remythologization "seeks to recover the biblical *mythos*, its theo-dramatic sense together with its theo-dramatic referent, and to provide a coherent and appropriate conceptual elaboration of the ontology of the divine *dramatis personae* in terms of communicative agency."[18]

These statements already suggest an agenda of problems and issues. But before identifying these we must note the contemporary setting in which Professor Vanhoozer places his project.

The Setting

As we have noted, in *The Drama of Doctrine* the author situates himself somewhere in between what Vanhoozer identifies as Charles Hodge's merely cerebral, cognitive, monologic theology (I do not here contest this eminently contestable claim about Hodge, but we shall consider it in chapter 6) and George Lindbeck's communitarian and instrumental (if not pragmatic) view of doctrine (which is not contestable), drawing from each. In the more recent book Vanhoozer offers a different sort of sandwich. I don't think that it's intrinsic to what Vanhoozer wants to say about remythologizing that he positions himself in this way, but what this positioning shows is that he has two audiences in view, at least. One is the American evangelical constituency, with its high view of Scripture but its relatively low view of systematic

---

16. Vanhoozer, *Remythologizing Theology*, 24.

17. Ibid., 25. The quoted words at the end are those of Gerald A. McCool. One might wonder whether a metaphysical account of the Triune God is a touchstone, a fully reliable sign, of the reality of a theological vision. Having such an account clearly does not ensure referential success, but it may be a necessary condition of it.

18. Ibid., 27.

theology. The idea here is to represent theology in theo-dramatic fashion because this is closer to the letter of Scripture than the "timeless abstractions" of CRT. The second intended audience is that of modern academic theology: Vanhoozer wishes to situate his positive theological proposals within this firmament of ideas. In order to do this he takes some time and trouble to sketch what are for him the two main, broad outlooks in modern theology.

Each outlook involves some form of Trinitarianism. One theme or set of themes arises from the loss of interest in the ontological Trinity, and the exclusive focus that has come to be placed on the economic Trinity. The ontological Trinity *is* the economic Trinity. God's being *is* his redemptive action, his identity is given through how his triunity is identified in creation and especially in salvation history. The thrust is both personalistic and panentheistic. Panentheism is the idea that the world and everything in it is not distinct from God its creator, but is in some sense an extension of him, or rather that the created order is situated within the divine reality, though yet somewhat distinct from it. The approach is panentheistic in that the account of God's being is intrinsically tied an account of the world and with how it goes.

This personalistic, panentheistic theme is developed in another way, through an emphasis on the social Trinity, understood as a Trinity of equal persons united in perichoretic (i.e., mutually interdependent) love. This is used both as a model for Christian relations and for God's relation with the world. Again, there are various variations on this theme: Vanhoozer cites Fretheim and Brueggermann, Catherine M. Lacugna, Elizabeth Johnson, and open theism.

Vanhoozer's own variant on such personalistic and panentheistic theological tendencies resists the proposal that the idea of personal relation should supersede the very idea of divine substance, and stresses the creature-creator relation of communication, an asymmetrical interpersonal relationship that also makes possible the exercise of divine and human freedom.[19] This asymmetry certainly moves the position in the direction of classical theism. But in considering who God is the emphasis still falls upon economic Trinitarianism, and especially upon personal action rather than "mechanical" causation, on dialogue, as we have already seen in the account he gives of one distinctively Augustinian and Reformed emphasis, divine effectual calling. This is the emphasis even though the parties are in an asymmetrical personal relationship, that of divine, loving self-communicative

---

19. Ibid., 215.

action accompanied by spoken commentary, and upon the response to that.[20]

A sign that Vanhoozer has not shaken himself free of the hyper-personal character of modern theology is that, along with the current theological culture that he cites, he employs the central dilemma of that theology, the same false dilemma: he thinks that personal language supplants the language of impersonal and mechanical causality,[21] and that there is no alternative to the mechanical or the personal.

But the alternative to this that is presented, the idea that otherwise God must deal with persons in an impersonal or mechanical manner, is a figment of the imagination. There is no dilemma to be faced, for there is a third alternative, and the resulting trilemma can be handled within the parameters of classical theism. This is not a mere debating point. For as we noted earlier, it is also clear that by insisting that divine action in relation to humans is exclusively personal (as he understands this), Vanhoozer cannot aid our understanding of effectual calling without also invoking causal notions of a distinctly asymmetrical and non-personal (in his sense) kind.

He claims that his remythologizing theology "scrutinizes language about causality in order to bring out a communicative sense to which the church has not sufficiently attended," that is, the personal and interpersonal sense.[22] But in fact the reverse is the case. As we saw earlier, so long as he restricts God's relation to the world primarily to that of communicative agency through dialogue he makes it impossible to do justice, for example, to the necessary emphasis on the passivity of the soul in regeneration. This failure arises because his account filters out non-conversational elements of divine communication given to us in the biblical revelation. Vanhoozer does not scrutinize the language about causality sufficiently thoroughly.

No significant theologian employs the idea of divine communication and the word "communicate" more than Jonathan Edwards. It is everywhere in his writings. As for example, this, taken from his *Observations on the Trinity*:

> For God's determining to glorify and communicate Himself must be conceived of as flowing from God's nature; or we must look upon God from the infinite fullness and goodness of His nature as naturally disposed to cause the beams of His glory to shine forth, and his goodness to flow forth, yet we must look on the particular method that shall be chosen by divine wisdom to

---

20. Ibid., 177.
21. Ibid., 205-6.
22. Ibid., 28.

do this as not so directly and immediately owing to the natural disposition of the divine nature, as the determination of wisdom intervening, choosing that means of glorifying that disposition of nature.[23]

There are references to the nature of God as communicating himself via an emanation of his goodness, not automatically, as a "natural disposition" but by an act of will. Does this suggest impersonality, mere mechanism? Clearly not. However, the Edwardsean idea of communication is much broader than Vanhoozer's, for it includes the creating, sustaining, and redeeming of the world. Yet these varied communications are personal through and through, the work of a personal agent, though not all are, nor could they be, "communicative" in Vanhoozer's sense, and some of them are what he calls "mechanical."

For in the business of creation, how could there be any cooperation from the human race or any other personal source? "Where were you when I laid the foundation of the earth? Tell me, if you have understanding" (Job 38:4). Interestingly, however, Vanhoozer appears to think that creation involved a struggle, so that creation itself is a drama, and the account of it is a narrative. It is ironic in virtue of his general disparagement of Greek ideas, that the Greek idea of creation as the activity of the Demiurge upon unformed matter should be thought to play a part in the biblical divine drama.[24] Even if it is allowed that such an account of creation may be thought to involve the struggle of overcoming the chaos, it is somewhat far-fetched to suppose that this is a case of "communicative agency" in Vanhoozer's sense. What seems even more far-fetched is the insistence that the divine relation to the inanimate creation is through and through that of an interpersonal dialogue. When Christ stilled the storm by a rebuke, was he actually conversing with the storm, as Vanhoozer seems to be proposing?[25] The "Let there be"s of creation are expressions of divine power. They are not divine speech acts understood as having a certain illocutionary force.

Or let us consider the pivotal act of the Christian drama, the incarnation. Any reader of the narrative is struck by the sensitive and gracious way in which Mary is addressed by the Angel Gabriel, who speaks to her as the highly favored one, words which caused her perplexity at what the greeting might imply. This perplexity and fear were no doubt both calmed and then further aroused by Gabriel's words of reassurance. But in regard to the momentous event that was to take place, the conception of the Mediator in

---

23. Edwards, *Observations on the Trinity*, 79.
24. Vanhoozer, *Remythologizing Theology*, 36–37.
25. Ibid., 186.

her womb, Gabriel did not seek Mary's cooperation. His was not on a diplomatic mission. Mary was not pregnant because she consented to be. Note the unconditional language: "The Holy Spirit will come upon you, and the power of the Most High will overshadow you, therefore the child to be born will be called 'holy'—the Son of God" (Luke 1:35). Was pregnancy caused? Obviously so. Was this mechanical, impersonal causation? Obviously not. Was her consent sought? Not in any way that is apparent. It makes little sense to suppose that Mary's words "let it be to me according to your word" expressed her free acceptance of the angel's word (as Vanhoozer suggests),[26] rather than submission to the unconditional purpose of the Lord for her that had just then been announced.

So the form of classical theism, and of divine sovereignty that Vanhoozer is seeking to reintroduce, is somewhat constricted. But more importantly for us here, in order to articulate his reinstatement of a form of classical theism, Vanhoozer first has to give a clear account of God as distinct from his creation in terms that approach those of classical theism, clearly delineating the metaphysics of "divine communicative agency" in such terms. If he does not favor a form of panentheism, then what? As Vanhoozer says, on this proposal the development of any divine metaphysics or ontology must be "after the fact."[27] God is more than a set of events or relationships, but what more? Who is God?

"God in act," "God's being is in his free, wise and loving communicative agency," "God is no other than he has revealed himself to be." We need to reflect on these forms of expression, for the words could be taken in various ways. For example, they could mean that in what he communicates, God is genuine. He is not faking anything. There is no façade. His communications have the backing of God himself, and in that sense are expressive of himself; they are not insincere or hypocritical. This would be a moral thesis about God's character. Or they could mean that we know of God only by means of his communicative action, by its character and scale. This would be an epistemological thesis. The author occasionally flirts with this idea, saying that we know of God's *identity* by what we *identify* regarding what he has done.[28] Or they could mean that though God is distinct from his creation he exhaustively reveals himself in it. But none of these suggestions would take us far enough to establish a metaphysical thesis about the being of God, a variant of classical theism, which is what Vanhoozer is after.

---

26. Ibid., 335.

27. Ibid., 217.

28. Ibid., 184. The discussion at this point seems to be marred by a conflation of "identity" and "identify."

We need to remind ourselves at this point that it is not possible to make genuine metaphysical proposals simply by introducing novel phrases or neologisms. In rejecting classical theism because it is, in Vanhoozer's judgement, impersonal, mechanical, and monological, and in rejecting modern panentheism because, for example, it collapses what God does and what God is, what other metaphysical option is this expression "God's being is in his free wise and loving communicative agency" intended to identify? Something between classical theism and panentheism, presumably. But what? Is there room for another alternative?

One possibility may be as follows. God is essentially Trinitarian, in a perichoretic relationship in which love is necessarily communicated among the persons. So being essentially communicative, he could not fail to communicate himself *ad extra*. Thomas Aquinas, though a "classical theist," says something like this. He says that God must create, even though the character of what he creates is at his free discretion. The Angelic Doctor puts it like this:

> Moreover, God, in willing His own goodness, wills things other than Himself to be in so far as they participate in His goodness. But, since the divine goodness is infinite, it can be participated in in infinite ways, and in ways other than it is participated in by the creatures that now exist. If, then, as a result of willing His own goodness, God necessarily willed the things that participate in it, it would follow that He would will the existence of an infinity of creatures participating in His goodness in an infinity of ways. This is patently false, because, if He willed them, they would be, since His will is the principle of being for things, as will be shown later on. Therefore, God does not necessarily will even the things that now exist.[29]

While at a number of places Vanhoozer endorses the idea that God is free,[30] as far as I can see he fails to address the consequences of this for his idea of God as a communicative agent. If God is necessarily a communicative agent, is he free to communicate in other ways than he has chosen to? Or more pertinently, could he have refrained from communicating? An attempt to answer such difficult questions is vital to providing an understanding of Vanhoozer's proposal as contrasted with panentheism, on the one hand, and classical theism, on the other.

---

29. Aquinas, *Summa Contra Gentiles*, 81.4. There is considerable discussion over whether this represents Aquinas's overall view, and of its implications for divine contra-causal freedom. For details, see Dolezal, *God without Parts*, 191–94.

30. E.g., Vanhoozer, *Remythologizing Theology*, 170, 215, 216. For discussion of divine freedom, see Rowe, *Can God Be Free?*

However, Vanhoozer attempts to move a critical step further than Thomas's idea of participating in the goodness of God, I think, by in effect arguing that since God's communicating agency is that of a speech agent, and since his being is in his communicative agency, then whatever he creates must be a dialogue partner. As he puts it *"the economic Trinity is a dramatic analogy (a being-in-temporal-act) of the light, life, and love that God is in himself (a being-in-eternal-act)."*[31]

Note that at what is a critical point in the exposition, unusual and unexplained expressions take the place of clarity of expression and the presentation of argument. What is "a-being-in-eternal-act" or "a-being-in-temporal-act"? Perhaps a being who is partly eternal, partly temporal? It looks are if these expressions are designed to span the metaphysical chasm between theism and pantheism, but without slipping into panentheism. It is clear that Vanhoozer wishes to stress that God is "in act" all the way down. So it seems that God is essentially active in this sense, whatever this sense is, though Vanhoozer does not say as much. He employs the time-honored distinction between God as he is himself and as he operates economically, but the basis of the distinction seems to be not statements in Scripture regarding the nature of God but the communicative activity of God disclosed in the theo-drama. This carries with it the dangers I have been suggesting, a doctrine of God without modality. The use of hyphenated expressions certainly cannot be the answer.

Besides this lack of clarity, insofar as it is possible to glean what, roughly speaking, Vanhoozer has in mind, there's both a logical objection to such a proposal, and a theological objection to it, if (that is) these expressions are intended to be statements about who God is and what he is like. The logical objection is that already discussed but which Vanhoozer totally ignores: how can we conclude (contrary to what Thomas holds, for example) from what God in fact does that his nature is such that he must do that? And the theological objection, already noted, remains: does this requirement that is placed upon God's agency, that his communicative agency must take the form of speech, etc., not place unduly restrictive constraints upon God? Who are we to say what God could and could not have done? Although Vanhoozer's procedure is necessarily "after the fact," is it not also somewhat prescriptive?

He reveals that he is beset by the same itch that afflicts the modern Trinitarians, to go beyond what either Scripture or logic warrant. Scripture tells us what God does and has done, but (by and large) it does not tell us what he could have done. It does not tell us that he must communicate with

---

31. Vanhoozer, *Remythologizing Theology*, 218. Italics in the original.

what he has created. However, if God is "in" what he does, and as a consequence he could not do other than he has done, then it is hard to resist the beckoning hand of panentheism. And far from such a concept of God being a recipe for free, interpersonal, non-mechanical, open-ended conversation between God and his intelligent creatures, it comes to look pretty fatalistic, for God at least. He is fated to communicate, to unendingly chatter, to be a divine Mr. Talkative.

It might be counter-argued at this point that Thomas Aquinas's understanding of God meets the same difficulties, at least if he is interpreted along the lines proposed by Norman Kretzmann. On such lines, though God must create, he is free to create one among many possibilities. So, for example, Thomas tells us that God could have redeemed us without incarnation.[32]

It may be that Vanhoozer believes his proposal is the best that can be done if we are to think theologically "after the fact." This itself is ambiguous: is it after the fact of God's redemptive action? Or is it after the fact of God's revelation as a whole? We have seen the importance of one-liners in that revelation for our understanding of God's being in itself. It is interesting to observe his attitude to those metaphysical proposals he regards as "before the fact," which have their being logically prior to any creative or communicative act. For example, he is somewhat dismissive of the perfect being theology of Anselm. He says that Anselm provides a schema by insisting that God is a being which no greater can be conceived for the identification of God with Being. "Thus was born the attempt to think about the nature and attributes of God with the aid of ontology (the study of being) as a generative conceptual scheme."[33] By this he means that Anselm generated a concept of God with the help of the concept of being, alone, thus theologizing "before the event."

Where does the writer of Hebrews (or the writer of Genesis) get the Anselmian idea from, that God is a being than which a greater cannot be conceived? (Heb 6:17). I suggest that he does not get it from the metaphysical shelf, as Vanhoozer suggests, but from reflecting on the biblical teaching that God is the creator of all that is. If he is the creator of all that is, then by definition no one thing other than himself is as great as he is, let alone greater than he. For there is one God, and he is the only creator of all that is. Everything depends on him. This conclusion is supported by the Second Commandment, which makes a sharp distinction between that which is in the heavens above, the earth beneath, or the waters under the earth—that

---

32. For Kretzmann's interpretation of Aquinas see "A General Problem of Creation." Scott, *Being and Goodness*. For Aquinas on the incarnation, see *Summa Theologiae*, 3a 1–6.

33. Vanhoozer, *Remythologizing Theology*, 86.

is, is a created something or other—and that which is God. Such created objects, wherever in time and space they may be located, are not fit objects of worship, any more than they are fit objects to swear by. The only such object is he who is uncreated.

Of course there are other biblical data to support the wonderful verses of Hebrews that we discussed in chapter 3, in their assertion of God's unsurpassable greatness. David refers to the greatness of God, and the fact that there is no God besides him (2 Sam 7 22); Nehemiah refers to the great, the mighty God (Neh 9:32, also Jer 32:18 and Titus 2:13). Besides, the Lord is a great God, and a great King above all gods (Ps 95:3); he is to be feared above all gods (Pss 96:4; 77:13); he is greater than all gods (Exod 18:11); his greatness is unsearchable (Ps 145:3). The sense here is not of one who just happens to be greater than all gods, but one who is *necessarily* greater than they.

There are other features of Anselm's perfect being theology that are worth emphasizing. It is far from being a dry, abstract, logic-chopping exercise, but is couched in the language of meditation. In fact, the entire work takes the form of a prolonged meditative prayer on the being and character of God. It begins, "Come, then, Lord my God, teach my heart where and how to seek you . . ." and it deplores the effects of the fall. And it ends "I pray my God, that I may know you and love you, so that I may rejoice in you."[34] The biblical references that adorn the text of the *Proslogion* are not there simply to provide decoration. It is an overtly Trinitarian work and the declaration of God's triunity forms the climax of Anselm's meditations.

> You are this good, O God the Father; this is Your Word, that is to say, Your Son. For there cannot be any other thing greater or lesser than You, in the order by which You utter yourself. . . . And You are so simple that there cannot be born of You any other than what You are. This itself is the Love, one and common to You and to Your Son, that is the Holy Spirit proceeding from both.[35]

A strong human intuition that tells us that none is greater than God, and that God alone is worthy of worship, arises from or is strengthened by reading the overall presentation of the being and character of God in Scripture. How could God be worthy of worship if he could have been greater than in fact he is? If there is a being greater than God then why is not he God instead? It is hard to see, from these data, and from the intuition, what

---

34. On this theme in Anselm, see Marilyn M. Adams, "Praying the Proslogion."

35. The quotations from Anselm are from chapters 1, 26, and 23 respectively, *Anselm of Canterbury: The Major Works*.

objections there can be to the idea of God as the most perfect being, or as that than which a greater cannot be conceived.

It is a great pity that Vanhoozer does not follow up his own later-expressed opinion that Anselm is intending to exposit the logic of the biblical account of God.[36] For that indeed is what Anselm is intending. In not taking up the Anselmian project, or employing the metaphysics of the tradition of which Anselm is perhaps a unique example, Vanhoozer has deprived himself of tools that would be useful, essential, in articulating the metaphysics of Christian theism.

As we have seen, he badly needs to allow himself the use of metaphysical modalities. By restricting himself, in his efforts to develop a theological metaphysics, to what God has in fact said and done via the one narrative that he has established—creation, redemption, and consummation through Jesus Christ—he is carried inexorably downstream by the rapids in the direction of panentheistic reductionism, despite his best efforts to swim upstream.

Modal Aspects

The gospel of Jesus Christ is free—liberal, undeserved, and also (we must never forget) not necessitated. It might not have been so; we might not have been so. To ignore such data is, I believe, not the way to achieve an advance in our understanding of Christian theism, but to slip backwards.

God's faithfulness to Abraham, it's being impossible for him to lie, and his inexpressible greatness, presuppose his possession of distinctive powers or properties—properties that is, that are not exhausted by what God does, but ones he possesses essentially. They express his essence, or are ways in which we express his essence. What are these properties? If we are thinking particularly of his covenant faithfulness, then I suggest three, though there are perhaps more. Firstly, his power, and particularly his power over the future, our future, the future of those to whom the word or warrant or covenant of God has come, and that to which (we are supposing) he is faithful. For God cannot be faithful if he cannot bring about his own actions in the future, and ensure in some way that he can suitably concur with the actions of creaturely agents, both benign and malign, distinct from himself, in order to bring about the fulfilment of his word or promise. This power has therefore to be very great power; it has to be omnipotence understood to include power over the future.

---

36. Vanhoozer, *Remythologizing Theology*, 94.

Secondly, besides power, great power, there has to be knowledge, very great knowledge; in particular, knowledge of the future, including knowledge of the actions of agents other than himself. For if God's promises are concerned with territory in which non-divine agents operate, then God, in order to be faithful, must know what these actions are, and be able to take the necessary action to cope with them. (I put the point deliberately vaguely, in order to avoid getting into the perfectly legitimate but thorny questions of the relation between the divine decree and human actions.)

Thirdly, besides power and knowledge there has to be goodness, including the element of veracity. Power and knowledge could, by themselves, be used in the interest of untrustworthiness; they could be used malevolently, so as to sow distrust. To be faithful to promises of goodness, of blessing, the giver of those promises also has to be good. Trustworthiness, as such, does not imply goodness, but merely consistency; though of course as conventionally used it has connotations of beneficence. Putting it crudely, God has to want to fulfill his covenant promises, and mere knowledge and power by themselves do not ensure such wantings. Such wanting has to be beneficent and efficacious wanting, wanting that is not subject to weakness of will or to frustration of any kind, wanting that carries through to the accomplishment of whatever is wanted. So while the impossibility of God's covenant failing is conditional upon his word of promise, it implies unconditional necessities, such as God's veracity.

The CRT theologian Stephen Charnock expresses the modal strength of God's goodness as follows:

> Goodness is not a quality in him, but a nature; not a habit added to his essence, but his essence itself; he is not first God, and then afterwards good; but he is good as he is God, his essence, being one and the same, is formally and equally God and good. . . . He is essentially good in his own nature, and not by any outward action which follows his essence. . . . If he were not good by his essence, he could not be eternally good, he could not be first good; he would have something before him, from whence he derived that goodness, wherewith he is possessed.[37]

Some centuries later, Bavinck writes in similar terms of God's immutability.

> But God who *is* cannot change, for every change would diminish his being. Furthermore, God is as immutable in his knowing, willing and decreeing as he is in his being. . . . As he is, so he

---

37. Charnock, *Discourse Upon the Existence and Attributes of God*, 542–43.

knows and wills - immutably. . . . Neither creation, nor revelation, nor incarnation brought about any change in God.[38]

These requirements do not entail the strictest possible immutability in the divine character, they do not entail that God cannot bring about changes in any respect, but they do entail that a promise, though made contingently, has nevertheless the strong immutability of the one who promises. It must come to pass if it has been promised. In order for the faithfulness expressed by the promises to be of the sort that is divine, the properties or attributes that are necessary conditions for it—and given a promise, sufficient conditions for the promise being trustworthy—must be fully *modal* properties or attributes. That is to say, the knowledge and power and goodness that God has essentially is knowledge or power or goodness that he *could in no circumstances lack*. It is not knowledge or power or goodness that might come and go, or change and decay.

It is one thing to have knowledge or power essentially. The knowledge or power that God has is not knowledge or power that he just happens to have, it is knowledge or power that he could not fail to have. And similarly with goodness or veracity. But, in addition, the knowledge or power or goodness that God essentially has is invariable omniscience and omnipotence and perfect goodness. He is not more powerful or knowing or good at one time than another, and there is no possibility of him ever being less than omniscient and omnipotent.

The reason for all this is obvious. If it were possible that God, having made a promise or established a covenant, not carry out his word faithfully, then for all we know to the contrary this is what might in fact happen. Even if God is trustworthy today he may not be trustworthy tomorrow. And even if we suppose that there is good inductive evidence that in this world God has, as a matter of fact, kept every promise that he has made, nevertheless, if he is not essentially invariably trustworthy, then for all we know to the contrary his power may give out, or his knowledge be inadequate, or his goodness falter, or all three may fail, just when he is most needed.[39]

But it may be objected that this requirement, which seems to be obvious, and is central to CRT, may be said by some to be unnecessarily strong. Why, in order to be trustworthy, does God need to be *essentially* trustworthy? After all, there are many cases of unreserved trust in which the objects of trust do not have their trustworthiness essentially or necessarily. I

---

38. Bavinck, *Reformed Dogmatics*, II:154.

39. "If God is true and just and unchangeable and almighty, we can have absolute confidence in his promises: otherwise we cannot, and there would be an end of Christianity," Geach, *Providence and Evil*, 9.

unreservedly trust the table on which I'm now leaning even though it could collapse or wobble uncontrollably even as I'm leaning on it.

Whether the requirement that God is essentially trustworthy is exaggerated or not depends upon what the object of trust is being trusted for. Trusting the table to bear my weight as I lean on it is one thing; the sort of evidence for its likely steadiness that we have is surely sufficient for such a case. But what if we need strong encouragement to hold fast to the hope set before us (as we saw earlier that the writer to the Hebrews believed his readers needed)? How can the great high priest be a steadfast anchor unless it is impossible for the promise of God to fail? Surely only a well-grounded trust in a God who is *essentially* trustworthy will be sufficient.

So, the argument is, the conclusions about God arising from the sort of theological treatment provided by Tom Wright (to take one example) and Kevin Vanhoozer (to take another) require more than history, more than sequence, and a narrative of that sequence, and more than communicative agency. They need God to have a nature consisting of features or attributes that are maximally modal, that hold in every possible eventuality in which God might figure, ultimately grounded in God's pure actuality. As we saw earlier, CRT utilizes such resources in articulating its doctrine of God in the Anselmian spirit. Much more would need to be said to provide a fuller account of God's features and their character, but this is the work of the systematic theologian proper, not that of a book about systematic theology. It is a shame that Vanhoozer is prepared to abandon this way of articulating the doctrine of God for such insubstantial reasons.

One particularly puzzling source of unease with CRT is that it is judged to be a theoretical, and so not a practical, endeavor. But whether some set of assertions is of theoretical or practical value depends upon what the set contains, and also upon the attitude of the reader or hearer of it. In theology exactness of thought should not be derided. We "participate in" sound definitions when they engender confidence that they have accurately identified the relevant bit of the conceptual skeleton. However, our attitude to what is exactly expressed depends entirely on whether what is clearly expressed is important or not. In the same way, we can stress the "participatory" nature of the language of Psalm 139 for all we are worth, but it remains on the page if no one sees the need to "engage" with it.

We noted earlier Calvin's high estimate of definitions. The prominence given to definitions in the *Institutes* is not merely testimony to the Calvinian love of order. Calvin shows that he thinks we ought to be moved by these definitions, not moved to admiration for the cleverness of the definer, but moved by the divine reality defined. For he notes more than once that an apt definition reveals the "force" of an idea. These realities, once defined, are not meant to be filed away, or simply to be argued over—they are not to "flit in the brain," but to move us.

This reminds us that, according to CRT, whether we like it or not, we are subjects who apprehend the set of sentences which comprise Holy Scripture. There is no way around such a subject-object "dichotomy," as we shall see in more detail later on. Systematic theology is (or aims to be) above all other things loving and obedient thought about God. Loving and obedient speech and practice may follow, but whether or not it does so depends upon other factors besides clear thinking. Dismissing exact, propositional theology as "theoretical" or "cerebral" does not alter anything. CRT recognized the sobering truth that the one gospel is to some a fragrance from death to death, to others a fragrance from life to life (2 Cor 2:16). But the definitions, and the realities they depict, are intended to help us to understand the faith better, or at least to protect it from misunderstanding.

God, Freedom, and Evil

Vanhoozer laudably wishes to uphold God's authorship of the grand narrative of the Christian story,[40] but at the same time he is apprehensive of doing so in terms that may suggest coercive action. He proposes a "robust" account of triune authorship that yields, he believes, divine sovereignty, human freedom, and the integrity of their relation.[41] This is most certainly a prize worth having: an account of divine sovereignty and human freedom harmonized in terms of a positive account of the relation between the two. Does Vanhoozer carry it off?

Since this book is a development of certain novel theological proposals in relation to the tradition of CRT I shall be rather selective in the way I try to answer this question. The focus will be those occasions where Vanhoozer appeals to the Reformed theological tradition, to Calvin, to Luther, and to the *Westminster Confession*, for example. So I pass over his account of God's and his creatures' relations to time, and even his account of God's passion. But before looking at his use of the tradition, which has to do with God and evil, I shall consider his position more generally.

Vanhoozer develops his account of the divine side of things using a variety of authorial analogies. These are drawn from the literary critic Mikhail Bakhtin, an author he earlier made use of in *The Drama of Doctrine*. But then he considers the obvious objection that human agents are not fictional persons on the page. Yet Bakhtin says that the independence and freedom

40. Vanoozer, *Remythologizing Theology*, 316.
41. Ibid., 317.

of a character is precisely what is incorporated into the author's design. So Vanhoozer thinks that if we take this seriously then our freedom is our answerability to God's first dialogic word in Christ.[42] Each of us is free to accept, or free to reject, his dialogic overtures. David accepted, Jonah rejected, Mary accepted. "So it is with every human being: the Author addresses each person and each freely responds and, in so doing freely realizes the voice-idea of the Author."[43] We are capable of self-determination, which "has its ground not in my own (monological) existence but rather in the potentially infinite dialogue with the Author God who alone calls me into being and who consummates my life and gives it meaning." So Vanhoozer concludes that there is "no contradiction between Authorial determination of a character's 'idea' and the character's own self-determination."[44] Would that this tangle of issues were that simple. Beyond the use of novel terminology not a single argument for this conclusion is offered, nor any allusion made to the vast literature on this area.

Some of the difficulties can be seen by pressing the issue of God's relation to evil. If God is the author of the world in which evil occurs, is he not ultimately responsible for what villains do? At this point Vanhoozer considers the language of the *Westminster Confession of Faith* about the divine decree, that in its execution, "neither is God the author of sin, nor is violence offered to the will of the creatures."[45] But he does not find much help from this. Why is this? He does not say, but perhaps it is because the language of the *Confession* is negative language; it tell us what the divine decree of evil does not imply, offering no explanation, while Vanhoozer is seeking to provide a positive account of God's apparent complicity in evil. Or maybe it is because he thinks that the Confession's approach is "monologic."

What of the particularly difficult case of Pharaoh's hardening? How does this fit into the dialogical scheme? It follows at once from Vanhoozer's account of God's nature that God cannot be the cause of Pharaoh's hardening. For that would be a case of mechanical, not of personal, agency. But he suggests that we may think of God as refusing to soften Pharaoh's heart, as a result of which Pharaoh self-hardens, so to speak. He considers Calvin's proposal that God, by withholding his Spirit, refuses to soften Pharaoh's heart. This is promising, he thinks, but only if it is developed in terms of God's triune communicative action.[46] He thinks that Luther's idea, that God

---

42. Ibid., 335.
43. Ibid.
44. Ibid., 336.
45. *Westminster Confession of Faith* III.1.
46. Vanhoozer, *Remythologizing Theology*, 340.

does not provoke Pharaoh to evil, but allows him to show his true colors "by thrusting at him through the word of Moses," is more promising because it places the hardening within the context of God's speech. For Pharaoh hears God's word, but instead of responding to it, he shows his true character by rebutting it.

Let us consider the other side of such a divine-human relationship: What happens when a person, with a potential for such hardheartedness, instead is addressed by the Author?[47] According to Vanhoozer, the answer is to be explained in terms of "soft power," persuasive, penetrative discourse. Such discourse evokes a response that comes from within rather than by coercion, from without. Turretin and other CRT theologians of that era would say that Vanhoozer has made a mistake of principle here: he has taken the character of effectual calling to be explicable only "from the event." Turretin quotes Bellarmine, who first makes "Effectual calling to consist in the assent and cooperation of man, so that it is called effectual from the event because it brings about its effect, and does because the human will cooperates with it; so that it is in man's power to render sufficient grace effectual." Turretin has no time for such a view. It "brings back the very error of Pelagius."[48]

To say that effectual grace is called such because it is in fact effectual in a particular instance does not go far enough for Turretin. It is effectual because it is designed by God, who calls, to be so. Vanhoozer most certainly asks the right question when he asks how divine communicative active works.[49] Jesus invites, he says "Come to me," he uses discourse. But not everyone is persuaded or accepts the invitation. There is division. Jesus has brought not peace but a sword. So Vanhoozer notes that there is the role of the Spirit, there is Spirit and word together, the Spirit is a minister of Jesus' words. This is surely an emphasis that CRT would welcome. He also notes Calvin's emphasis on the internal testimony of the Spirit.[50] The Spirit writes the word on the heart. But as we noted in our earlier discussion of effectual calling in the previous chapter, such writing on the heart is pure monergism, though utterly congruent with the nature and personality of the patient. Such monergistic, non-dialogic influences may respect the contours of the personality, going with the grain, and in that sense they are non-coercive, but nevertheless such work is in accordance with the good pleasure of God and does not seem to respect the contours of Vanhoozer's idea of communicative agency.

47. Ibid., 361.
48. Turretin, *Institutes of Elenctic Theology*, II:517.
49. Vanhoozer, *Remythologizing Theology*, 364.
50. Ibid., 365.

So, to refer to Turretin again, he states that efficacious grace

> [v]aries according to the diverse circumstances and qualities of the subject and so with the motion which is congruous with respect to one, is incongruous with respect to another and vice versa. But it brings with it that help which is called efficacious and which on that account is distinguished from the inefficacious.[51]

And, more pointedly, citing Augustine's phrase "delightful conqueror," he says:

> Thus neither that strength nor efficacy compels the main unwillingly, nor sweetly moves him now running spontaneously; but each joined together both strengthens the weakness of man and overcomes the hatred of sin. It is powerful that it may not be frustrated; sweet that it may not be forced. Its power is supreme and inexpungable that the corruption of nature may be conquered, as well as the highest impotence of acting well and the necessity of doing evil. Yet still it is friendly and agreeable, such as becomes an intelligent and rational nature.[52]

There are further aspects that Vanhoozer's model of dialogue does not address. In dealing with the problem of evil it is simplistic. For example, it does not consider that God, the leading conversation-partner, may have multiple intentions in entering into dialogue. And the theology of communicative action has no way of addressing other questions that necessarily arise: What is freedom? What is voluntariness? What is involuntariness? CRT is capable of carefully reflecting on these questions with help from the philosophers, and of offering definitions. Were the sailors who had to jettison the ship's cargo in a storm, famously discussed by Aristotle and also by the Reformers, acting freely?[53] Was Paul, who kicked against the pricks? Or Peter, who left everything to follow Jesus? And ultimately, the most basic question: since we are all hard of heart, as Vanhoozer says, to what is a positive acceptance of the divine overtures due? Is the favorable response due to free will or free grace? These basic issues go undiscussed, because they fall outside the terms of reference of Vanhoozer's theology of communicative agency, and there seems to be no way of ensuring them a place on his agenda.

---

51. Turretin, *Institutes of Elenctic Theology*, I:520.
52. Ibid., II:524–25.
53. See, for example, Peter Martyr Vermigli's *Lectures on the Nicomachean Ethics*.

What has gone wrong? I am tempted to suggest that in *Remythologizing Theology* the dialogue model itself has been employed unilaterally. In confining God's communicative action to speech it imposes a pattern that does not do justice to the richness and diversity of God's ways highlighted in CRT, especially to his uniqueness as creation's redeeming Lord. For all Vanhoozer's protestations against the malign influence of the Enlightenment, his own approach turns out also to be somewhat *a priori*, and so is in this sense dogmatic. This same spirit is also seen in his lack of caution—as in the spurning of negative theological expressions, as seen in his rejection of the *Westminster Confession's* phrasing on the divine decree.[54] In all these respects Vanhoozer's neglect of the CRT tradition in the interests of presenting a model of divine communicative action results in loss. The theology of communicative agency, at least as he forges it, is a blunt instrument, and wielding it is a backward step.

---

54. Vanoozer, *Remythologizing Theology*, 339.

5

Speech Acts, Propositions, and Assertions

So far it has been argued that the nature of narrative sequences, if developed consistently as the only or chief kind of theological data, prevents the reception into systematic theology of statements about natures and essences, the nature of God, the nature of man, and so on. For a narrative is simply a sequence of events, made intelligible by the speech actions of the participants, accompanied some of the time by a running commentary, making clear the significance of why event A was followed by event B, why event P preceded event Q, and so on. If carried out consistently, it delivers to us only a "bundle" account of God's being, of mankind, and of everything else. So, as Vanhoozer makes clear, on this view the logic of revelation is nothing but the logic of *mythos*, or of drama.

When Vanhoozer speaks theologically, God is a communicative agent. But I've been arguing that this is only papering over the cracks and leaves us with a strangely remote God. It leaves us with a serious and an unbiblical impoverishment of the task of systematic theology, taking us quite away from CRT. It ties the hands of the systematic theologian behind his back. But it may be worse than this. If pressed, it may actually render narrative or theo-dramatic or remythologized theology unintelligible. It may be that such theological intelligibility as narrative and theo-dramatic theologies possess is because practitioners of them have for some reason appealed to systematic theology in the CRT sense, even while they pursue the objective of supplanting it.

The Problem with Propositions

In this chapter we shall see that much of what drives the projects of theo-drama and remythologizing—a fear of propositional theology, of a theology which is nothing other than lists of propositions—is not warranted by the presence of propositions in Scripture. To see this requires us to focus attention on another area of disquiet for post-foundationalists. The innovators argue (or at least claim) that traditional systematic theology is seriously deficient in its neglect of the actual language of Scripture. It is said that traditional CRT constricts or reduces the Bible to a series of propositions, statements of fact that are (typically) of a general and abstract and "timeless" kind. From these it formulates doctrine that is correspondingly static and abstract, that is purely cerebral and has no applicatory force. It is claimed that to do theology in this way is to fly in the face of the obvious fact that the Bible has a variety of literary forms, and particularly that its central theme comes to us in the form of real-time narratives. The canon of Scripture consists not only of statements, but of a wide variety of speech forms, and of material of widely differing genres. In a word, while CRT expresses its claims about God and man in terms of *propositions*, Scripture itself communicates to us through a wide variety of different kinds of *speech acts*.

Here are some examples of such verdicts upon CRT from *The Drama of Doctrine*:

> The main defect of propositionalism is that it reduces the variety of speech actions in the canon to one type: the assertion. This results in a monologic conception of theology, and of truth. To think of theology as a monologue, even a truthful monologue, is to reduce theo-drama—in which dialogical action is carried by a number of voices—to mere theory.[1]

> [P]ropositionalism tends to see all of Scripture in terms of revelation, to see the essence of revelation in terms of conveying information (e.g., truth content), and to see theology in terms of processing this information (e.g., *scientia*). In the words of one contemporary propositionalist: the "Scripture contains a body of divinely given information actually expressed or capable of being expressed in propositions."[2]

So it is argued that the "static" view of propositional revelation must give way to the "dramatic" view of revelation as God's acts, especially God's speech acts. Hence the need for a "post-propositionalist theology,"[3] theology that is cognitive, but not propositionalist. Understanding the language of Scripture in terms of speech acts, it is said, holds one key, if not *the* key,

---

1. Vanhoozer, *The Drama of Doctrine*, 266.
2. Ibid., 268. The quotation is from Carl F. H. Henry.
3. Ibid., 266f.

to a much-needed re-shaping of systematic theology; theology as speech set apart for and bound to its object, the gospel of Jesus Christ.[4] Speech acts and theo-drama fit snugly together, as can easily be seen. We shall begin our consideration of such claims by first looking at the idea of a speech act.

Speech Acts

The term "speech act" arose from the work of the Oxford philosopher J. L. Austin in the 1950s. *How To Do Things with Words*, published in 1962 after Austin's early death, is the seminal work. However, we must not confuse the term with the thing. Appreciation of speech acts and their forces is by no means a novelty in biblical interpretation, any more than it is in grammar, as we shall see in due course.

First we need to note a couple of things about speech acts. In his work Austin focused upon what he called *performative* utterances; forms of utterance in which the saying of something is to perform an act more than the mere act of speech. The standard example is the wedding ceremony. The saying of "I do" uttered at the appropriate points in the ceremony *is* the wedding of the groom and the bride. Their words constitute the action of two people becoming man and wife. Such acting by speaking occurs because of words uttered with the appropriate intention, and also because of the existence of certain conventions; in the case of marriage, certain legal and moral conventions that govern the marriage service or ceremony, making it the sort of occasion that it is. A more theologically central example is the nature of justification. When God justifies a sinner he does so by *declaring* that person righteous. It is law-court language, as when a judge pronounces a person to be innocent of the charge against them. By his declaration the judge is not making a person innocent, nor is he describing what innocence is, nor (in the first instance) is he informing the man that he is innocent, nor infusing him with innocence. Rather, he is declaring the man to be innocent in the light of the evidence presented to the court (and as a consequence, indirectly informing the defendant that he is innocent). What is noteworthy about such cases is that there is an identifiable framework that confers on certain authorized people—a judge, a minister, and so on—certain powers, or recognizes inherent powers, so that in appropriate circumstances their speaking becomes the performing of an action.

However, such conventions may be very informal and tacit. In the course of a conversation to say "I promise" is usually taken to be the very act of promising, as saying "I resign" is, in certain circumstances, to resign,

---

4. Ibid., 265.

saying "I apologize" is the making of an apology, and so on. But, of course, the mere utterance of these words need not be cases of promising or resigning. Suppose a person uses the words "I promise" merely to clear his throat, or for pronunciation practice, or in the course of reciting a poem, then the words "I promise" are not a true performative. So not only do certain conventions, formal or informal, need to be in operation, but also the speakers must have a certain intention in speaking, and the hearer (or hearers), the ones addressed, must understand that intention in order for what is said (such as "I promise") to have a certain *illocutionary force*, for someone, say, the force of being promised to. As noted, there are many types of speech act: they include asking questions, giving orders, and (most importantly for us) making assertions.[5]

Speech-act types do not exactly correspond to grammatical mood. A question may be used to perform the speech act of commanding, as in "Is it not time you did the washing up?" or an expression of thanks may be used to make a request, as in the rather irritating notice, "Thank you for not smoking." But in the appropriate circumstances, saying "The cat is on the mat" is asserting that the cat is on the mat, as the expression "Is the cat on the mat?" is standardly used to ask a question.

Arising from such reflections, Austin distinguished between the *locution* (for example, the words that are spoken or written on a sign, such as "Beware of the dog") and the *illocution*, that is the force of the words, what is intended by them in the circumstances in which they are uttered. The sign "Beware of the dog" may be used to warn people about the presence of the fierce dog. Finally, as we noted earlier, an illocution may (or may not) have *perlocutionary effects*. The sign may or may not be successful in bringing it about that a reader of the sign is warned of the dog. (Incidentally, the example of the warning sign shows that speech acts do not need to be precisely dateable events, they can have a permanent or at least an enduring character. This will be significant in what follows.)

Speech Acts and Scripture

So the focus of the proponents of a speech act approach to Scripture, as opposed to a propositionalist approach, is to stress the interrelation of divine and human activity through speech, to stress divine-human dialogue. We

---

5. "Take away assertions, and you take away Christianity. Why, the Holy Spirit is given to Christians from heaven in order that He may glorify Christ and in them confess Him even unto death—and is this not assertion, to die for what you confess and assert?" Luther, *The Bondage of the Will*, 67.

conduct conversations through speech, and speaking involves us in making speech acts. So, it is claimed, speech acts indicate the potential for dialogue, whereas propositions only allow for monologue. On some views, Scripture is the record of such speech and its interactive effects; on other, stronger views, of a more "theo-dramatic" kind, we ourselves may be caught up in this interaction; we ourselves may be (or become) the conversation-partners of God, participants in the drama. Either way, the point is that Scripture is not reducible to a set of propositions, but divine and human speech is recognized for what it is. Scripture has cognitive content, but that content is not to be understood in terms of the truth of certain propositions, but of the significance of certain speech acts.

There are reckoned to be at least two other advantages of this speech act approach. One is to make clear that Scripture is richer than the propositionalist view leads us to believe; it is not simply "lists of propositions," but it contains a great variety of types of speech, associated with different genres. Scripture consists not only of statements or assertions, but of questions, commands, vows, exclamations, and so forth, and both the exegete and the theologian need to take account of all such forms, and not to reduce Scripture to one form, the proposition, or to pay exclusive attention to that form, neglecting all else as mere "packaging."

> The propositionalist temptation is to regard narrative simply as the pretty packaging of historical content to be torn off and discarded. But the point of narrative is not merely to assert "this happened, and then this happened." Narratives make another kind of claim altogether: "look at the world like this." Narratives do more than chronicle, they *configure*. Configuration is the act of grouping people and events together in a meaningful whole and is, as such, an act of the narrative imagination, a power of synoptic vision.[6]

A second advantage of using the speech act approach to the language of Scripture is to help us to identify the genre of particular books or parts of Scripture. The idea here is that particular books or parts of books in Scripture are written with different conventions or rules, though perhaps not consciously or explicitly so. The rules that govern the writing of apocalyptic, such as parts of the book of the Revelation, or parts of Daniel and Ezekiel, are different from the conventions of a Chronicle, or of prophecy, or of New Testament letter-writing, or of a historical narrative, or of the telling of a parable. These diverse forms, properly grasped in terms of their associated conventions, set up different kinds of expectations in our minds as to how

---

6. Vanhoozer, *The Drama of Doctrine*, 282.

the language is to be taken, the place of repetition (in Hebrew poetry, for example), the nature of a greeting (in Paul), the use of numbers and symbols and weird animal forms (in apocalyptic), and of story-telling (as in Jesus's parables).

What are we to say to these proposals? The basic idea that God's word is God's speech, the word of our creator and redeemer, certainly echoes an important biblical theme. Through the various divinely appointed human agents, through prophets and apostles, through his Incarnate Son, God speaks to his people of the Old and New Testaments in various ways, and the entire record of this may be deemed to be his speech, the living word of God. In addition, the whole of divine revelation in Scripture, in which the Lord records the speech of some, inspires the speech of others, and he himself speaks, is confessed by the Christian church to be God's speech, God's word. We might, then, think of the whole of Scripture as being enclosed within one set of speech marks, with other sets of speech marks occurring within Scripture. The entire Bible is in these various senses "God's speech."

However, there is one general disadvantage to placing exclusive or the main emphasis on the idea that Scripture is God's speech. As we have noted, though speaking is an event, not all speech acts are events. The words, "Beware of the dog," may be a warning, and have that illocutionary force for as long as the sign is hung on the gate. Yet typically a speech act, like any human action, occurs at a time, lasts for so long, and then stops. It is an event every bit as much as coughing or raising one's arm is an event. The general danger is that, with this in mind, we approach Scripture in an overcontextualizing frame of mind, a tendency to think that the occasions of divine speech pass, and are replaced by others, and that the words of Scripture have a correspondingly fleeting significance. While, obviously enough, there are original situations in which the words of Scripture were uttered, spoken or written down, it is does not follow that what was uttered has to do with that situation alone. This is what earlier we referred to as the Utterance Fallacy. The one sign may warn countless passers-by over many years; and many of the assertions of Scripture retain their original illocutionary force centuries after they were first uttered. We shall take up the question of how the significance of a speech act may endure in the next chapter.

Earlier we saw that besides locutions and illocutions, speech-act theory in the hands of J. L. Austin posits perlocutions or perlocutionary effects. These are the effects on those who understand the meaning of a locution, through appreciating its illocutionary force, or who fail to understand it. Vanhoozer occasionally mentions the significance of perlocutionary effect[7]

---

7. Ibid., 66–68.

but it does not seem to have any substantial consequence for who misunderstand it. But the fact is that in the New Testament, the effect of the word, or what it means, is of fundamental importance for our understanding of Christian doctrine, and especially when doctrine is understood in speech act terms. For example, the perlocutionary effect can be that a person leaves the company of Jesus, as in the case of those who sought to arrest Jesus, but who recognized that he taught against them, and so left him alone (Mark 12:18). The same teaching may have a variety of different effects, as Jesus shows in the parable of the sower, and as Paul stresses in his recognition that the same gospel may be to some a fragrance from death to death, to others a fragrance from life to life (2 Cor 2:18).

Propositions and Speech Acts: A False Antithesis

Kevin Vanhoozer has an ambivalent attitude to propositions. On the one hand, he resists what he calls "propositionalist theology," as exemplified in Thomas Aquinas and Charles Hodge, for example. On the other hand, he wishes to think of some speech acts as having "propositional content." Propositionalist theologians allegedly see the Bible as a book of factual propositions[8] and nothing more. More generously, perhaps, he sees such theologians as "abstracting" propositions from the multi-genred library of books we call the Bible. The unacceptable price that is paid is that figurative language of Scripture is discounted. In behaving in this way propositionalist theologians show themselves to be modernistic (even Aquinas!) in their reduction of knowledge to information,[9] and in being committed to the modernistic view that rationality is universal. Above all, they de-dramatize Scripture. Yet Vanhoozer wishes to affirm that some of that propositional content is necessary for theology.[10] Later on we shall examine his effort at preserving propositional content without propositions. And we shall see that his estimate of Charles Hodge as a "purely cerebral" theologian is factually incorrect.

But we can accept the idea of Scripture as divine speech as accurate and helpful. However, to claim that in view of Austin's work on speech acts we are faced with a new choice about the nature of divine revelation, an exclusive choice to take *either* a speech act view of divine revelation *or* a propositional view, won't stand up to scrutiny. There are a number of reasons why this is so.

8. Ibid., 83.
9. Ibid., 87.
10. Ibid., 89.

Behind the polarization between speech acts and propositions lies a misunderstanding of the terms "proposition" and "propositional" as used in standard accounts by proponents of propositional revelation. The word "proposition" can be used as a term of art equivalent to an expression that conveys a thought to which a truth value may be assigned. So the sentence "The cat is on the mat" can be employed as a proposition in this sense. It can be given a truth value, or believed to have one, and uttered to express the truth that the cat is on the mat. Or it can be assigned a truth value, true or false, in an arbitrary way and then be used in the testing of logical arguments. It can be assumed, for the sake of argument, that *the cat is on the mat* is a true premise of an argument, or assumed that it is false. We may call this the logician's sense of proposition.

So, a thought can have a truth-value because it describes the way the world is, or fails to; or it can be assigned a truth value by the logician for the purpose of illustrating some point of logic. When used in this special sense the "proposition" is considered in a way that abstracts from particular occasions of utterance. We may say such propositional language is occasion-neutral or occasion-indifferent. But a proposition in the sense of a statement of fact cannot be so easily jettisoned.

Despite the charge that the propositionalist view of revelation and theology considers propositions to be "timeless"—a matter to be discussed more fully in the next chapter—no practitioner of the allegedly dark art of "propositional theology" believes that "proposition" in "propositional revelation" is being used in this logicians' or grammarians' way. The propositions of Scripture are not declarative sentences to which a truth value has at some point been arbitrarily assigned. Rather, such propositions, it is claimed, are as a matter of fact conveyed in Scripture and some of the most important are summarized in the creeds and confessions of the church.

Many of the sentences of Scripture, and of the theology drawn from Scripture, express not simply declarations that may possibly be true, but true thoughts. Such sentences have their occasions of utterance, whether the words were first used in speech or writing, or to report speech actions indirectly, as in the language of a narrator, or of a commentator such as we find in the New Testament letters. Asserting, narrating, and reporting are familiar and fundamental types of speech act. In Scripture the expression of truths standardly has this form, the form of assertion. So, since "assertion" is a central type of speech act, a fundamental type, there is no need to polarize propositions against speech acts. If the term "proposition" offends the sensibilities of some, let us substitute the speech act term "assertion" for it.

This account of propositions or assertions is borne out in CRT in obvious ways. One way is in the frequency with which the New Testament writers refer to Old Testament Scripture as "saying." "The Scripture *says*, 'In you all the families of the earth shall be blessed'" (Gen 12:3); "The Scripture *says* to Pharoah, 'For this very purpose I have raised you up'" (Rom 9:17). Sometimes the Scriptures are referred to as if they were the voice of God; at other times, God and Scripture are brought together to show that they carried the same authority. But in each case these are instances of "saying," instances of performing a straightforward speech act. B. B. Warfield, a favorite example of a "propositionalist" theologian, in his learned review of these passages, does not make any effort to diminish the force of the word "say," to "de-dramatize" it.[11]

Indexicality

But in our stress on the direct speech in Scripture, and in thinking of Scripture as itself constituting God's direct speech to us, we must note some other important features of speech, especially the use of speech to speak about things as they happen and about places from the point of view of the speaker. Much of our everyday speech is not only an event, an act of speaking at a time, it is an act of speaking in which what is asserted is something that is contemporaneous with the speaking, or past or future measured by the temporal position of the speaker. If I make the true assertion at 5:38 am on 9th May 2013, "The sun is rising," that utterance is true *only at that time*, just as if I say "The sunrise is clearer today than yesterday" I am comparing something that is contemporary with the utterance with something that occurred the day earlier. There are many such assertions in Scripture such as: "My time has not yet come," "Today you shall be with me in paradise," "Let us go hence," and "Now is our salvation nearer than when we first believed." This is the phenomenon of *indexicality*, the fact that language may be about the very time (or the very place) of its utterance. Indexical expressions can be transformed by turning them into reported or indirect speech, as in "Jesus said to the thief on the cross that he would be in paradise that day," which, once its indexicality has been eliminated, expresses a truth that can be reasserted an indefinite number of times.

Why is it necessary to draw attention to indexicality? Because, by and large, indexical speech acts have a short shelf-life. They are soon spent, the point of uttering them in the first place passes as the occasion of their utterance passes. Jesus's assertion "My time is not yet come" can be reported and studied, but it cannot now be asserted to express the same truth as Jesus uttered. We may translate such indexical speech into non-indexical

---

11. Warfield, "'It says': 'Scripture says': 'God says.'"

equivalents by replacing words such as "now," "today," "tomorrow," "next week," and so on, with dates and times, and spatial uses of "here" and "there" with grid references or place names. Modified in this way we can continue to re-issue these assertions in non-indexical ways. While we can retain the cognitive truth that way, obviously the immediacy of the original utterance cannot be retained. But there is no avoiding this. Even a theo-dramatic construal of the utterance "My time has not yet come" has to recognize that the time of the original utterance is in the past, and so irreversible. Using the language of drama cannot alter or revitalize what has happened, resurrecting or in some other way causing the words to breathe their old life again. The equivalent non-indexical expressions have a longer shelf-life. But the transposition from the indexical to the non-indexical results in a loss. Reported speech loses some of the force of the original.

By contrast, very many of the different speech acts to be found in Scripture presuppose abidingly true assertions about God and his ways that provide the bedrock of theological reflection on which systematic theology is based. Such assertions may be re-used without loss. For the speech of Scripture to be understood theologically, its indexicality must be framed by sets of non-indexical assertions the purpose of which is to give us the abiding theological significance of the original indexical speech, or to provide data which help us to build up an understanding of the speaker.

We can put this slightly differently, in terms of what Scripture reports. Besides the assertions that we have been considering, it reports direct speech ("Are you the only visitor to Jerusalem who does not know the things that have happened there in these days?") and uses indirect speech ("They all with one consent began to make excuse"). Besides this it reports events and states that are wordless ("The stone was rolled away from the tomb"). Other statements it reports simply by reproducing them. So the scriptural statement that God is love is reproduced as a text: "God is love."

"Lists of Propositions"

A simple inspection of its text shows that the Bible cannot simply be "lists of propositions," nor even lists of assertions, and if ever there were people who thought differently then they were clearly mistaken. The Bible records that Jesus wept, that he was angry and tired, that he rebuked and invited. In some of what he did he used words. He asserted that his Father is greater than he. He rebuked Peter with the words "Get you behind me, Satan," and invited sinners with the words "Come unto me all you who labor and are heavy laden and I will give you rest." On one occasion he wept without saying anything, and this action had an effect, though not a perlocutionary effect. So, on the one hand, Jesus used words to rebuke and to invite, while on the other hand, he did things that did not involve words. The words he used in rebuking and inviting are of course not statements or assertions, any more than are promising and requesting. To rebuke or to invite is not to assert or state anything. Jesus did and suffered all these non-assertoric things, and many more besides.

In what it reports, Scripture presents actions performed through language, such as assertings and promisings, and actions and states of affairs that are done or that occur wordlessly. But are these non-propositional data merely the packaging of what is of real value, the proposition?[12] Obviously not. Such data may be vital in building up an understanding of what the New Testament teaches us about the person of Christ. Was Jesus a Stoic? No, he wept. Was he only a stern teacher? No, he graciously invited the weak and heavy laden to come to him. Was Jesus likely to be deflected from the course that he had set himself, the work that his Heavenly Father had given him to do? No, he rebuked as satanic temptations any suggestions that he might deviate from that path. Such information, the information conveyed to us in the speech acts of Jesus other than by his assertions, and in his wordless states, such as his weeping, or the occasions of his being tired or angry, are vital for enabling us to build up a faithful doctrine of the person and work of Christ.

According to the caricature, the CRT view is of Scripture as merely "lists of propositions." But such an attitude to Scripture is impossible to defend. It is supposedly impossible to draw conclusions from goings-on in Scripture that are not propositions. For according to the caricature, the Bible is simply nothing but packaged propositions. But it is obvious that weeping and rebuking and inviting and having a stone rolled away from the mouth of a grave, are not propositions, even though the reports of them *are* in the form of assertions. But we must not confuse the report or narrative, which is in the form of one or more assertions or statements, with what is asserted or stated, which is often not another assertion, but a wordless state or event.

What Has Gone Wrong?

What has gone wrong in this repudiation of propositionalist theology? Two things. The first of these is a straightforward mischaracterization of what the likes of Aquinas and Hodge intended. A *Summa* or a volume of systematic theology does not replace the Bible, nor is it intended to. It provides and

12. Vanhoozer, *The Drama of Doctrine*, 88.

defends a framework for the understanding of Scripture, no less and no more. Another charge is that the propositionalist devalues Scripture; systematic theology displaces the Bible. Theology becomes positivistic prooftexting. But there is nothing to suggest this. As it happens, both Aquinas and Hodge wrote commentaries on books of the Bible.

Where is the source of such serious misunderstandings? I believe that they are due to misunderstandings about the language of Scripture. One part of the answer is this: that although requests or rebukes or invitations, a resurrection and an ascension, and so forth are not propositions or statements or assertions, the language used in such activities, including the reports of wordless events, if it is intelligible language, embodies *thoughts*. (Vanhoozer uses the phrase "propositional content" to refer to such thoughts,[13] but he does not seem to see the point.) Suppose I invite you to shut the window by saying "Please shut the window." In order kindly to comply with my request, why do you go over to the window and not to the door? Because the request I make contains or implies the thought that the window is open and not the thought that the door is open, even though the door may in fact be open. The point may be put in terms of informativeness. Why were commands, or invitations, or promises of Jesus informative to those to whom they were originally addressed, and why do they continue to be so for us? How is it that we can cue into them, to obey or disobey the commands, to accept or reject the invitations, or believe or disbelieve the promises? Simply because the words of these types of sentence express or imply distinct *thoughts*, which we are capable of understanding. Sometimes the thought implied is simple, at other time it is more complex. "Jesus was convinced that attempts to persuade him not to go to Jerusalem to fulfil the will of his Father were Satanic temptations," or something like it, is the thought that is implied in (and so, in a metaphorical sense, it is what "lies behind") Jesus's rebuke of Peter.[14]

Similarly, words are necessary in order to report the wordless fact of Jesus weeping. But the words don't take the place of the weeping, or get in its way, functioning as an opaque linguistic film between the reader and the

---

13. Ibid., 279.

14. Note the following remarks of Carl Henry, whose views of Scripture are often regarded as only expressive of a crude propositionalism: "In common philosophical parlance today, a proposition and a command (imperative) are no doubt viewed as two entirely different things. Commands are not said to be true or false and are often treated today simply as non cognitive uses of language. But the commands and promises of Scripture are only part of the problem; in no way do they undermine the essential claim that the primary concern of the revelation is the communication of truth." Henry, *God, Revelation and History*, III:477.

event itself. The words "Jesus wept" *report* the state of affairs of Jesus weeping, they don't supplant or distort it.

So it is plainly false, demonstrably false, to suppose that the view of Scripture presupposed by CRT is the view that the Bible is nothing other than a list of propositions, or that all that is important in Scripture are only the propositions or assertions or doctrines[15] that we find there. There are, besides assertions, the *thoughtful* content of types of sentences that are usually used to make requests, to rebuke, and to report in words states of affairs that themselves are wordless.

The response to such non-propositional sentences as they were originally uttered cannot simply have been to believe them. The appropriate response of Peter to the rebuke of Jesus was to be rebuked, and to take the necessary action to avoid further rebukes, which he was rather slow in doing, of course. The proper response of his hearers (and of countless others down the Christian centuries) to Jesus' invitation "Come unto me . . ." is to go to him. Rebukes and invitations are not so much to be believed as to be complied with. Isn't that how the church down the ages has seen this?

Reductionism?

Now compare that with this:

> The main defect of propositionalism is that it reduces the variety of speech actions in the canon to one type: the assertion. This results in a monologic conception of theology, and of truth. To think of theology as a monologue, even a truthful monologue, is to reduce theo-drama—in which the dialogical action is carried by a number of voices—to mere theory.[16]

> *Propositionalist theology views the Bible as revelation, revelation as teaching, teaching as propositional, and propositions as statements susceptible of truth and falsity.*[17]

On a high view of Scripture such as that endorsed by CRT it is true that Jesus wept, and that he slept in the back of the boat, and that he was hungry, and weary, even though we know these things about Jesus not because we saw him, but because of the testimony of witnesses. Weeping, or sleeping,

---

15. In his treatment of B. B. Warfield's use of Scripture, David H. Kelsey, in *The Uses of Scripture in Recent Theology*, uniformly assumes that Warfield's high view of Scripture leads him to regard it as having no other value than teaching doctrines.

16. Vanhoozer, *The Drama of Doctrine*, 266.

17. Ibid., 267, author's italics.

or being hungry, or being weary are not propositions, but are reported by assertions.

To illustrate further. People are saved by the cross, not by words about the cross, though words about the cross are vital if we are to understand what occurred on it. Such words do not interpose themselves between the readers and the wordless facts and somehow prevent us from ever being acquainted with these facts as they are. On the contrary, the words (so the classical view of Scripture avers) give us a wholly true account (as far as the account stretches) of the facts. "Jesus wept" is true if and only if Jesus wept. Did he weep for a minute or for five minutes? Scripture does not tell us. "The stone was rolled away" is a fact if and only if the stone was rolled away. Was the stone granite or limestone? Scripture does not tell us.

Now compare that with this:

> [P]ropositionalism tends to see all of Scripture in terms of revelation, to see the essence of revelation in terms of conveying information (e.g., truth content), and to see theology in terms of processing this information (e.g., *scientia*).[18]

> Proof-texting assumes a uniform propositional revelation spread evenly throughout Scripture: one verse, one vote. Not only does this approach risk decontextualizing biblical discourse, it also leaves unclear just how the texts cited in support actually lend their support to the point in question.[19]

No evidence is provided for the presence of such tendencies and risks, but that hardly seems to matter to the writer. Post-conservatives tend to be fairly dogmatic in their dismissal of classical Christian dogma and its scriptural basis. But of course the classic view does not reduce, does not "monologize," does not "decontextualize" (whatever precisely those words mean). In fact, the reverse. It endeavors to protect and to express the variety of biblical states of affairs—some of which are statements, some questions, some exclamations and the like, and some of which are reports of wordless events—in the appropriate language.

There is one more element to this. Scripture also records what is false. In the transcript of a trial it may be recorded that Joe Bloggs, the accused, said "I was fifty miles away from the scene of the crime when it took place." But the transcript, in faithfully and accurately and truly reporting that claim, may be reporting what is false, and so the (let us suppose) inerrant report of the trial contains a falsehood. David once said "Now I shall one day perish

18. Ibid., 268.
19. Ibid., 271.

by the hand of Saul" (1 Sam 27:1). This turned out to be false. He did not perish by the hand of Saul. The friends of Jairus said of his daughter, "She is dead" (Mark 5:35), when this was not true. So the Bible contains falsehoods.

Why, one wonders, do the vocal critics of "propositionalism" not see this? Why do they make it difficult for those who hold, as part of CRT, the classic view of Scripture and of theology to make that view clear? Why do they put barriers of misunderstanding in the way? Perhaps because of the confusions that we have been considering, the idea that speech acts supplant propositions, and that the classical view of theology and especially of systematic theology, promotes an exclusively cognitivist attitude to the Bible, *scientia* at the expense of *sapientia*. But if so, then the matter is easily remedied, as we have seen. The revisionist proposals of theo-drama are not required.

Genre

Associated with the charge of a purely cognitive attitude to Scripture are Vanhoozer's remarks on genre. He says:

> Just as no one voice dominated the canon, neither does any single literary form or genre. Scripture is composed of many different kinds of literature, including narrative, legend, genealogy, law code, prayer, song, proverb, parable, prophecy, letter, Gospel, sermon, confession of faith, hymn and apocalyptic. The diverse nature of the canonical texts suggests that no single interpretative approach will be adequate to all types.[20]

But the diversity of genre in Scripture has been standardly recognized. It is worth quoting a passage making this clear, in full.

> Comparatively little of Scripture consists of systematic theological exposition; most of it is of a different order. Broadly speaking, the Bible is an interpretative record of sacred history. It reports God's words to Israel, and His dealings with them, down the ages. It includes biographies, meditations, prayers, and praises, which show us how faith and unbelief, obedience and disobedience, temptation and conflict, work out in practice in human lives. It contains much imaginative matter—poetical, rhetorical, parabolic, visionary—which sets before our minds in a vivid,

---

20. Ibid., 273.

concrete and suggestive way great general principles, the formal statement of which has often to be sought in other contexts.[21]

And what of this, from Carl F. H. Henry, allegedly an arch-propositionalist?

> By its emphasis that divine revelation is propositional, Christian theology in no way denies that the Bible conveys its message in many literary forms such as letters, poetry and parable, prophecy and history. What it stresses, rather, is that truth conveyed by God through these various forms has conceptual adequacy, and that in all cases the literary teaching is part of a divinely inspired message that conveys the truth of divine revelation. Propositional disclosure is not limited to nor does it require only one particular genre. And of course the expression of truth in other forms than the customary prose does not preclude expressing that truth in declarative propositions.[22]

Henry by no means advocates the denial of genre, the presence of diverse literary forms, in Scripture, even though he regards these forms as vehicles of propositional teaching in a way that would not commend itself to Vanhooozer.

At the time of the Reformation, discussions of the four-fold sense of Scripture showed familiarity with ways in which a passage of Scripture may be given one or more other senses.[23] Further, the curious beasts of Ezekiel and the Revelation are not like lions and tigers, the streets of Jerusalem are not paved with real gold, and so on. It has been noted from time immemorial that apocalyptic literature was a special case, with its own rules. And it has long been recognized that Jesus's parables are not to be taken as accounts of what actually happened. Further, as Calvin long ago insisted, God accommodates himself to us in Scripture; there is metaphor, analogy, anthropomorphism, and the like. This is part of the entire approach of the Christian theological tradition to human language, particularly human language about God, though it is true that writers of Hodge's era, for example, did not agonize or panic about whether or not "religious language" is cognitive, in the manner of a post-logical positivist theologian.

Since Charles Hodge's name in particular has been linked with critiques of "propositionalism," and with an implied disregard of genre, we might at this point have him in mind. Here are two or pieces of evidence that

---

21. Packer, *"Fundamentalism" and the Word of God*, 93–94.
22. Henry, *God, Revelation and History*, III:463.
23. Turretin, *Institutes of Elenctic Theology*, I:150, 153.

appear to go entirely the other way. To suppose that Hodge is a theological empiricist, assembling biblical data by naïve induction, and so disregarding differences of genre, does not withstand serious examination.

It must be remembered that before he became a systematic theologian at Princeton, Charles Hodge was the Professor of Exegetical Theology there. Besides publishing commentaries on Romans, Ephesians, and 1 and 2 Corinthians he lectured, for example, on the prophecies of Isaiah. It is not likely that he carried out these activities without being aware of issues of genre.

Further, a glance at his *Systematic Theology* reveals appreciative references to the symbolism and figurative language of the apocalypse,[24] and of visions, and the figurative language of prophecy.[25] There is a sophisticated discussion of anthropomorphic language about God, a sense in which, Hodge thinks, it is valid and expresses truth about God, since human beings are made in the divine image. Hodge claims that such language is indeed essential to true theism.[26] He notes the importance of promises in the covenant of grace, and of the commands that accompany the covenant promises.[27] The idea that such a theologian seriously thought of divine revelation as consisting of nothing but lists of propositions, or as reducible to such lists, or thought of the non-propositional elements of Scripture as mere adornment, is frankly ludicrous.

It's not a case of the "propositionalist" favoring prose and disparaging poetry, either. The poetry of Psalm 139 is full of propositions, of assertions. Of course it is full of questions too, and of exclamations, and so there's the danger here of a false polarization between propositions (or assertions) and other linguistic forms. Also, the very fact that some of the psalmist's language is regarded as rhetorical ("Where shall I go from your Spirit? Or where shall I flee from your presence?" Ps 139:7) implies that the psalmist knows what the answers are, even as he is asking the question. So, as noted earlier, other forms of speech are often intelligible, and have their force, only because they imply (either logically or conversationally) certain assertions or propositions.

While reflecting on genre, it is worth noting that there is also one characteristic New Testament genre that, so it seems to me, Vanhoozer and other critics of "propositionalism" fail to recognize or to give the appropriate place to. That is, a type of writing that is of the form *teaching + application*. Vanhoozer finds it difficult to give due recognition to such writing because of his

24. Hodge, *Systematic Theology*, III:828.
25. Ibid., I:492–94.
26. Ibid., I:339, 343.
27. Ibid., III:343.

strong theo-dramatic impulse. As we saw earlier, he uses the idea of theo-drama not as an illustration of the nature of doctrine, but as what the nature of doctrine consists in. For him, doctrine is directional and functional in character, and (therefore?) not only or chiefly intellectual or cerebral. CRT gives due recognition to both the distinctness and the connectedness of *doctrine* and *application* as it appears in the teaching and applicatory writings both of Jesus and of Paul, a distinction that (as we noted in chapter 2) gives a number of Paul's letters, for example, their characteristic literary form. According to Paul it is in view of what they are "in Christ," including of course what they believe about him, that Christians ought to live in certain ways and not live in other ways. "Shall we sin that grace may abound? Certainly not! How can we who are dead to sin live any longer therein?" (Rom 6:1–2). Doctrine is truth-asserting. Properly understood and appreciated, the doctrine may enjoin action, as Jesus and Paul teach, and as Scripture shows, and as CRT teaches. Doctrinal divinity leads to practical divinity.

This fundamental point is well expressed by Richard Muller:

> The division between "systematic" and "practical" is nothing more or less than a statement that the life of the Christian community can be distinguished into categories of faith and obedience, of what is believed and what is done. It should also be clear that this distinction of aspects of the religious life or of elements of a theological curriculum does not permit a radical separation of fields of study or aspects of church practice: what is believed not only ought to relate to what is done, it ought also to govern and guide it; what is done or, better, what is learned from what has been done ought, likewise, to draw consistently on and occasionally, modify the expression of belief, though not the substance.[28]

The emphasis upon the difference between locutions and illocutionary force is relevant here. That distinction is presented as one important feature of the emphasis upon speech acts. But it is not a novel distinction. It was widely recognized in the study and teaching of rhetoric long before the distinctions were made in a self-conscious way by Austin in the 1950s. The same form of words can be used to make different and incompatible speech acts. In the case of the language of Scripture it may not always be easy to determine what is the force of the original speech act, partly because its original force as an illocution depended on tone, and on other non-verbal cues such as body-language, which as interpreters of Scripture we are largely ignorant of, though not wholly so. When we learn that Jesus wept, or that

---

28. Muller, *The Study of Theology*, 123.

he was angry, this is important in helping us to "fix" the illocutionary force of his accompanying speech. When Jesus said, "Martha, Martha, you are anxious and troubled about many things, but one thing is necessary" (Luke 10:41–42), what was his facial expression? Was Jesus serious or jocular? Was he angry or winsome? Did Vermeer correctly catch Jesus's mood by having him extend his arm, palm open, to Mary? Does the context, and what else we know about Jesus—our Christology—answer this question without us needing to know his tone of voice? Would a video-clip have helped? Perhaps it would. But perhaps we have sufficient information from the words on the page and what else we know from Scripture to enable us to interpret the passage accurately, though naturally enough we'd like to have some more.

With the help of John Calvin we can reflect on another biblical incident, the drama of Hezekiah's sickness and recovery (Isa 38), and note the conditions in which some of the language of the drama occurs, and understand the language accordingly, seeing for instance that the Lord's words, "Set your house in order, for you shall die; you shall not recover," not as having the illocutionary force of a *prediction*, but that of a *warning*. Commenting on the Lord's response to Hezekiah's prayer, after the Lord had prophesied that he would die, Calvin says:

> It may be thought strange that God, having uttered a sentence, should soon after be moved, as it were, by repentance to reverse it; for nothing is more at variance with his nature than a change of purpose. [How does Calvin know this? Because he takes from elsewhere in Scripture its teaching about the immutability or steadfastness of the Lord.] I reply, while death was threatened against Hezekiah, still God had not decreed it, but determined in this manner to put to the test the faith of Hezekiah. [So the Lord's words had a particular force, not the force of a decree or infallible prediction, but of a threat. His intention was to threaten or warn Hezekiah, and so to test his faith.] We must, therefore, suppose a condition to be implied in that threatening; for otherwise Hezekiah would not have altered, by repentance or prayer, the irreversible decree of God.[29]

The distinction between a prediction and a threat is of some importance here for the doctrine of God. If the prophet's words were an eternal decree from God, or an infallible prediction, then how are we to understand his countermanding of the decree or the prediction a short time later? Did God change his mind? No such issue arises if God is not decreeing or

---

29. Calvin, *Commentary on Isaiah*, ch. 38 v. 4. There is more of Calvin's treatment of this incident that is relevant. See the discussion in Helm, *John Calvin's Ideas*, ch. 7.

predicting, but rather threatening or warning in order to put Hezekiah to the test. Calvin pays particular attention to the flow of the narrative, the very thing that has allegedly been lost by the church's "static" and "timeless" approach to the Scriptural text. But he also tacitly recognizes that for all our adherence to the narrative, and our appreciation of it, we cannot ourselves be Hezekiah, or be back in his time. After all, the story, with all of its original indexical features, is in front of us, and we have read it through endless times and know how it goes. Vanhoozer's idea that we come closer to the nature of God's revelation by adopting a kind of "real time" approach to the text is jejune. The events were pretty dramatic for Hezekiah, much less so, if at all, for us. But the teaching of the text, that in these dramatic incidents God was putting Hezekiah to the test, abides. It teaches us that sometimes God tests his people, which I guess is a rather unfamiliar theme. The idea that focusing on speech acts will make the Bible more dramatic for us, and so encourage our participation in its drama, is not likely to prove very successful as a way of appreciating large tracts of biblical narrative.

It's only because we know (from elsewhere in Scripture) that Hezekiah believed that God is utterly trustworthy and unchangeably true, and that we already know, as we re-read the story, how it turns out, that it is reasonable to believe that the Lord's words to Hezekiah have the form of a threat or warning, a test to elicit faith, and not a prediction that fails or may fail, or a decree that the Lord quickly countermands by another decree.

So—as is usual in thinking theologically—we need a historical perspective, in this case about biblical interpretation, if we are not to be bowled over by the latest big words. This perspective gives us a sense of proportion. More importantly, we need a little philosophy, in this case the idea of propositions and assertions, what accounts for their meaning, and their fundamental character as truth-bearers.

Interestingly, in the course of his treatment of divine sovereignty at the end of *Remythologizing Theology* Vanhoozer briefly refers to the Hezekiah episode and to Calvin's treatment of it. He notes that in this dialogue with Hezekiah, God is not informing Hezekiah of his death but testing him and working a change in his heart.[30] With Calvin, Vanhoozer reckons that Calvin's initial words to Hezekiah are tacitly conditional, not a prediction but a warning or a challenge, rather along the lines of our own discussion. Ironically Vanhoozer does not note that, those many years ago, Calvin was already working with a speech act view of language.

30. Vanhoozer, *Remythologizing Theology*, 495.

The "Flattening" of Scripture

Finally, what about the repeated charge that in CRT the Bible is (in the words of Andrew McGowan) "flattened and reduced to a set of propositions that are then deemed to be inerrant."[31] This is an expression of McGowan's view (which we have already met in Kevin Vanhoozer), that there is a reductionism at work in the minds of the theologians of CRT, particular the Princeton theologians. So McGowan says that the theological method of Princeton was "founded on the notion that Scripture can be reduced to a set of 'facts' or 'propositions', which are then collected and arranged into a systematic theology. This rationalist approach, however well intentioned, actually undermines the authority of the Scriptures."[32] Here we touch upon a kind of confusion in the mind of Dr. McGowan and those who think like him.

For those who allege that there is a "flattening" effect when a theologian incorporates a revealed truth in his system are faced with a dilemma. Either this effect, or perhaps a "distorting" effect, occurs whenever material from Scripture is directly incorporated into some other human production, such as a book of theology, a sermon, or a statement of a person's faith, or it does not. If it does then it is not CRT or Princeton theology or Thomas Aquinas who is at fault, but it is a consequence of the very activity of relocating the material. So theological discussion courts distortion. The only way to avoid this would be to adopt a pure biblicism, in which passages of Scripture are recited and no more. Paraphrasing and summarizing forbidden!

But such an attitude is surely confused. The practice of relocating Scripture for the purposes of discussion, in confessing the faith, and so on incurs loss and gain. Provided that the re-locators are aware of this, the danger of distortion can be minimized. To illustrate the confusion, let us take these three propositions, drawn from a well-known nursery rhyme. In the nursery rhyme:

1. (It is true that) Miss Muffet sat on a tuffet

2. (It is true that) Miss Muffet ate curds and whey

3. (It is true that) A Big Spider frightened Miss Muffet away

Let us suppose that the three statements are abstracted from the rhyme. Nevertheless they each express truths about Miss Muffet. According to McGowan's suggestion, in being set out as above, as three distinct

---

31. McGowan, *The Divine Spiration of Scripture*, 117.
32. Ibid., 116.

propositions, the nursery-rhyme story of Little Miss Muffet, is reduced or flattened into something cold and clinical, for it is now presented in a form that disregards the "genre" of nursery rhyme. It has to be conceded that the three propositions do not convey the rhyme or lilt of the original. They are not as entertaining, not easily recited or sung to children as is the nursery rhyme itself.

Biblical language is no different from other language; it can be used to express the emotion of the reader and to evoke emotion in the listener, through repetition, alliteration, cadence and so on, as well as by rhyme. But then nothing but the original, said or sung, will convey the original rhyme or lilt and have these effects. Even these effects wear off if the use is of the wrong kind. Such effects are largely muted by any second-order commentary or paraphrase, whether by a "theo-dramatic" or "propositionalist" rendition, or by being incorporated into a book about theo-drama. As Robert Frost has it, "Poetry is what gets lost in translation."

So *all* theologies—including both CRT and the "post-propositionalist" theology of Vanhoozer *et al.*—have a difficulty here. For as a theologian reflects upon a text, and offers a gloss on it or proposes a way of integrating it with other data, the first-order datum of the text is considered apart from its original context. Is there a solution, something that will preserve the pristine freshness and impact of the first-order text for the theologian? No, there is not. In the biblicist strategy of endeavoring to use nothing but the original words, each successive recital is likely to reduce the impact of the original, and in any case will not solve any of the difficulties in understanding that the reader or hearer may have. The eunuch's question "Of whom, I ask you, does the prophet say this? About himself or about someone else?" would have to remain unanswered, and Philip would not have been doing the correct thing in going on to tell him the good news about Jesus (Acts 8:34–35).

Despite first appearances, however, McGowan cannot be defending a pure biblicism, since elsewhere in *The Divine Spiration of Scripture* he offers a high view of preaching and of confessions of faith. So the precise point being made is not clear.

Where does this idea of "flattening" come from? Frankly, it is not easy to say. But here's a suggestion. It may arise from the idea that putting a piece of literature into explicit propositional form (as in (1)–(3) above) emasculates or reduces its content to some lowest common denominator. The idea seems to be that a series of propositions, simply in virtue of being a set of propositions, has a content that is all on the same level, and so all (or much) that is distinctive in the original text is removed or diluted. As a botanist, using the language of his science, may classify flowers and so may miss their beauty and fragrance, or a doctor in talking easily about a migraine may fail to appreciate its killing pain, so a systematic theologian of the Princeton school (and of theology more generally, as we have just noted) must miss those features of Scripture that are intended to move the emotions and energise the will, and so be blind to features that are crucial to the proper appreciation of these documents.

To see how confused such a suggestions must be, let us adopt the convention of expressing the content of each of (1)–(3) in italics. Then the content of (1) is *Miss Muffet sat on a tuffet*, the content of (2) is *Miss Muffet ate curds and whey*, and that of (3) is *Miss Muffet was frightened by a spider*. The italicized expressions relate three facts about Miss Muffet, three truths. But, other than the loss of rhyme and rhythm, and the change of genre, where's the flattening? In the evocative power of the original. Yet does asserting that it is true that Miss Muffet sat on a tuffet (as opposed to reciting "Little Miss Muffet sat on a tuffet . . .") interfere in any way with the distinctiveness of this fact, and so make it more or less equivalent, say, to the fact that she was frightened by a spider? (1)–(3) are, after all, nothing other than expressions used to record or report bodily states, (like sitting) or actions (like eating) or reactions (like being frightened). Of course the report of someone being frightened is not necessarily a case of being frightened, and it may not even have a frightening effect on those who hear the report. A report of someone being frightened that uses language that rhymes is different from a report without rhyme. But then a recipe for haggis is not itself haggis, nor a photograph of Edinburgh Castle itself Edinburgh Castle.

The examples we have used are of course trivial ones. But we can substitute for them assertions of some of the constitutive facts of the Christian faith, such as

(4) (It is true that) The Word became flesh (John 1:14)

(5) (It is true that) Jesus wept (John 12:35)

(6) (It is true that) Jesus asserted "One of you will betray me." (John 13:21)

It is now, I hope, easy to see that prefixing these first-order biblical expressions with "it is true that" does not flatten each of them, nor make them cold and clinical. What does it do? It acts as a device for enabling us to assert (4)–(6) as facts. (It is not the only such device, of course. Speaking in a certain tone of voice would often do the trick.) However, if they are all facts, if they are true, they most certainly do not each express the same fact, nor are they truths of equal importance. But who seriously can think that an assertion of Jesus's to the effect that one of his disciples will betray him comes to be on the same level as the assertion of a particular reactive state of Jesus, his weeping at the tomb of Lazarus, or as the deeply mysterious assertion that the Word became flesh?

But perhaps this is not quite the problem. Perhaps it is that by extracting the kernal from the husk of Scripture, violence is done to Scripture itself, because the form and content of Scripture are inextricably connected so that to express the content of Scripture in other ways than by Scripture itself is necessarily to mis-state that content, to lose some of it or to distort it.

No doubt there is something in this. Scripture is Scripture, and anything that isn't Scripture is something distinct from it, even if it is intended to reproduce some of the content of Scripture. Every thing is what it is and not another thing. But provided that it is clear that certain statements are meant to reproduce the propositional or cognitive content of Scripture, and to do nothing more than that, then would this not be sufficient to meet Dr. McGowan's fears? Otherwise it may be that in all doctrinal construction and all attempts to teach the Bible, in preaching or in catechesis, the losses must inevitably outweigh the gains.

To express the propositional or cognitive content of Scripture is important, and to feel the emotional impact of its language is not the only way in which Scripture can be appreciated. It provides us with an account of human lives, of Abraham and Job and Samson, say. When we read of the largely self-inflicted ills of Samson, or the other-inflicted afflictions of Job, these may be expressed propositionally. But the "feltness" of the temptations, what it was like to be Samson in this situation, cannot be reproduced propositionally, any more than the significance of the afflictions of Job can be appreciated as he first appreciated them. Nothing reproduces the softness of the breeze on the skin, or the terror of a thunderstorm. There is knowledge by acquaintance and there is knowledge by description. All this is true. But reminding ourselves of this only amounts to an argument against "propositionalism" if we also have the mistaken belief that an account of an event may take the place of the event or even improve on it in some way. As far as I am aware, no propositionalist has ever thought that.[33]

There is a further, connected matter. McGowan claims that a high view of Scripture, such as that associated with CRT, only makes sense in relation to what he refers to as "propositional statements."[34] Hence, no doubt, his claim that such as Charles Hodge or B. B. Warfield reduce the Bible "to a set

---

33. For an at-length development of these points, in connection with the appreciation and understanding of suffering, see Stump, *Wandering in Darkness*.

34. McGowan, *The Divine Spiration of Scripture*, 213.

of propositions," becoming "mere data to be processed by the theologian."[35] But from what we learned earlier in this chapter we are in a position to see that this charge, too, rests upon a simple misunderstanding. To illustrate this, let us take two or three biblical sentences at random: "They took up the broken pieces left over, seven baskets full" (Mark 8:8); "Who do people say that I am?" (Mark 8:27); "Get behind me, Satan!" (Mark 8:33). Let us add the usual prefix:

(7) (It is true that) they took up the broken pieces left over, seven baskets full.

(8) (It is true that [Jesus asked]) "Who do people say that I am?"

(9) (It is true that [Jesus said]) "Get behind me, Satan!"

These three prefixed sentences, (7), (8), and (9), are, we may assume, true. But the three sentences that are prefixed are not all true, nor are they all capable of being true. Only one of them, (7), has a truth-value, for it is a report in the form of a statement, or an assertion. Questions and commands are not "propositional statements." Nevertheless, as we saw earlier, in agreeing with Vanhoozer, questions, commands, exclamations, aspirations, vows, and so forth, as well as statements, all may have propositional content, and all find their way into the text of Scripture. For questions, commands, and so forth, can each be inspired, delivered unerringly by their speakers, and/or unerringly recorded. Likewise, distinct scriptural genres ought to hold no fears. The idea that CRT reduces the Bible to a set of doctrinal statements or assertions, and that all questions, commands, vows, etc., are eliminated, or that the CRT view of the Bible in some way supplants the importance and efficacy of the events that it reports, are all claims that are wide of the mark, as I hope this chapter has shown.

---

35. Ibid., 117.

6

Propositions, Time, and Truth

The last chapter considered linguistic and literary issues arising from the claim that CRT (as exemplified by Charles Hodge, for example, or B. B. Warfield) has a "propositionalist" view of Scripture. Now we will reflect on the more philosophical critique of "propositionalism," that it promotes a "timeless" view of truth and an exclusively theoretical, cognitive interest in the Bible. It is a central part of Vanhoozer's project to *"rehabilitate the cognitive propositional approach to theology by expanding what we mean by 'cognition' and by dramatizing what we mean by 'proposition.'"*[1] Part of this requires that he tell us what is the matter with propositions, and develop his account of cognition. This chapter will take us into this territory.

This claim about the evils of "propositionalism" comes from two directions; first, from the idea that truth is not (and perhaps cannot be) propositional in character, and then the contention that propositionalism is a gross distortion of scriptural language and of the character of Scripture more largely, ignoring genre and emasculating its "theo-dramatic" character, its appeal to the imagination, the emotions, and the will. Hence Vanhoozer's stress on the "canonical-linguistic" basis of Christian doctrine, on speech acts, and on God as essentially a speaker, a communicative agent, in the drama.

Vanhoozer does not think that truth is propositional in form, that is, that truth is a relation between a proposition and that which it propounds,[2] though he holds what William Alston calls a "minimalist realist theory of truth," and Alston's is a propositionalist account of truth.[3] I think that he

---

1. Vanhoozer, *The Drama of Doctrine*, 88. Italics in the original.
2. Ibid., 286.
3. Ibid., 287, fn. 68. The reference is to Alston, *A Realist Conception of Truth*, ch. 1

may mean this account of his own outlook to cover all truths of matters of fact, including, say, truths in natural science, but it is most certainly meant to characterize all theological truth. What makes a non-propositional character of truth attractive for him, and gains support from his view that Scripture is polyphonic, is that it offers its readers a plurality of genres and aspects, and so underlines his view that Scripture is not simply "lists of propositions" and "monological" or a presentation of timeless truths. This in turn leads him to favor what he calls "aspectivalism" in epistemology, and therefore in the understanding of Christian doctrine. In this chapter we shall look at each of these in turn—propositions and truth, propositions and knowledge, and propositions and time. We shall consider "aspectivalism" in chapter 8.

Propositions and Truth

According to Vanhoozer, Christian doctrinal belief is not primarily a propositional attitude. Rather, beliefs are to be built up of from the awareness of a set of different aspects of what God has revealed, rather like the aspects of a building—the front, the back, the inside, the roof. (It is not altogether clear how literally the visual connotations of "aspect" are to be taken. I have taken them fairly literally in this account.) Our beliefs are thus multifaceted, built up as they arise from an experience and an appreciation of more and more of these different aspects. The idea is that these viewings, taken together, complement and support each other, giving us a better all-round appreciation of the "building" of Christian theology than a mere list of propositions can do. (But surely since each aspectival belief has propositional content, isn't such a belief one that such and such an aspect is true?) Vanhoozer is a metaphysical realist and he thinks that our beliefs are not, or some of the time are not, a human construct.[4] Rather they may faithfully realize or "render" reality to us,[5] though not in such a manner that the structure of reality is *pictured* in the structure of language.

As a consequence he seems to reject a correspondence theory of truth, though it's not clear why, any more than his aspectivalism should lead him to reject belief as a "propositional attitude." Instead, as we have noted, he subscribes to what he calls Alston's "minimalist realist theory of truth," but as Alston makes clear, this is a version of a correspondence theory, a minimalist account of truth as correspondence, where "correspondence" is

---

4. Vanhoozer, *The Drama of Doctrine*, 287.
5. Ibid., 286.

understood in the way that he explains.⁶ For Vanhoozer, there is a relationship between language and reality in respect of truth, but he is not willing to specify what that relationship is. Instead he refers to the Scripture bringing us into "covenantal contact" with the truth.⁷ Here once again Vanhoozer exhibits the tendency of thinking that replacing one word by another changes a theory. Language "renders" reality, not by "corresponding" to it but by being in "covenantal contact" with it. He never tells his readers what these differences amount to. He also takes pains to say that he rejects a picture theory of meaning, at least in a very strong, literal version of that theory. So he thinks that propositions can "render" reality, without picturing it but by being in "covenantal contact" with it. He tends to exaggerate the views he rejects; in the case of the picture theory of meaning as a way of understanding the correspondence theory of truth he refers exclusively to the form it took in the logical atomism of Bertrand Russell and others, almost a century ago.⁸ This is part of his case against the view that our language can yield "a complete and exact knowledge of the world." Such an outlook has, he says, "been called into question by postmodern thinkers"⁹ as well as, he might have added, by distinctly pre-modern skeptics and fallibilists of various stripes, and by anyone who has a robust sense of human finitude. Clearly, Vanhoozer's aim here is to dissipate any idea that there is only one way of expressing the truth by means of language, and that these ways are inexact.

Nevertheless, though he raises doubts about truth as picturing in any sense, he accepts the idea of true belief as polyphonic or aspectival *representation*. So, being a realist, he accepts that there is truth in the objective sense, something independent of our consciousness and of our perceptual powers, to which these powers may be successfully directed. This is what he refers to as "aspectival realism."¹⁰ In this minimal sense, and allowing for anachronism in expression, his view accords with that of CRT. In the case of the place of Scripture and its relation to Christian doctrine, aspects do not arise from vision, of course, as in the example of the building, but from the various aspects of God's ways that Scripture provides for us. "*The one truth can be variously figured and configure,*"¹¹ through complementary accounts, as it is through the particular literary forms of the canon of Scripture. So "A

---

6. For details see Alston, *A Realist Conception of Truth*, chapter 1.

7. Vanhoozer, *The Drama of Doctrine*, 286, 301.

8. Russell, *The Philosophy of Logical Atomism*; Wittgenstein, *Tractatus Logico-Philosophicus*.

9. Vanhoozer, *The Drama of Doctrine*, 286.

10. Ibid., 289.

11. Ibid., 287.

postconservative theology affirms a *plurality of normative points of view in Scripture*, each of which is authoritative because each discloses a particular *aspect* of the truth."[12] Not only is Vanhoozer a theological realist, but the "points of view" that he notes are not at all our own intellectual constructs. They are given, in normative fashion, in Scripture,[13] and as best we can we are to faithfully convey what is given. This is one reason why the Scriptures transcend particular cultures.[14] Finally, as we have already seen, the plurality of such points of view is very strongly tied to the diverse literary forms of Scripture.[15] We shall consider some of this material in a rather different way when we discuss Vanhoozer's attitude to foundationalism in chapter 8.

Propositions and Knowledge[16]

Yet in spite of the fact that some of his own proposals involve merely changes in verbal expression, it should be emphasized that on his own estimate of things his view is quite self-consciously a novel and a radical theological departure from centuries of theologizing, a break with the "aristotelianizing" of epistemology. For "Western philosophical and theological thinking about truth has more or less been a series of footnotes to Aristotle." According to Vanhoozer, Aristotle's epistemology held that knowledge is gained when our ideas are equivalent to what they are ideas about, "a perfect representation, a re-presencing of the thing in one's mind," providing a "complete and exact knowledge of the world," a "perfect, complete equivalence between language and world, formulation and fact." This view is seductive, since "it is tempting, all too tempting, cavalierly to assume that our system of thought has indeed attained the philosophical ideal of *adequatio*; that we know the truth, wholly and completely. That way idolatry lies."[17] This is the familiar postmodern warning, that knowledge claims are but claims, and are claims to power, which when exercised leads to idolatry.

Here I shall not consider the question of how accurate Vanhoozer's sketch of Aristotle's view is. But whatever exactly that view is, it obviously must recognize that a representation of some fact or state of affairs is distinct from what is represented, as Vanhoozer himself does, as we have just seen. Other than this, let us suppose that he is correct about Aristotle, that for

12. Ibid., 289.
13. Ibid.
14. Ibid., 328, 348.
15. Ibid., 289.
16. I am indebted here to Mark Talbot for several suggestions that were a great help.
17. Vanhoozer, *The Drama of Doctrine*, 286.

him the knowledge that *p* provides a whole, perfect, and complete understanding of *p*. Nevertheless, Vanhoozer cannot surely be suggesting that the entirety of Western theological thinking (at least, since the twelfth century until now) has been in thrall to the view that (say) when Scripture teaches the truth that God is perfect goodness, as a result we have a whole, perfect, and complete understanding of the reality of the divine goodness. Such an exaggerated view would totally ignore, for example, the contrast that CRT theologians routinely drew between the finite and the infinite, between God *in se* and God *quoad nos*, a distinction they took from the medievals. Such theologians affirmed the fact that the finite cannot grasp the infinite, and maintained the distinction between archetypal knowledge, the knowledge that God has of himself, and ectypal knowledge, the knowledge that we are granted. What of those scriptural data that point to divine incomprehensibility, the unfathomable ways of God, including the unspeakable love of God? Are these ignored by "propositionalsm"? Surely Vanhoozer's remarks, at least as they apply to the Christian tradition of theologizing, are somewhat one-sided, to put it mildly. Maybe what Vanhoozer is suggesting is that the tradition took the Aristotelian view as an ideal, but even then this neglects the important place played by *opinio* and *assensus* in Reformation and pre-Reformation accounts of certitude and faith that lie at the basis of Christian theologizing.[18]

In order to make his case, that in propositionalism there is a view of knowledge that is justifiably called into question by postmodern thinkers,[19] Vanhoozer has to stress that aspect of the Western theological tradition that readily recognizes that the ways of God are past finding out, that we see through a mirror darkly, and so forth, *at the expense of* the confident affirmations of knowledge found in scriptural accounts of those who believe the promises. Furthermore, he passes by the ways in which standard thinkers such as Augustine or Aquinas or Calvin think of language about God as analogical, metaphorical, and accommodated. He does not mention the prospect of approaching an understanding of God in negative terms. He does not think of at least some of the expressions of knowledge in Scripture as aspirational, of efforts to approach a knowledge of God that at present the Christian does not reach. He finds no room for implicit faith. To polarize the main spine of Christian theological tradition, a tradition that includes CRT, as claiming to provide "perfect and complete understanding" against

---

18. According to scholastic epistemology, faith is not a form of *scientia*, but of *assensus*. For discussion, see Turretin, *Institutes of Elenctic Theology*, II:564f.

19. Vanhoozer, *The Drama of Doctrine*, 286. It is not clear how exactly he intends to be taken here. Western Christian theology was significantly influenced by Aristotle only from the twelfth century onwards.

his more modest "aspectival realism" in order to provide an argument to support the latter is to create a straw man.

Vanhoozer is on something of a knife-edge at this point. To see this, we must note again his remarks on Scripture, remarks such as: "Aspectival realism insists that theo-dramatic reality is independent of what we say and think about it, even though it is indescribable and unknowable apart from the diverse canonical forms and only partially accessible to any one form."[20] Here we have epistemological realism; our thinking and saying things about a reality that exists independently of our minds. It is hard to see how this does not commit him to a form of propositionalism, though not a propositionalism of the sort that he so emphatically decries. Granted, our knowledge requires us to add aspect to aspect in order to gain fuller knowledge. But the various aspects are represented to us in language. How could that be in any other way than by us believing certain things? Of course, the object of our belief may not be an isolated proposition but the vision of a prophet or the psalm or the story of the parable, and it may have tacitly as well as explicitly recognizable features. Not all aspects of the objects of faith may be or can be spelt out. A vision may render speechless those who see it, leaving them dumbfounded, just as on one occasion the hearing of a sound but seeing no man did. But insofar as the vision means anything, it has propositional content.

If, on the other hand, Vanhoozer were to say that what are believed are not propositions but directions to enable us to enter into the drama of redemption, even then, participants in the drama need to believe the directions before they can follow them, and so these beliefs must also have a propositional character. We must be taking certain things to be true. For we do not enter into the drama mindlessly. It is hard to see how, for all his anti-propositional sentiments, he himself can altogether avoid being a propositionalist himself.

Apart from the fact that he is (rather strangely) tying these different aspects exclusively to the distinct literary forms in Scripture, is his "aspectivalism" any different in principle from saying that "God is love" is a different yet complementary aspect of the truth from "God is a consuming fire"? There is need to keep in mind, at a fundamental level, the distinction between partial descriptions being complementary, and partial descriptions being contradictory. As we have stressed earlier, and as any reasonably intelligent Bible student can see, certain biblical expressions complement other such expressions, others act as contrasts. "God is love" complements and is complemented by "God is a consuming fire," while "I and my Father are

---

20. Ibid., 289.

one" contrasts with "My Father is greater than I." But neither of the pairs is a contradiction, and each pair may quite fairly to be said to provide aspects of the sum of revealed truth about God, expressed as assertions or propositions by the various biblical authors. Similarly, Jesus's parables enhance his teaching, the Psalms give expression to faith and hope, as well as to doubt and fear. At this point, is there any substantive difference from the tradition? Yet we must recognize that the singer of a psalm, say, may not only believe the words being sung, but they may become her words, she may live through them and they may be a perfect expression of her own state of mind and heart. In highlighting the propositional element of faith we must not neglect such other strands of religious experience.

What is different, perhaps, is Vanhoozer's linking of the various aspects with correspondingly different literary forms of Scripture. He makes quite a bit of the idea that the variety of aspects that Scripture provides corresponds to and arises from the variety of literary forms that the canon contains.

> That the truth of Jesus Christ comes clothed in the form of narratives, songs, parables, fulfilled prophecies, pastoral epistles, and apocalyptic says something about the *nature* of that truth, namely that it is a truth that must not only be believed, but *felt, done and loved*. Scripture enjoins us to receive the propositional content of testimony in a variety of ways that correspond to the variety of its forms; as something to be believed by me, done by me, hoped by me. To repeat, the testimony in Scripture is doing more than conveying information: it is training our thinking and perceiving to understand what God is doing in Jesus Christ and in the Scriptures themselves.[21]

This is an argument against the purely "informational" account of truth which, according to Vanhoozer, the propositionalist view engenders, but for which (as far as I can see) he has provided no evidence. The diverse literary forms of the language of Scripture tell us something about the nature of the truth that the propositional content of that language conveys, and he thinks that propositionalism cannot convey these, the truths that Scripture expresses that are meant to affect us in certain ways, to prompt the imagination and to stir the affections.

As we saw in the previous chapter, there is certainly something in the idea that Scripture conveys more than information, though this also is not a novel idea. In accusing others of the Utterance Fallacy we must not fall into another fallacy, the *Propositionalist Fallacy* as we might call it. Because propositions or assertions are central and essential to the identity of the

---

21. Ibid., 288, emphasis in the original. See also ibid., 419–20.

Christian faith, and nature of its revelation, this does not mean that in our apprehension of that revelation assent to propositions is the first and distinct event in the life of faith. Relationship with God-in-Christ may engage the whole person, faith, delight, and obedience, in worship and devotion, and so on. It is no part of a propositionalist approach to insist that the believing apprehension of Scripture is a distinct act or event, which is then followed by an affective response. The whole person may be engaged from the start. Besides, it is a time-honored view that understanding Christian doctrine ought to lead to its application.

The point is, the intellectual core of such a holistic response is capable of being articulated in propositions, some of which are "tidier" than others. Vanhoozer's canonical approach to theology, involving aspectivalism, is neither necessary nor sufficient to make and enforce that point, that we are to be doers of the word and not hearers only. And it is rather odd to say that the alternative view being proposed tells us something about the *nature* of the way in which we apprehend the truth. What it tells us is something that goes beyond the nature of the truth, namely that the truth conveyed is intended to be affective and directive. The core warrant for this arises, for example, from the character of Christ's teaching about eating the living bread, and hearing and doing, and the New Testament letters in which truth, Christian doctrine, is intertwined with emotional engagement, and faith with works.

In the case of Paul's letters, sometimes the flow of argument is interrupted by a practical command, or some exclamation such as "What shall we say then? Are we to sin that grace may abound? By no means!" (Rom 6:1–2); "Thanks be to God for his inexpressible gift!" (2 Cor 9:15). More commonly, the letter is structured as first doctrinal exposition and then application. In other cases (as in 1 Peter, say, or James) there is a closer intertwining of the two. The existence of this all-important literary genre, the *teaching + application letter* (as we might call it), is strangely neglected by Vanhoozer, as we noted earlier. Why do we sing the praises of God? Not simply because the canon contains examples of psalms and songs, for these might simply be museum pieces, just as what it records about the dietary prescriptions for ancient Israel are now museum pieces. Rather, it is because we have the example of Christ the psalm-singer, and there is normative apostolic teaching to sing. As Hodge puts it, according to Paul the Holy Spirit produces a joy that expresses itself in psalms and hymns and spiritual songs, and which is coupled with thanksgiving to God.[22] While some of Vanhoozer's proposals in this area fall outside CRT, and he believes that he is offering a radical

---

22. Hodge, *A Commentary on the Epistle to the Ephesians*, 303–5.

departure from what he regards as age-old mistakes, often he is in fact, if not in intention, echoing some of its characteristic emphases.

So far, both the novelty and efficacy of Vanhoozer's proposals about truth appear somewhat exaggerated when set against the tradition from which they are supposed to be principled departures. We must now turn to his strictures on the very idea of a proposition to see if the argument here offers more persuasive reasons for his rejection of CRT. We shall do this in two stages, first by considering the exclusive concern with cognition that he thinks that such propositionalism engenders, and then with the dismissal of propositions themselves.

Exclusive Cognitivism?

Besides these rather exaggerated proposals regarding the nature of truth and belief, Vanhoozer has a further set of objections to "propositionalist theology," aspects of which we have already touched on, which we must now consider more directly. Propositionalist theology should in his judgment carry a health warning about the alarming dangers that one may be tempted into by it.

> What is *tempting* in propositionalist theology is the idea that one can "master" divinity by learning the system of truths communicated through the language and literature of the Bible. What is tempting is the thought that one can package the Bible in a conceptual scheme that is tidier than the original. What is tempting is that it is enough to *know* the information thus packaged. . . . Cognitive-propositionalist theology risks deflecting doctrine from its proper role in drawing us into the drama by turning it into an ossified, formulaic knowledge that will either wilt on the vine or, on another plausible scenario, be used as a shibbolethic instrument of power.[23]

The language here is rather unfortunate; the idea that propositionalism promotes the mastery of divinity, the tidy packaging of the untidy Bible, and that it encourages a purely theoretical and detached approach to doctrine and to theology. Furthermore, it is inherently unsatisfactory for the reader to have to assess and then to respond to unsubstantiated temptations and tendencies, and to engage in measuring risks and assessing the plausibility of scenarios, when not a shred of evidence is provided to support any of them.

23. Vanhoozer, *The Drama of Doctrine*, 87–88.

Since we are dealing with Vanhoozer's repudiation of a mode of doing theology that, on his own account of things, has persisted for hundreds of years, at least since the rediscovery of Aristotle by the Latin West in the twelfth century,[24] no doubt it would be possible to find instances of men and women falling into such tendencies and temptations. This unfortunate state of affairs would hardly be surprising, but it would not be sufficient to provide persuasive empirical support for Vanhoozer's case against an entire tradition, or to make that case remotely plausible.

Calvin on Religion

A more tractable question is, do those well-known and influential systematic theologians that Vanhoozer has in mind—particularly, of course, Charles Hodge—invariably foster or give countenance to such temptations, tendencies, and risks? In other words, do the proponents of such a theological method think of the theology that it delivers in purely cerebral terms, and celebrate it for that reason? Do they also believe that simply by learning a series of truths one can gain mastery of divinity? Is not Christian theology rooted in mysteries that far exceed our grasp? Do not CRT theologians recognize that revealed truth should appropriately affect the emotions and the will, and, so to speak, master us? Are they totally preoccupied with the intellect, and so ignore or give no place at all to the intended impact of such theology on practice? Do they disavow such an impact or downplay it?

Although Vanhoozer makes his serious assertions about the irreligious and impious effects of "propositionalism" without providing any evidence for his charges, I shall offer an outline answer to these charges that does provide some evidence.

It is clear, for one thing, that this charge could not fairly be levelled against one of the fountainheads of CRT, John Calvin. No one can fail to be struck by the leading motif of his *Institutes*, that true wisdom consists in the knowledge of God and of ourselves. Note the stress upon "religion." Calvin was wary of the term "theology" on account of its speculative connotations. It was the word used by the Sorbonnistes as they sought to undermine the work of the Reformation in France. And so Calvin routinely repeats the following refrain:

> Such is pure and genuine religion, namely, confidence in God coupled with serious fear—fear, which both includes in it willing reverence, and brings along with it such legitimate worship

24. Ibid., 268, 286.

as is prescribed in the Law. And it ought to be more carefully considered that all men promiscuously do homage to God, but very few truly reverence him. On all hands there is abundance of ostentatious ceremonies, but sincerity of heart is rare.[25]

So faith and knowledge are meant to have more than cerebral effects, important though those effects are. This view of Calvin and of the other Reformers of what faith and knowledge are became codified in the following formula: faith is awareness of what God has revealed, which is assented to and relied upon. So Francis Turretin writes, in the more formal language of Reformed Orthodoxy, that

> The objects of justifying faith, proper and specific (as will be proved afterwards), are the promises of the gospel, which cannot be received except by trust because they are proposed not only as true, but also as good. The gospel is not only the object of contemplation of the intellect, but also the object of consolation of the heart (which faith cannot apprehend except trustingly).[26]
>
> The properties and effects ascribed to faith cannot be bare assent, but necessarily suppose antecedent trust as the cause: such as peace of conscience, access to God and to the throne of grace, boldness by which we address God as our Father, confidence as to the hearing of our prayers, a holy boldness, by which we are confident in all evils, glorying in the Lord, and in adversity. All these cannot be in the believer, except on the supposition of trust from which they spring.[27]

Maybe Vanhoozer thinks that this account of faith as a virtue, something that is certainly more than cerebral, is nevertheless characteristically held by its proponents in a merely cerebral fashion; a purely cerebral attitude to an account of faith which is itself more than cerebral; an exercise in hypocrisy, or double-think. It could happen, of course. But then if we believe that it has happened and does happen, and in a routine way, to the detriment of "propositionalism," some evidence for this allegedly widespread phenomenon is certainly required. In any case, may not the same thing be said of doctrine as theo-drama? May one not act the part as a routine? May one act the part without being the part?

---

25. Calvin, *Institutes*, I.2.2.
26. Turretin, *Institutes of Elenctic Theology*, II:569
27. Ibid., II. 569–70.

Hodge on Religion

And then there is the very case that Vanhoozer takes, that of Charles Hodge. We shall look at two places, the first chapter of his *Systematic Theology*, which (as we shall see later) Vanhoozer has also given considerable attention to as part of his critique of Hodge as a child of the Enlightenment. And then, for a second piece of evidence, at two passages, taken at random, from Hodge's *Commentary on the Epistle to the Romans*. Finally we shall note an anecdote of B. B. Warfield's about Hodge's teaching. I focus on Hodge because of Vanhoozer's interest in him.

This is what Hodge says in chapter 1 of his *Systematic Theology*, the chapter that allegedly gives the game away regarding his strong connections with Enlightenment rationalism.

> The effort is not to make the assertions of the Bible harmonize with the speculative reason, but to subject our feeble reason to the mind of God as revealed in his Word, and by his Spirit in our inner life. It might be easy to lead men to the conclusion that they are responsible only for their voluntary acts, if the appeal is made solely to the understanding. But if the appeal be made to every man's, and especially every Christian's inward experience, the opposite conclusion is reached. We are convinced of the sinfulness of states of mind as well of voluntary acts, even when those states are not the effect of our own agency, and are not subject to the power of the will. We are conscious of being sold under sin; of being its slaves; as being possessed by it as a power or law, immanent, innate, and beyond our control. Such is the doctrine of the Bible, and such is the teaching of our religious consciousness when under the influence of the Spirit of God.[28]

What impression do these word convey? Do they suggest that, as he enters on the development of his *magnum opus*, Hodge is about to demonstrate to his readers that he has the mastery of Christian divinity, and that it is enough for Christian faith and life to have in one's head the "packaged" information that will now follow? They do suggest, it is true, the importance of human reason, and the need to subject reason to the word of God. However, as Hodge stresses, the appeal is not to be made solely to the understanding, but to every Christian's inward experience. As a result of subjecting our feeble reason to the word of God, and coming under the influence of the Spirit, Hodge says, people come to be conscious of the power of sin in their lives. The example that Hodge uses is merely illustrative, of course, but it

---

28. Hodge, *Systematic Theology*, I:16.

carries a point of principle: that word and Spirit together bring illumination to the consciousness, with all the affective and volitional changes that this implies. This does not suggest that Hodge is about to launch into developing a system of ossified or formulaic knowledge, a plaything of the cerebrum.

Hodge the Commentator and Teacher

Now Hodge the commentator. His commentary on Paul's letter to the Romans divides it into sections. For each section there is a brief Analysis, followed by the Commentary, then the Doctrine taught in it, and then Remarks. Here, taken at random from the book, are some of the Remarks on Romans 3:1–8.

> 2. It is a mark of genuine piety, to be disposed always to justify God, and to condemn ourselves. On the other hand, a disposition to self-justification and the extenuation of our sins, however secret, is an indication of the want of a proper sense of our own unworthiness and of the divine excellence.

> 3. Beware of any refuge from the fear of future punishment, founded upon the hope that God will clear the guilty, or that he will not judge the world and take vengeance for our sins.[29]

And consider these two of the Remarks on Romans 10:20–21.

> 4. It is the first and most pressing duty of the church to cause all men to hear the gospel. The solemn question implied in the language of the apostle, HOW CAN THEY HEAR WITHOUT A PREACHER? should sound day and night in the ears of the churches.

> 6. If "faith comes by hearing" how great is the value of a stated ministry! How obvious the duty to establish, sustain and attend upon it![30]

And so on throughout almost every set of Remarks. What these show is that in his commentaries Hodge habitually takes his readers beyond mere understanding and acceptance of a doctrine, to the fostering of Christian virtues and duties, the application of which may involve self-examination and careful self-discipline. Doctrine, and then application.

Finally, in a short paper "Dr Charles Hodge as a Teacher of Exegesis," in which he is not altogether uncritical of his former teacher, B. B. Warfield

---

29. Hodge, *Commentary on the Epistle to the Romans*, 76.
30. Ibid., 51–52. Emphasis in the original.

notes, writing of Hodge's expository method, that "Now and then he would pause a moment to insert an illustrative anecdote—now and then lean forward suddenly with tearful, wide-open eyes, to press home a quick-risen inference of the love of God to lost sinners."[31]

So here is Charles Hodge, the main half of the "Hodge-Henry hypothesis"[32] that Vanhoozer forcefully dismisses, the author of a work of systematic theology that is allegedly the product of the rationalism of the age of Enlightenment, whose work carries with it the temptation to use theological knowledge as a shibbolithic instrument of power! But when we actually take the trouble to consider the evidence, what do we find? We find Hodge using a part of the New Testament to promote "genuine piety," a concern for the state of one's soul, the imperative need to proclaim the gospel to all and to establish a stated ministry to do so. And, when teaching biblical exegesis, not being able to hide from his class the way in which the truth of the gospel affects him. Doctrine is to affect the emotions and the will.

Vanhoozer needs vacant space in order to construct his own theological contribution, and so Hodge is bulldozed out of the way. George Lindbeck, his other obstacle, seems to receive a much gentler treatment. But it is nothing less than scandalous that in order to justify this he offers what is intended as a damning condemnation of the method and bad effects of Hodge's "propositionalism." He does not take the trouble to offer even a shred of evidence to support that critique, despite evidence for precisely the opposite conclusion lying open to the most cursory inspection.

Propositions and Time

So far we have been considering Vanhoozer's concept of truth, and some of the grounds he offers for his departure from "propositionalism." We now consider what is the most persistent criticism of it by him and others, that it conveys the idea that theology is a set of timeless, abstract ideas.

One of the main failures of the "monologic" account of revelation, according to Vanhoozer, is that it is "reductive." Appropriating the criticism of theoretical systems made by the literary critic Mikhail Bakhtin, he claims that for the monologist, "it does not matter *whose* thoughts they are or in *what situation* these thoughts are held; all that matters is their propositional content (i.e., propositions that are either true or false, regardless of the speaker or the situation) that it tries to combine into a 'system of thoughts'

---

31. Warfield, "Dr Charles Hodge," 438.

32. Vanhoozer uses this expression in "Lost in Interpretation?" 101. "Henry" is, of course, C. F. H. Henry.

(i.e., separate thoughts that can be contained by a single consciousness)."[33] In a word, on such a monologic account of revelation, it consists of propositions that are abstracted from their situation; and so context-free and timeless, a "system of universal truths."[34] Taking Scripture in this way leads to positivistic proof-texting.[35]

It is not easy to count the number of times that the idea of propositional revelation has been alleged by theologians to express the Christian faith as "timeless truth," or as "timelessly true," or as "abstract," or even as "eternally true." But the connection between propositional revelation and timeless truth certainly goes back quite a few years.[36] Writing in 1975 of B. B. Warfield's view of Scripture, David Kelsey claims that "If the texts [of Scripture] serve to teach, then when used in theology they are construed as a text-book of doctrine having the force of *asserting* some eternal truths about objective states of affairs."[37] Those who say such things clearly regard timeless or eternal truth as a bad thing, something to be avoided at all costs. (It is easy to imagine that this charge, like others we shall consider later, is passed from hand to hand rather unreflectively.) What follows is an attempt to discover why it is that "timeless truth" is associated with the idea of revealed propositions.

Despite the repetition of the charge, the claim that propositional truth is "timeless" is hard to fathom. It is impossibly difficult to find a critic of revelation as timeless truth who will clearly state what the problem is. What would it be for a theological assertion to express a timeless truth, and then, if a particular instance is produced, who will tell us what's so bad about it? So the following reflections are offered in an effort to put into words what the "timelessness" objection amounts to, in the interests of furthering communication among those interested in systematic theological method.

Timelessness

Timelessness is often associated with God himself. In the mainstream Christian tradition—say, Augustine, Boethius, Anselm, Aquinas, Calvin, and Edwards—God's existence is timeless, in the sense that he is outside time, without a past or future, existing in a timelessly eternal present. But

33. Vanhoozer, *The Drama of Doctrine*, 269-70, emphasis in the original.
34. Ibid., 87.
35. Ibid., 270-71.
36. I discussed the issue as long ago as 1972. Helm, "Revealed Propositions and Timeless Truths."
37. Kelsey, *The Uses of Scripture in Recent Theology*, 100. Emphasis in the original.

it's surely not in this sense of timelessness, the timelessness of the eternal life of God himself, that some people think that "propositionalism" delivers a system of "timeless truth."

Still, if God is timelessly eternal then at least some propositions about him will be timelessly true in this very robust sense. Presumably the timelessness of God is itself an example of a timeless truth in this sense, if it is a truth. And whatever else is essential to God will, in turn, be robustly timeless in this sense—God is just, God is love, God is one nature in three persons, and so on. Of course it may be that narrative theology and theodrama entail that God is not timeless, but in time. But even then the fact that God is just, that God is love, and that God is three persons in one godhead, if not timelessly eternal, would be true for all times, and so at least they would be everlastingly true.

Vanhoozer on Time

In general, on the question of God and time, Vanhoozer wishes to retain much of the language of the tradition, God's fullness, his not being subject to time, his being (using Barth's expression) the Lord of time. Yet it is obvious that his controlling idea of God as a communicative agent in dialogue with his creatures, pulls him in the other direction. Here, as in his treatment of other parts of the catholic and Reformed theological tradition, there is an evident desire to try to find some "third way." Unkindly, one might say that he wants to have his cake and eat it, using words enclosed in inverted commas to aid the process of swallowing, if not of digestion. As in, "Time I submit, is the 'space' or medium in which persons communicatively relate."[38]

Does God himself inhabit this medium? I think it is fair to say that Vanhoozer does not give a clear answer to this question. In one of the longest discussions in *Remythologizing Theology* he offers these general statements: "Eternity is the form of God's triune communicative action *ad intra*, and God creates time in order to communicatively relate to creatures other than himself."[39] "Time is the medium of personal self-presentation to human others. At least, such is the nature of time in a theo-dramatic metaphysic for which the spatio-temporal existence is a predicate of God's dialogical interaction with the world."[40] So if God is in dialogical interaction with those in time must he himself be in time, even though "eternity is the form of God's

---

38. Vanhoozer, *Remythologizing Theology*, 254.
39. Ibid., 321.
40. Ibid.

life"?⁴¹ In occupying territory in which he could give an answer to that question, he chooses not to. "God's eternity is the form of his own life and hence the medium of his own being in communicative act. As such, eternity is not timelessness but 'eminent' (Barth) or 'supra' (Von Balthasar) temporality."⁴² Is there a "third way" between temporality and timelessness? His own position obviously favors divine sempiternity, or maybe a "double aspect" view of God and time such as that offered by William Lane Craig. God is eternal *sans* creation. But in creating he himself "becomes" sempiternal.⁴³ For it would seem to be necessary for communicative agency in Vanhoozer's sense that God forms new intentions to facilitate communicative dialogue with his creatures. But perhaps not. I think it is fair to say that Vanhoozer does not go as far as to say this, but nor does he appear to offer one consistent account of God and time.

These ruminations are in stark contrast to CRT, which maintains the eternality of the creator and the temporality of the creation. So Bavinck,

> For God did not become Creator, so that first for a long time he did not create and then afterward he did create. Rather, he is the eternal Creator, and as Creator he was the Eternal One, and as the Eternal One he created. The creation therefore brought about no change in God; it did not emanate from him and is no part of his being. He is unchangeably the same eternal God.⁴⁴

So while for Vanhoozer timeless eternity is closely associated with de-dramatization he does not claim that it entails it, any more than he claims that de-dramatization entails timeless eternity.⁴⁵ But he may think that the catholic tradition of timeless eternity has bequeathed to the church a timeless theology, and with it a view of divine revelation as being nothing but timeless, "static" truths, though he does not say this in so many words. Logically speaking, one could have a sempiternal God and a de-dramatized (in Vanhoozer's sense) theology. And, for all that he suggests to the contrary, one could hold to both divine timeless eternity and a theo-dramatic theology.

As we've seen, such doubters about the viability of propositionalism who nevertheless believe that God is timeless will, like it or not, be committed to some timeless truths—perhaps to an infinite number of them.

---

41. Ibid.
42. Ibid., 254.
43. Among several expressions of this view by Craig, see his *Time and Eternity*. For discussion see Helm, *Eternal God*, chapter 12.
44. Bavinck, *Reformed Dogmatics*, II:429.
45. Vanhoozer, *Remythologizing Theology*, 75.

Nevertheless, I don't get the feeling that the excoriation of revealed "timeless truth" is due to the thought that propositionalism commits one to the view that the entire body of theological truth is timeless as the eternal God is timeless.

Other Options?

What are the other options? In the Reformed tradition especially, there is emphasis on the idea that everything that comes to pass is timelessly (and yet freely) decreed by God. So all events, including all divine assertions, may be said to have an eternal character, albeit in a rather stretched sense. Events occur in time, assertions are made in time, but each such occurrence is eternally decreed to happen. Does a particular view of Scripture, that of regarding it basically and essentially as propositional revelation, entail such a view of God's will, of his plan? Clearly not. Does the "timeless" charge amount to saying that it does? I certainly hope not. There have been many who uphold the view that revelation is propositional who would vehemently deny that everything is eternally decreed by God. And it is possible that there are those who deny propositional revelation who nevertheless think that all things, including all dramas, are decreed by God. So it's hard to see that the charge is that propositionalism leads to the view, or entails the view, that everything is eternal or timelessly decreed by God. In any case, in the literature the issue of revelation as timeless truth has never, as far as I can tell, been introduced by reference to God's eternal decree.

Propositions and Permanence

So what are we to think? Here's what I have come to believe is behind the "timeless truth" charge. In saying that propositionalism is committed to "timeless truth" what the objectors have in mind is not the robust timelessness of God's eternal existence, the sort that Vanhoozer may be committed to, nor that associated with eternal divine decrees, but with *tenselessness*. "Copper expands when heated" is a tenselessly true proposition. Besides, it is a general or universal truth about copper. So it is not surprising to find objectors to propositions also criticizing them for turning theology into a system of "universal truths."[46] At any and every time it is true that copper expands when heated. So my surmise is that what the objectors object to is timeless truth in the sense of tenseless truth that (they think, for reasons that

---

46. Vanhoozer, *The Drama of Doctrine*, 87.

are not precisely clear) propositionalism is saddled with. So what "timeless" may boil down to is "true at all times" or perhaps or "true at any time." So propositionalism is the view that the propositions of Christian theology are context-irrelevant, or context-neutral. If they are true, then they are true at all times.

But if this is what they mean, that the truths of the Christian gospel are distorted by propositionalists into something that is true of all times, tenselessly true, then this charge is also wide of the mark.

The reason is obvious. It is that events in time, and statements about these events, are crucial to the Christian faith. The creedal statement that "Jesus Christ our Lord was conceived by the Holy Ghost, born of the Virgin Mary, suffered under Pontius Pilate, was crucified, dead, and buried . . ." is true, and integral to the Christian faith. This set of sentences is about what occurred at some particular time, or times, the times of the birth, suffering, crucifixion, and burial of the Savior, whenever exactly these times were.

So the idea that propositionalism, because of its timeless character, commits one to eliminating all references to events from true statements about the Christian faith is simply false. A glance at the text of any systematic theology in the CRT will immediately show how plainly false such an idea is. For example, in his discussion of the incarnation, Louis Berkhof states, "His [the Son of God's] active participation in this historical fact is stressed, and His pre-existence is assumed."[47] Or take what Charles Hodge has to say about the gospel dispensation.

> The old dispensation was temporary and preparatory; the new is permanent and final. In sending forth his disciples to preach the gospel and in promising them the gift of the Spirit, He assured them that He would be with them in that work until the end of the world.[48]

And this about the incarnation "God gave his Son for the redemption of man. He came into the world to save his people from their sins, to seek and to save those who are lost."[49]

Clearly, for Hodge, "The Son came into the world" is not a timeless truth, at least not a timeless truth about the world. It is certainly not a necessary truth, for, Hodge says, it refers to an event that was an act of voluntary humiliation.[50] We might say that it is a *dated* truth, a truth about an event

---

47. Berkhof, *Systematic Theology*, 333.
48. Hodge, *Systematic Theology*, II:377.
49. Ibid., II:455.
50. Ibid.

that occurred at such and such a time and place in history. But how, for Christian theology, could it be otherwise? It is a dated truth about an event that may well be true for all times, in the sense that its significance is never to be countermanded or in some way spent. Its importance may reach back, to times before the event concerned, and reach forward to the end of time. But it does not have such efficacy in virtue of being a sempiternal truth such as "copper expands when heated." It has a sempiternal value because it is the will of God that it will never be countermanded.

As we have already noted when discussing what I call the Utterance Fallacy, although p may be true about a time or times when certain events occurred, either presupposing these times or expressing them, the truth of p does not depend upon when p is uttered or asserted. It is equally true for men and women living at any time, and in any place.

The same is obviously true about what Berkhof and Hodge say about the incarnation. The sort of involvement that the event has with time is not that associated with *indexicality*. The statement "The sun is now beginning to shine" may be true at the time when this expression is uttered to make a particular statement, and only about that time. But the statements about Christ that Berkhof and Hodge (and countless others) make, or those recounted in the Apostles' Creed, are not utterances that are true only when they are first uttered. Whenever people recite part of a creed, and in whatever natural language they choose, they make a statement, or set of statements, which Christians believe to be true. Christians down the centuries, reciting that creed, have expressed the same truths. We may say this, then, as regards the central affirmations of the Christian faith, the very business of systematic theology, that their truth is bound up with the occurrence of certain events, and that truth was not altered or modified, by when they are subsequently asserted, or by any other subsequent events. We might say of such assertions: once true, always true, permanently true, true everywhere, true at every time.

So revelation has permanent truth. But it does not have permanent force. For it is now true that the revelation of Old Testament dietary laws are commands, but they are done away with, for the coming of Christ has taken away their original force. They no longer have the force of commands, and so they do not have illocutionary force for us. This is part of the "withering away" of the Mosaic order. It had the illocutionary force of a command, but no longer has it. Nevertheless, it is still true that the dietary laws were given. But the revelation of the faith in its New Testament fullness still has (the church maintains and CRT emphasizes) the force it first had. And it is part of the New Testament ministry to remind people of that force, and of the office of the Holy Spirit to bring the various forces—commands, covenant promises, and the like—to men and women today, that they are appropriated (as J. L. Austin might have said) with the appropriate "perlocutionary uptake." The language of the old order has lost much of its illocutionary force and the new order, the new covenant, has supplanted it.

Can it be that those who hold that "propositionalism" engenders "timeless propositions" are worried that the truths of the Christian faith are now forever true? Are they bothered by the thought that it is now true that the Apostles Creed is true, and that it will always be true? Surely not. Heaven forfend! What would have happened to the character of the Christian faith if it were not true for as long as time lasts that the Savior was born of the Virgin Mary? Jesus stopped being born, he stopped suffering, and so on, but the assertions "Jesus was born of the Virgin Mary," "Jesus suffered under Pontius Pilate," etc., never stop being true, and their importance and efficacy are undiminished by the passage of time.[51] In stressing this, the permanent truth of the report of an event that occurred in the past, we are of course stressing a commonplace. We can express it in various ways: the past is over and done with; what is now past cannot now not be past, what is true in the past is now unchangeably true, and so on. It should be clear that the upholders of propositionalism are not, therefore, making a plea for any special status for the central theological claims of the Christian faith. They are merely saying that *Christ suffered under Pontius Pilate* is permanently true. We see here, incidentally, another temptation that those who are fond of the current emphasis may fall into. Not quite the Utterance Fallacy, but a near relation. Current emphases on speech acts, theo-drama, and the rest focus our attention upon an event or a series of events. Are events true? They happen, but are they true? Clearly not. Paul asserted *Christ Jesus came into the world to save sinners*. Paul's asserting this proposition was an event. In this speech act or act of writing he expressed a part of the significance of the incarnation. But his asserting this at the particular time that he did does not *make* it true. Paul's statement did not give the incarnation a significance that it did not already have. What makes Paul's utterance true is Jesus coming into the world to save sinners. To focus on the fact that Paul uttered *p*, that uttering *p* is a linguistic act, and by concentrating upon its theo-dramatic performance, while at the same time downplaying propositional revelation, and the permanent truths that may be expressed in such a revelation, distracts us from the matter of truth. According to CRT and to creedal Christianity more generally, the great thing about the Christian gospel is that it is permanently true, true as long as time lasts, and so it can

---

51. Indeed, following Scripture itself, Christian theologians have frequently reflected on the fact that the death and resurrection of Christ are retroactive, their efficacy extending to the men and women of faith depicted in the Old Testament.

be freely reproduced and reiterated, by translators, teachers, and preachers the world over.

It is in this sense that such propositions are used in creeds and confessions and in the construction of systematic theological claims. Isn't this how it should be in our systematic understanding of the faith? Of course, it is not without interest that Paul made the assertion, that this is a statement having apostolic authority, that he uttered it (by writing) when he did and in the context that he did. Paying attention to these matters is part of the process of establishing what he wrote. No doubt all these factors affect the meaning of what he asserted, and so help us to determine what the truth is that he uttered. But none of this affects the point of principle. For in systematic theological endeavors we must repeatedly move from the assertions of Scripture and the conditions under which they originally occurred to what is asserted in them, the theological truth-content.

When we focus on the truth of what Paul asserted, rather than upon the fact that he asserted it, or on facts about the fact of his asserting it, are we abstracting? Is what Paul asserted, that Jesus Christ came into the world to save sinners, abstract? As we have been seeing, there is a clear sense in which it is: it is abstracted from the original occurrence of the speech act, the original assertion: it is the truth content of that assertion, and so may become the content of countless other assertions. When the preacher asserts it, or the congregation recites it, then its truth is being "re-issued," reaffirmed. Those who reissue it in such ways may not know much about its original setting. Does that stop them from presently asserting it, or from asserting it again and again? We may not have a notion about when the so-called Apostles' Creed was formulated. Having abstracted this creedal content from Scripture, the fact of the matter is that Jesus was born of the Virgin Mary, and came into the world to save sinners. These statements or assertions then become available for re-asserting.

We can see from this that abstracting the cognitive content of the event from Paul's assertion is not a failing. It is not a weakness of the idea of propositional or informational truth that such truths are "abstract" or "abstractable" in the sense discussed. Rather, their being abstract in this sense is a part of their strength and underpins their abiding theological significance. Such abstracting is necessary if we are to be in the position to consider the truth of such assertions, and of asserting them today and tomorrow. But is our abstracting of them an act of detachment? Are we, in abstracting them, and then confessing them, detaching ourselves from them? Are they then of merely theoretical interest, merely cerebral? Whoever would think such a thing? Cannot one's conscience be bound to the word of God when one makes such affirmations? Cannot one be energized by them, or moved to tears? So propositions may be abstracted from their original context of utterance and reissued, and they may nevertheless bind the mind, affect the emotions, and energize the will.

But in another sense such assertions are not abstract or timeless, for they are about a particular individual and about a particular time. The informational content of the original assertion has not been watered down nor does it become smoothed away by frequent repetition. It is not vague, as "Someone called" is vaguer than "Peter called" and "Peter called" is vaguer than "Your brother Peter called." Judged in this way, "Jesus Christ came into the world to save sinners" is a concrete, not an abstract, assertion. It is about a particular person, what he did, and what happened to him. Of course, it leaves other questions to be answered, and many of the questions that occur to us cannot now be answered. But this is true of every similar utterance. There is always more that could be known, and more that could be said. So, once more, it is hard to see what the charge that propositionalism turns divine revelation into "abstract propositions" means. Until the meaning of the charge is made clearer I suggest that it may be safely disregarded.

A Puzzle

There is something extremely puzzling about this entire discussion. The critics of propositionalism, it seems, are not worrying about whether or not God is timelessly eternal, nor about whether he timelessly decrees everything that comes to pass. Or if they are worrying about these things, these worries are clearly separate matters from the question of the nature of divine revelation. They may be concerned about "abstraction" in the sense of "abstractness," but as we have seen this worry is either unfounded or unclear. Maybe what really concerns them is that propositionalism is committed to the elimination of events from Christian theology. Certainly this is a concern one may have over theological liberalism's view that as far as understanding the Christian faith is concerned, historical events, being contingent in character, are dispensable. But why should propositionalism as such be tarred with that particular theological brush? For dateable events are at the heart of Scripture as they are of the creedal formulae of the church.

I hope and presume that the critics are not worrying about the fact that the historical events that Christians claim are at the heart of their faith, expressed in creedal formulae and in other such ways, are, once they are formulated, forever and so time-indifferently true. They are available for confession, for praise and worship and for much else, at any time. If there is agreement about that, what are those who are concerned about the connection between propositional revelation and timeless truth worrying about? Can anyone say?

7

Meaning and Reasoning

We noted in the first chapter the importance of reasoning for the CRT systematic theologian. He has a concern with the meaning of theological statements, with the drawing of inferences from them, with questions of consistency and with organic and narrative connectedness, as well as having a sense for the limitations upon intellectual investigation imposed by the mysteries of the faith. And he has a concern for gauging the performance of reason itself, bearing in mind that it has not escaped the effects of the fall.

At this point we turn to consider issues raised by some of the new proposals for the form that Christian doctrine is to take and the necessary conditions for theologizing. In the first place we shall examine Vanhoozer's account of concepts and propositions in *The Drama of Doctrine*. Then we shall give an account of his sustained attack on the theological method of Charles Hodge, and offer a defense of Hodge against certain misunderstandings. Finally, we shall look at the logical character of Vanhoozer's own way of understanding the informational content of Scripture that is apparent in his later work, *Remythologizing Theology*.

Concepts and Propositions

In *The Drama of Doctrine*, as part of developing his "middle way" between the cognitive propositionalist theology of Charles Hodge and the expressive communitarian theology of George Lindbeck, Vanhoozer provides a brief account of concepts and propositions. He wishes to give propositions their proper place, but not to overvalue them, as he believes Hodge did, or undervalue them, as he believes that Lindbeck has.

It may seem that a theo-dramatic account of doctrine, with its emphasis on action, would have no need of propositions at all. Vanhoozer's demurs. His account of propositions is to focus on propositional content. "A proposition *is a thought pattern whereby a speaker or author weaves two or more concepts together for some communicative purpose.* Every speech act, even the joke, has such propositional content; but not all speech acts make informative statements."[1] Propositions are nothing other than the informational content of diverse speech acts and literary genres. So every speech act that is informative has propositional content, and so we need an account of that content, and this requires an account of a concept.

Vanhoozer's view is that concepts are habits of mind by which we order human experience into patterns. Vanhoozer uses the idea of "Christmas" as an illustration, and claims that for one user the word will have one set of associations, for another user another set of associations. But the concept of Christmas has sufficient associations in common for the purposes of successful communication among such users. Earlier, in chapter 1, we saw how CRT placed a premium on definitions and that these definitions identified realities, providing us, in standard cases, with an account of the essence or nature of a thing. We can see from what Vanhoozer says that he has a very different approach. It is perhaps unfortunate that he has chosen "Christmas" as his main example, because Christmas is a cultural artifact. Another example he offers is "house," another artifact of course. There is a strong element of personal or societal construction in such cases, as well as a strong functional aspect. For some "Christmas" in nothing more than a secular holiday, "Winterlude." A barrel may be a table, and a teaspoon may be a small trowel. By contrast, concepts of natural kinds, such as those of a dog or an apple tree, have both essential and accidental properties. For animals and trees have natures. But Vanhoozer does not consider these, any more than he considers the concept of God, and that is a pity.

Nevertheless, Vanhoozer thinks that a theoretical term such as "the speed of light" is precise, though even here it must follow from what he says in general about concepts, that what I associate with that phrase may be very different from what you associate with it. It is usual in philosophical logic, at least since the time of Frege, to distinguish between the meaning of a concept and any psychological associations that it may have, but Vanhoozer makes such associations intrinsic to the meaning of a concept. So for him a concept is a highly personal, even a biographical, idea.

More significantly, he goes on to claim that the concepts of the Bible, such as father, king, salvation, or sin, all have fuzzy edges. Their meaning is

---

1. Vanhoozer, *The Drama of Doctrine*, 90. Italics in the original.

inexact, and so they are not "susceptible to unambiguous and univocal definitions." This is because they are not mental pictures of reality, but mental habits connecting reality with our experience of it. "A concept is a habitual way of experiencing and interpreting the world. We do not think about but *with* concepts."[2] So when question fourteen of the *Westminster Shorter Catechism* defines sin as "any want of conformity unto, or transgression of the law of God," the question for Vanhoozer is not whether this is a good definition of sin or not, but whether "sin" or any other biblical term can in principle be defined. We shall return to the significance of this later on, but it is already clear that Vanhoozer's philosophy of language makes exact theology impossible. You may mean something radically different by "sin" than I do. The possibility of reforming our ideas by the word of God, or the claim that Scripture provides us with a definition of sin, seem remote.

Propositions are concepts in a kind of articulated combination: a subject, which picks out some object, and a predicate or predicates, which ascribe a property or properties to the subject. "The cat is sick" may pick out a definite feline animal, and ascribes a property to it, the property of being sick. It is rather odd that, with his stress on action, Vanhoozer says nothing about verbs. Nevertheless, the basic point is clear. A proposition, considered in isolation, is "de-dramatized." Its proper home is as the propositional content of some speech act or other.

In *Remythologizing Theology*, which presents the idea of a theology to match the dramatized version of doctrine depicted in the earlier book, Vanhoozer says a little more about reasoning, or rationality. How are we to move from the Bible, the drama, to the theology, to the account of God? The answer is, it is necessary to reason about God on the basis of Scripture. Reasoning in this way makes a Christian theology "reasonable," or reasoned. So theology, particularly the doctrine of God, which Vanhoozer has in mind, arises from the judgments about God that we make on the basis of what we take to be God's part or place in the drama. These thoughts bear a strong relation to the propositions that we have just been thinking about, for the judgments use meaningful sentences composed of subjects and predicates. These sentences are necessarily "de-dramatized" (though Vanhoozer does not make this point) if only because they endeavor to express in present-day conceptualities the biblical conceptualities that may no longer be used in present-day natural languages.[3]

Such a procedure is obviously inductive in character, or at least involves induction, a gathering together of the dramatic data of Scripture in

2. Ibid. Italics in the original.
3. Vanhoozer, *Remythologizing Theology*, 186.

order to make judgments about the being of God from them. In various places in the book Vanhoozer offers us examples of such inductions.[4] The very form of the question that Vanhoozer regards as being fundamental to the theological task—what must God be like if he is actually the speaker depicted in the Bible?[5]—is a question that can only be answered by the adducing of evidence that is inductively acquired from the depictions of God's activity in Scripture. We must bear in mind, however, that our thought and the judgements that we seek to make are, according to Vanhoozer, already theory-laden, and as we noted in the last chapter, the data that we assemble are multi-aspectival in character.

What is much more serious, as far as the success of Vanhoozer's theological project is concerned, is the account of concepts that we noted earlier. The consequences of this account now come home to roost. For the theological endeavor, whether or not it is inductively based in Scripture, is afflicted by a two-fold indeterminateness or "fuzziness," to use his word. The theologian's task is first burdened by the indeterminateness of the concepts in the text of Scripture. No word of Scripture can be understood with exactitude, and my concept of God's speech may be different from yours, each having different complexes of association. But there is worse. For the concepts of the original text of Scripture (not to mention its various translations) may, for all we know, have different sets of associations for the original utterer than they do for me, or for you. How would we now know what associations were in John's mind when he wrote, "The Word was made flesh"?

A further consequence is that we may be sure that we never grasp any biblical concept exactly, for no concept is exact, and the inexactnesses can vary from speaker to speaker, and from interpreter to interpreter. The task of theologizing must therefore be in a permanent state of double jeopardy. Some theologians may choose an inexact style on purpose, but on Vanhoozer's account no theologians can ever give an exact account of any Scriptural matter or of any theological proposal. Here it is not the social context that gets in the way, as later on we shall see John Franke claiming, but it is the private, highly individual sets of associations of the original writer and the present-day interpreters, that prevent clarity and exactness of expression. Vanhoozer pays a very high price for his preference for a "meaning is use," language-games theory of meaning, with its stress on the "open-texture" of language. For while it is an exaggeration to say that his philosophy of language leads to theological skepticism, it nevertheless promotes an endemic tentativeness in any theological reasoning.

---

4. Ibid., 313.
5. Ibid., 23.

The Attack on Hodge

In a number of places we have noted the rather low view that Vanhoozer has of the "propositionalist" theology of Charles Hodge and the Princeton tradition. In a piece from which we have already quoted, "On the Very Idea of a Theological System: An Essay in Aid of Triangulating Scripture, Church and World," and in the course of his advocacy of theology as involving "theo-dramatic triangulation" between Scripture, church, and world, Vanhoozer has much more to say about Hodge.

To start with, Hodge's inductive method betrays certain tell-tale marks of its time, though this alone is hardly an argument against it. In particular, the method presupposes a subject-object dichotomy in which the interpreter's mind observes and analyses its object: the facts of the Bible. The direction of theological reasoning is bottom up: from biblical foundations to doctrinal formulation. The location or situation of the interpreter is irrelevant: the glory of the inductive method is that close observation allows the facts to emerge, regardless of who is doing the observing. Second, Hodge works with a dichotomy between fact and theory that has been called in question by philosophers of science who insist that data are always "theory-laden." Third, Hodge's decision to read the Bible as a book of divinely revealed facts predisposes him to focus on the Bible's content and to construe this content as propositional teaching. Such a focus on revealed content runs the risk of neglecting the larger canonical context and literary form of the biblical "facts," perhaps the inevitable result of biblical empiricism.[6]

These claims also bear certain familiar tell-tale signs, expressed in three charges against Hodge: that he presupposes a "subject-object dichotomy" in which the mind observes facts (which are in some sense mind-independent) and in which the situation of the interpreter is irrelevant. According to Vanhoozer, according to Hodge anyone can do the observing necessary for being a systematic theologian. It could be done by machine. Second, Hodge is said to work under the influence of the further "dichotomy" just noted, that between fact and theory. He does not take any account of the theory-ladenness of data. Thirdly, in virtue of the first and second of these proposals, in focussing on the content of the Bible, Hodge is predisposed to construe that content as propositional teaching.

It is tautologically true that Hodge was a child of his time. No doubt he could have benefited from the philosophy of science of children of later times, notably the claim that scientific theories are falsifiable hypotheses, not inductive generalizations from the data. No doubt Hodge's account of

---

6. Vanhoozer, "On the Very Idea," 136-37.

scientific procedure is naively Baconian. No doubt he would have learned things from Karl Popper, or N. R. Hanson, or Imre Lakatos, or even from Thomas Kuhn.[7] But this is not, I think, the main point. For Hodge the main reason for invoking induction is to endorse a method that gives Scripture theological priority in doctrinal construction or doctrinal correction, allowing Scripture to address us rather we addressing it. One imagines that for Hodge any methods that ensured this outcome would be regarded as equally valid. For example, he might well have endorsed the view that every doctrinal hypothesis must be falsifiable by Scriptural data, thus giving the power of veto to the biblical data, a power to be exercised regarding any theological proposal that is judged not to be sufficiently or appropriately grounded in Scripture.

We have just noted that any inquiry about the meaning of a document must involve induction, as Vanhoozer sees. His criticism of Hodge, in a nutshell, is not that he employs induction, but that he has a naively inductivist view of science, and that he applies this to his understanding of the relation between Scripture, which is a "storehouse of facts," and to the construction of systematic theological doctrines. It is alleged that this approach, besides expressing a primitive view of scientific method, does not make sufficient allowance for context, or presupposition, or for having due regard to the organic character of Scripture. It is said to be unacceptably positivistic, objectivistic, and empiricist, a brainchild of the Enlightenment.

Bavinck and Kuyper

Surprisingly, perhaps, part of the story, at least, appears to begin further back, not however as far back as the era of the Enlightenment, but in a very similar set of charges that were levelled at Hodge in brief discussions that the Reformed theologians Herman Bavinck and Abraham Kuyper have of his views. Perhaps this is the taproot of present-day criticisms of Charles Hodge and others, though this is not likely, bearing in mind that Bavinck's *Reformed Dogmatics* (1895–1901) has only recently been translated. The source may be Abraham Kuyper's *Encyclopaedia of Theology* (1898), the second volume of which has been available in English for quite a while.[8] The two theologians have very similar ideas about Hodge. We shall look first at Bavinck and then more briefly at Kuyper.

---

7. For an informative and provocative recent discussion of the relation between religion and science that takes account of modern developments in the philosophy of science from Popper onwards, see van den Brink, *Philosophy of Science for Theologians*.

8. Kuyper, *The Principles of Sacred Theology*.

In the section on theological method dealing with the "scientific" character of theology in Volume I of his *Dogmatics*, Bavinck contrasts what he calls the "synthetic genetic method" of establishing the "scientific" character of theology with the "experimental" method of Charles Hodge. This is part of a discussion about whether, following Schleiermacher, the subject matter of theology ought to be the scientific study of human religious states or the study of an objective revelation. This leads to the question, if Christian theology is distinct from religious studies, what ought to be the method of systematic theology, and is that method "scientific"?

Bavinck proceeds to outline the synthetic genetic method, which he himself adopts. He describes it as follows. While receiving the content of his faith from the hands of the church,

> the theologian is positioned in Scripture itself as the foundation of theology (*principium theologiae*) and from there develops dogmas. What a theologian does in that case is to replicate, as it were, the intellectual labor of the church. We are shown how dogmas have arisen organically from Scripture—that the firm and broad foundation on which the edifice of dogmatics rises is not a single text in its isolation but Scripture as a whole.[9]

Presumably the term "synthetic-genetic" is used because ideally the theologian derives data "organically" from the entirety of Scripture and generates theology from these data.

Bavinck makes a point of sharply distinguishing this method from the "empirical or experimental method" of Charles Hodge. He understands Hodge to be applying to Scripture the Baconian experimental method of first collecting the facts, then of framing an explanatory hypothesis for them, and finally testing the hypothesis experimentally. Actually, although in the *Dogmatics* he cites Hodge as the chief offender he does not take these points directly from Hodge himself but from an article by Robert McCheyne Edgar.

> Correspondingly, he [Edgar] says, the first task of Christian dogmatics is to gather the facts, say the facts of the moral world order, sin, the person of Jesus, holy Scripture, etc. The second task is to attempt to explain these facts by the presupposition of creation, fall, the deity of Christ, the inspiration of Scripture. And, finally, the theologian must verify them by what Scripture teaches concerning these presuppositions.[10]

---

9. Bavinck, *Reformed Dogmatics*, I:94.
10. Ibid. Edgar's article is, "Christianity and the Experimental Method."

According to Bavinck, this method does not stand up under examination. He offers three connected reasons for rejecting it. But first he draws an implicit contrast with his own approach, in which the "dogmatician . . . lives in communion of faith with the church of Christ and confesses Scripture as the only and sufficient basis (*principium*) of the knowledge of God," and aims "to replicate, as it were, the theological labor of the church."[11] Accordingly, the dogmatician receives the content of his faith from the hands of the church. Here are Bavinck's three reasons for rejecting the Hodge-Edgar approach.

First,

> In divine revelation, word and fact are always connected; it does not merely convey facts that we have to explain, but itself clearly illumines those facts. Scripture does not show us some facts that we then summarize under the rubric of sin, but it tells us itself what the essence of sin is. It not only tells us what Jesus has done but also who he was. Without this explanation we would not understand the facts at all and would give them a totally wrong interpretation.[12]

Secondly,

> Accordingly, the term *hypotheses* is completely inappropriate here. In the first place, the doctrine of the origin and essence of sin, to cite an example, or the doctrine of the deity of Christ, is not a hypothesis we have conceived but part of the witness of Holy Scripture. Furthermore, that doctrine, based as it is on this witness, is not a human hypothesis but a word of God that as such demands faith.[13]

Finally,

> If God has spoken in his Word, there is no longer any room for "experiment." Subsequent to the witness of Scripture, verification is in the nature of the case impossible in this area.[14]

Insofar as it involves Hodge, Bavinck's account is rather compressed. There is no direct citation from Hodge, though Hodge is clearly in view, and only a brief summary of the McCheyne Edgar article. In a work such as the *Reformed Dogmatics* this summary approach is understandable.

---

11. Ibid., I:93.
12. Ibid., I:94
13. Ibid.
14. Ibid.

Nevertheless it leaves the reader with a seriously misleading and even unintelligible account of the Princeton theologian's method. For each of the three points made by Bavinck, insofar as they are intended to implicate Hodge, seem to be off their target.

The impression Bavinck conveys is Hodge thinks Scripture simply consists of a set of facts, for which the theologian then provides an interpretation, the interpretation coming from the hypothesis that the facts suggest or indicate. So it is a fact that on a certain date three men hung on crosses, and said various things. What do these facts mean? The theologian offers an interpretation.

But as an account of the procedure that Hodge recommends, this is very wide of the mark. As the Princeton theologian understands matters, the "facts" that the systematician assembles are the clauses and sentences and collections of sentences—narratives and arguments—of Scripture, and only those facts. In other words, the "facts" with which the systematician deals are not raw data but already carry a theological load.

> It is a fact that the Scriptures attribute omniscience to Christ. From this it was inferred that He could not have had a finite intelligence, but that the Logos was clothed in Him with a human body with its animal life. But it is also a Scriptural fact that ignorance and intellectual progress, as well as omniscience, are ascribed to our Lord. Both facts, therefore, must be included in our doctrine of his person. We must admit that He had a human, as well as a divine intelligence.[15]

We see from these words what Hodge means by a fact: "Christ is omniscient," "Christ was ignorant of certain matters," "Christ made intellectual progress," are all facts ascribed to our Lord by Scripture, according to Hodge. And "Christ could not have had a finite intelligence" and "the Logos was clothed with a human body" are examples of inferences about the nature of the incarnation drawn from an incomplete induction of such facts. Though the word "hypothesis" may be absent, the idea of a hypothesis tested by the facts is clearly present, as we have just seen. But the facts from which the inferences are drawn are not facts apprehended apart from words, but facts that are expressed in words. The idea that the data of Scripture are like the data of a natural scientific kind, sets of events or other regularities occurring in the natural world for which an explanation or interpretation is sought, is not one that Hodge ever entertained.

In the case of the third objection there is straight misunderstanding. Hodge is not proposing an experimental or verificationist procedure that

---

15. Hodge, *Systematic Theology*, I:12.

will test the claims of Scripture by reference to data outside or apart from Scripture, but the very reverse of this. Such verification as there is is not a case of testing the statements of Scripture by natural scientific data from outside Scripture, but testing them by other data from within Scripture.

Despite these criticisms of Hodge, it is clear that Bavinck's own theological method is itself strongly inductive. That is, Scripture is given theological priority as the *principium* of Christian theology. This becomes clear in his account of his own "synthetic genetic" method, which (as we have seen) he rather mistakenly contrasts with Hodge's inductivism. What is the synthetic method? It "receives from revelation, both fact and word, word and fact, and the two in conjunction with each other" and the dogmatician can thereby "show the unity and organic interconnectedness of dogmatics."[16] After all, what is the alternative to this *a posteriori* approach? For Hodge at least the alternative involves approaching Scripture in a speculative or rationalistic manner. But both Bavinck and Hodge are united in their opposition to such methods, and also united in affirming the organic connectedness of the various elements in Christian theology

Abraham Kuyper briefly discusses Hodge's method in his *Principles of Sacred Theology*.[17] Unfortunately this also contains some inaccuracies: Hodge does not say, as Kuyper clams, that Scripture offers us no "scientific theology," but rather that parts of such theology are to be found in the New Testament epistles. "[A]lthough the Scriptures do not contain a system of theology as a whole, we have in the Epistles of the New Testament, portions of that system wrought out to our hands."[18] That is, such passages of Scripture are already theological in character, offering precedents for how the systematic theologian is to work. Nor does Hodge say that the theologian must authenticate the truths of the Bible that are not truths until he authenticates them. In fact, just the reverse. And as for Hodge being brought back "under the power of naturalistic science," that would be to treat the data of Scripture as no more than data of human religiosity. Kuyper seems to have regarded Hodge as somewhat Schleiermachean in his approach to theology. He does not seem to have realized, either, that for Hodge the appeal to induction is purely methodological in character.

So Hodge's references to induction should not be misunderstood. He cannot be referring to the procedures of general induction characteristic of natural science, for the inductions of the theologians are drawn from the bounded set of expressions in the canonical Scriptures. Suppose we attempt

---

16. Bavinck, *Reformed Dogmatics*, I:94.
17. Kuyper, *Principles of Sacred Theology*, 318–19.
18. Hodge, *Systematic Theology*, I:3.

by induction to determine whether all swans are white. We discover that some are black. Are all swans either white or black? Perhaps there are pink swans in remote and unexplored regions. And what about past swans? And future swans? Induction in the natural world is necessarily unbounded in time and unrestricted in space. But inferences from the biblical data are the precise opposite; there is a fixed set of data the boundaries of which are known and agreed.

Secondly, the inferences drawn from such data are not mere generalizations taken from the experiences of natural regularities in the world, but they arise from data that have meaning, the clauses and sentences of Holy Scripture as these leave the exegetes' hands. So induction may be followed by deduction, as the consequences of the meaning of the canonical sentences are addressed, and the logical implications of such sentences are part of those data. Similarly, the organic connectedness of one doctrine with another may be exhibited. The inferences from texts and the recognizing of connections between doctrines are ways in which the "internal relations" (as Hodge puts it) of the facts of Scripture are exhibited. And he emphasizes that systematization involves the "reconciliation" of data, that is, the establishing of their consistency and connectedness, the "relation in which the separate truths contained therein stand to each other."[19]

So Hodge's appeal to scientific induction is an *analogical* argument: as natural facts are to scientific induction, so the facts of Scripture are to the inductive reasoning of the theologian. But it does not follow that the theology *is a case of* natural science.

Theology, Biblical and Systematic

Geerhardus Vos, in his inaugural lecture for the newly-established Chair of Biblical Theology at Princeton Theological Seminary (1894), "The Idea of Biblical Theology," at first seems to offer some support for the Bavinck/Kuyper view of theology and theological method. Vos views biblical theology as a part of exegetical theology, which deals with the revelation of God in its historical continuity and stresses its organic character, and he explains it as follows.

> Biblical Theology exhibits to the student of the Word the organic structure of the truth therein contained, and its organic growth as the result of revelation. It shows to him that in the Bible there is an organization finer, more complicated, more exquisite than

---
19. Ibid., I:2.

even the texture of muscles and nerves and brain in the human body; that its various parts are interwoven and correlated in the most subtle manner, each sensitive to the impressions received from all the others, perfect in itself, and yet dependent upon the rest, while in them and through them all throbs as a unifying principle the Spirit of God's living truth.[20]

And in the case of the interrelationship between fact and interpretation he has this to say:

> And in the second place, we must remember that the revealing acts of God never appear separated from His verbal communications of truth. Word and act always accompany each other, and in their interdependence strikingly illustrate our former statement, to the effect that revelation is organically connected with the introduction of a new order of things in this sinful world. To apply the Kantian phraseology to a higher subject, without God's acts the words would be empty, without His words the acts would be blind.[21]

> ... the mighty creation of the Word of God furnishes the material for Theology in this scientific sense, but *is* no Theology. It is something infinitely higher than Theology, a world of spiritual realities, into which all true theologians are led by the Spirit of the living God. Only if we take the term Theology in its more primitive and simple meaning, as the practical, historic knowledge of God imparted by revelation and deposited in the Bible, can we justify the use of the now commonly accepted name of our science. As for the scientific elaboration of this God-given material, this must be held to lie beyond the Biblical period.[22]

Despite all this, however, comparing biblical theology and systematic theology, and in no way disparaging the latter, Vos has this to say

> The very name *Biblical* Theology is frequently vaunted so as to imply a protest against the alleged un-Biblical character of Dogmatics. I desire to state most emphatically here, that there is nothing in the nature and aims of Biblical Theology to justify such an implication. For anything pretending to supplant Dogmatics there is no place in the circle of Christian Theology.

---

20. Vos, "The Idea of Biblical Theology," 21–22.
21. Ibid., 9–10.
22. Ibid., 21.

. . . Dogmatic Theology is, when rightly cultivated, as truly a
Biblical and as truly an inductive science as its younger sister.²³

So Vos, writing sixteen years after the death of Charles Hodge, is not opposing induction to the stress he places on Systematic Theology as an organically related set of revealed truths, or to the interconnectedness of fact and interpretation in the biblical revelation. This can only mean that he takes induction to be a method of pursuing a resolutely *a posteriori* approach in gathering and understanding the biblical data, and not as covering the entirety of the theological method. As I am arguing, this is Hodge's view as well.

So it is possible that in claiming that Hodge thinks of systematic theology as being on all fours with natural science, Bavinck and Kuyper were at least one source of the criticism of Hodge as thinking of systematic theology as the result of a positivist, verificationist attitude to "the facts." These two (perhaps together with others) may have started that particular ball rolling, and since then it has gained momentum. So in the present day numerous theological critics may have understood (or rather misunderstood) Hodge by interpreting him through a Kuyperian lens, though perhaps without realizing this, and nevertheless accepting the criticism in a thoroughly uncritical fashion.²⁴

Another nineteenth-century American Reformed theologian, W. G. T. Shedd, takes a rather different view from that of Hodge. For him theology is the science of God and his relations to man and the universe. As such, it aims at the development of a profound and self-consistent understanding of these relations. ²⁵ In his opinion, such a view of science, theological science, is to be contrasted with the natural sciences in that it delivers absolute knowledge, true for all rational intelligences, whereas natural science can only be developed relatively to the intellect and senses of the investigator.²⁶ However, despite the contrast he draws between natural science and

---

23. Ibid., 23 Interestingly, Vos notes that he would have preferred the term "history of special revelation" to "biblical theology" but that usage triumphed over accuracy (*Biblical Theology*, Preface). This is a pity. The term "biblical theology" encourages a rivalry with systematic theology, and there have been those who have set up an antithesis between the two of the sort that Vos himself would clearly not have approved of.

24. See, for example, Murphy, *Beyond Liberalism and Fundamentalism*; Grenz, *Renewing the Center*; Marsden, "The Collapse of American Evangelical Academia"; Clark, *To Know and Love God*; McGrath, *A Passion for Truth*; Sparks, *God's Word in Human Words*; McGowan, *The Divine Spiration of Scripture*.

25. Shedd, *Dogmatic Theology* I:19.

26. Ibid., I:27.

theological science, Shedd is forced to recognize that though God himself is necessary and immutable,[27] nevertheless

> Christian theology differs from every branch of knowledge, by being the outcome of divine revelation. Consequently the interpretation of Scripture is the very first work of the theologian. When man constructs a system of philosophy, he must look into his own mind for the data: but when he constructs the Christian system he must look in the Bible for them. Hence the first procedure of the theologian is exegetical. The contents and meaning of inspiration are to be discovered. Christian dogmatics is what he finds, not what he originates.[28]

So theological science, however different from natural science, nevertheless proceeds *a posteriori*, by a careful examination of the biblical data.

In the light of the chorus of contemporary scholarly voices raised in unison against Hodge's mistakes, it is important that a careful examination is made of what Hodge actually said and the spirit in which he said it. So we shall now look at the opening pages of his *Systematic Theology* before examining the charges levelled against them by one of the more outspoken of his critics.

Hodge's Seventeen Pages

The seventeen pages in view are those that comprise the Introduction (chapter 1) of his *Systematic Theology*. Before we look at Vanhoozer's three detailed charges against Hodge in turn, it is worth noting that in the article in which he makes them,[29] Vanhoozer says little if anything directly about Hodge's inductive approach to the data of Scripture (though he does mention it in his article cited earlier.)[30] Nevertheless, a further word or two about Hodge's inductive approach are in order.

Hodge distinguishes what he believes to be the correct systematic theological method from two other methods that he calls somewhat imprecisely (as he acknowledges) the "speculative" and the "mystical." The speculative method, Hodge says, "assumes, in an *a priori* manner, certain principles, and from them undertakes to determine what is and what must be. It decides on all truth, or determines on what is true from the laws of the

---

27. Ibid., I:28–29.
28. Ibid., I:11.
29. Vanhoozer, "On the Very Idea of a Theological System."
30. Vanhoozer, "Lost in Interpretation?" 100.

mind, or from axioms involved in the constitution of the thinking principle within us. To this head must be referred all those systems which are founded on any *a priori* philosophical assumptions."³¹ He then proceeds briefly to examine three forms of this Method: the Deistic (the natural religion of Herbert of Cherbury, no doubt), the Dogmatic (Hodge cites the method of Anselm's *Cur Deus Homo*), and the Transcendentalistic (including the romantically tinged rationalism of the New England of Hodge's day, and more widely, Hegelianism). The second main method, the mystical, in its supernatural form holds that the Spirit of God is in direct communion with the soul, granting otherwise unattainable knowledge. Such mysticism is to be distinguished from the internal testimony of the Holy Spirit in his role as illuminator of the Scriptural truths. Mysticism in its natural form appeals to natural religious consciousness.

To these methods, very broadly sketched, Hodge opposes "the inductive method."³² This method is similar to induction in the natural sciences in assuming the trustworthiness of sense perceptions, of our mental operations, and of truths not learned from experience but which are given in our human constitution. By induction the scientist perceives, gathers, and combines the facts, taking care as far as possible to collect only the facts and all the facts. From these he draws certain general conclusions. So it is a case of first induction, and then deduction.

The Christian theologian proceeds in a parallel way. For him the Bible is the "store-house of facts."³³ Besides the mental principles used in natural science, the theologian appeals to other naturally implanted principles. For example, to the essential distinction between right and wrong, that sin deserves punishment, and other similar first truths, "which God has implanted in the constitution of all moral beings, and which no objective revelation can possibly contradict."³⁴ Using these principles the Christian theologian must "ascertain, collect and combine all the facts which God has revealed concerning himself and our relation to Him."³⁵ But even though Hodge may at this point gain some assistance from Thomas Reid, were no such help available he notes that the Bible itself clearly reveals what is

31. Hodge, *Systematic Theology*, I:4.
32. Ibid., I:9.
33. Ibid., I:10.
34. Ibid. It is at such a point perhaps that Hodge's sympathy with Thomas Reid's Common Sense Realism most clearly reveals itself. If he were alive today perhaps Hodge would express these ideas in terms of proper basicality or reliable truth-acquiring mechanisms. On the supposed influence of Scottish Common Sense Realism on Hodge and Princeton more generally, see Helseth, *"Right Reason" and the Princeton Mind*.
35. Hodge, *Systematic Theology*, I:11.

otherwise dimly perceived, the character of the external works of God, our consciousness and the laws of our nature, and our religious experience. So Hodge holds that this is a position that the Bible simply assumes to be true. Further, "the Scriptures teach not only the truth, but what are the effects of the truth on the heart and conscience, when applied with saving power by the Holy Ghost."[36]

Like the scientist, the theologian ought to carry out his induction as thoroughly and as comprehensively as possible. Hodge believed that in theology a partial induction of particulars has led to serious errors, as we saw earlier.

The facts induced

> [M]ust not be willfully denied or carelessly overlooked, or unfairly appreciated. We must be honest here, as the true student of nature is honest in his induction. Even scientific men are sometimes led to suppress or pervert facts which militate against their favorite theories; but the temptation to this form of dishonesty is far less in their case, than in that of the theologian. The truths of religion are far more important than those of natural science. They come home to the heart and conscience. They may alarm the fears or threaten the hopes of men, so that they are under strong temptation to overlook or pervert them. Science cannot make facts; it must take them as they are. In like manner, if the Bible asserts that Christ's death was a satisfaction to justice, the theologian is not allowed to merge justice into benevolence in order to suit his theory of the atonement. If the Scriptures teach that men are born in sin, we cannot change the nature of sin, and make it a tendency to evil and not really sin, in order to get rid of the difficulty.... We must take the facts of the Bible as they are, and construct our system so as to embrace them all in their integrity.[37]

Finally (at least as far as we are concerned), according to Hodge, "principles are derived from facts, and not impressed upon them."[38]

> It is . . . unscientific for the theologian to assume a theory as to the nature of virtue, of sin, of liberty, or moral obligation, and then explain the facts of Scripture in accordance with his theories. His only proper course is to derive his theory of virtue, of sin, of liberty, of obligation, from the facts of the Bible. He should remember that his business is not to set forth his system

36. Ibid.
37. Ibid., I:12–13.
38. Ibid., I:13.

of truth (that is of no account), but to ascertain and exhibit what is God's system, which is a matter of the greatest moment. . . . So long, however, as the binding authority of Scripture is acknowledged, the temptation is very strong, to press the facts of the Bible into accordance with our preconceived theories. If a man be persuaded that certainty in acting is inconsistent with liberty of action; that a free agent can always act contrary to any amount of influence (not destructive of his liberty) brought to bear on him, he will inevitably deny that the Scriptures teach the contrary. . . . It is the fundamental principle of all sciences, and of theology among the rest, that theory is to be determined by facts, and not facts by theory.[39]

Summarizing, two things are to be noted. The first is to underline the point that in setting out his views Hodge is *prescribing* a set of ideals, not *describing* what actually goes on. And it is obvious, in reading his words, dated in certain respects as they must be, that his overriding concern is to preserve and protect the *a posteriori* character of theology in its relation to Scripture, by being resolutely *a posteriori* in his construction of Christian doctrine. This is the point of the emphasis upon induction. And so we come to Vanhoozer's three charges against Hodge that go a long way, he thinks, to explain his cerebral, purely cognitive, "propositonalism," making it imperative that it should be supplanted.

Vanhoozer's Three Charges

Vanhoozer's first charge alleges that Hodge presupposes a subject-object dichotomy. If by this phrase is meant a distinction between the mind, the subject, and what the mind thinks about, including itself, the objects of its awareness, then such a distinction is fundamental to all thought, or at least to all non-mystical thought. For this reason the distinction has been recognized with near unanimity in Western philosophy.[40] But perhaps Vanhoozer takes it to mean that the mind does not influence what it thinks about. His use of the term is not very clear. Let us suppose that he does mean this.

But as we have noted, Hodge is not *describing* what actually goes on in carrying forward the science of theology, but giving his views on what *ought to* happen. His words are not descriptive, but normative or prescriptive. So of course, Hodge insists on the importance of taking into account the

39. Ibid., I.13-4
40. "Subject-object Dichotomy," in Audi, *The Cambridge Dictionary of Philosophy*, 773-74.

situation of the interpreter. He refers to it time and again. Rationalists and dogmatists and mystics bring principles to the interpretation of Scripture that they are unwilling to test by its data. Everyone is tempted to do this. Because of the importance of the issues at stake, we are tempted to pervert or overlook the teaching of Scripture, to "press the facts of the Scriptures into accordance with our preconceived theories," as he puts it. Hodge says:

> It would be easy to show that in every department of theology, in regard to the nature of God, his relation to the world, the plan of salvation, the person and work of Christ, the nature of sin, the operations of divine grace, men, instead of taking the facts of the Bible, and seeing what principles they imply, what philosophy underlies them, have adopted their philosophy independently of the Bible, to which the facts of the Bible are made to bend. This is utterly unphilosophical.[41]

In making these observations (so it seems to me) Hodge was far from being the fuddy-duddy that he is nowadays reckoned to be, but instead had his finger firmly on the pulse of things. If by a miracle we could introduce him into contemporary discussions we may imagine him having a word or two to say about the relativizing and skeptical consequences of viewing Scripture through the lens of postmodernity. What Hodge affirmed is that it is possible, by careful attention to the data, and by the help of the Holy Spirit (another vital factor about the theological situation which makes it distinct from the procedures of natural science), to come to a true understanding of the teach.ing of Scripture, even though there is also a sense in which the theologian is involved in a never-ending process of revisiting the data.

Whether Vanhoozer succeeds in showing that Hodge failed to avoid a "subject-object dichotomy" depends on what exactly is meant by this phrase. "Dichotomy" means "a sharply defined division." Is there a sharply defined division between the subject, the human senses and intellect, and the object, the data of Scripture? Don't most of us make such a "dichotomy"? Aren't most of us "guilty" of what Hodge was guilty of here? In the last chapter we noted Vanhoozer's own representational, "aspectival" realism appears to presuppose a dichotomy between subject and object. Except in certain forms of idealist and constructivist thinking, or certain kinds of mysticism, the subject and the object, though they are related, are distinct. Hodge can only make the important distinction between the principles that we may wrongly bring to Scripture and the principles that we may rightly take from Scripture, by making a distinction between principles and facts. Any process involving the testing of theories must do the same.

41. Hodge, *Systematic Theology*, I:14.

Contrary to what Vanhoozer claims, then, for Hodge the situation of the observer matters a very great deal. It matters whether or not the observer is a speculator, or a dogmatist, or a mystic, or some of each. Operating with preconceived theories was not a situation that Hodge himself is exempt from, nor (he would say) is anyone else. He saw the operation of such preconceptions as a danger that obstructed the full impact of the data of Holy Scripture on the mind. He was certainly not setting himself up as some kind of paragon. The point is that, according to Hodge, we should strive with might and main—by checking and rechecking, by taking expert advice, and by prayer for the Holy Spirit's guidance—for an objectivity based on a thoroughly *a posteriori* approach to the data of Scripture.

Secondly, Vanhoozer charges that in Hodge's approach there is another dichotomy, that between fact and theory. For Hodge (it is said) did not take any account of the "theory-ladenness" of data. "Theory-ladenness" was a term coined by N. R. Hanson[42] to convey the idea that all factual statements, but particularly those that enter into scientific reasoning, imply some theory or other. "There is a table over there" is "laden" with the theory of the spatio-temporal location of middle-sized artefacts; "I am aware of a red sense datum" is laden with the theory of phenomenalism; "He has an Oedipus complex" is laden with psychoanalytic theory. Some words, like "gene" and "electron" are theory-laden terms. Was Hodge aware of this point? Decidedly so. His *Systematic Theology* begins as follows

> In every science there are two factors: facts and ideas; or, facts and the mind. Science is more than knowledge. Knowledge is the persuasion of what is true on adequate evidence. But the facts of astronomy, chemistry, or history do not constitute the science of those departments of knowledge. Nor does the mere orderly arrangement of facts amount to science. Historical facts arranged in chronological order, are mere annals. . . . If, therefore, theology be a science, it must include something more than a mere knowledge of facts. It must embrace an exhibition of the internal relation of those facts, one to another, and each to all.[43]

What Hodge here referred to as an internal relation between each fact to another, and each to all, once it is being developed, may very well give rise to something very like theory-ladenness or may even be theory-laden. For "the facts" will then be understood in their relations to one another. The idea of sin involves the idea of law, and of guilt, for example. The idea of Christ involves the Trinity, as well as economic subordination and submission; it

---

42. Audi, *The Cambridge Dictionary of Philosophy*, 797.
43. Hodge, *Systematic Theology*, I:1.

involves two natures, human and divine, and so on. It is not surprising, therefore, that the seventeen pages of the Introduction end with the words "It is also assumed [viz. by the inductive method applied to Scripture] that the relation of these Biblical facts to each other, the principles involved in them, *are in the facts themselves* . . ."[44]

As Hodge shows, collecting together the facts of Scripture is not like collecting pebbles from a beach and sorting them. Rather, Hodge claimed that the facts of Scripture are related conceptually and organically. They are "internally" related, as he put it.[45] In a Christian view of Scripture "God was in Christ reconciling the world unto himself" is consistent with "God created the heavens and the earth" and "Our God is a consuming fire." Each of these sheds light on the other, forming part of an organic whole, and it is the task of the systematic theologian, as far as he is able, to display this consistency and interrelatedness.

As we have already noted, for Charles Hodge systematic theology builds on the results of biblical theology.

> So the Bible contains the truths which the theologian has to collect, authenticate, arrange and exhibit in their "internal relation" to each other. This constitutes the difference between biblical and systematic theology. The office of the former is to ascertain and state the facts of Scripture. The office of the latter is to take those facts (viz. the facts ascertained and ordered by the biblical theologian), determine their relation to other cognate truths, as well as to vindicate them and show their harmony and consistency.[46]

So for Hodge the facts to which the systematic theologian attends are already "laden" with the conclusions of the biblical theologian, that is, the exegetical theologian. It is because of his work that Hodge was able to say, "Although the Scriptures do not contain a system of theology as a whole, we have in the Epistles of the New Testament, portions of that system wrought out to our hands. These are our authority and guide."[47] So it would be a mistake to think that Hodge believed that the Bible is nothing but sets of facts and that all theological reasoning is "bottom up," as Vanhoozer thinks.[48] No, the Bible implies general conclusions too, and employs concepts, as the biblical or exegetical theologian teaches us. The language of the Bible

---

44. Ibid., I:27. Emphasis added.
45. Ibid., I:1–2.
46. Ibid.
47. Ibid., I:3
48. Vanhoozer, "On the Very Idea of a Theological System," 136.

is laden with them. Perhaps Hodge would even be inclined to say that in the Bible "God" and "sin" and "redemption" are, like "electron" and "gene," theory-laden terms.

So besides facts, the Scriptures, especially the Pauline letters, also provide us with portions of systematic theology. This is why Vanhoozer is inaccurate in supposing that Hodge made a principled distinction between the facts of the Bible and the systems that theologians devise.[49] The Bible already contains valid samples of such a system. "It is no less unscientific for the theologian to assume a theory as to the nature of virtue, of sin, of liberty, of moral obligation, and then explain the facts of Scripture in accordance with his theories. His only proper course is to derive his theory of virtue, of sin, of liberty, of obligation, from the facts of the Bible."[50] The theologian is the focus of the influence of competing theories. Those he brings to the Bible which may well distort it, and those he obtains from the Bible after proper induction, involving inquiring into, summarizing, and connecting up its teaching, accurately represent it. Unsurprisingly, therefore, Hodge asserted that systematic theology "is not an easy task."[51] The idea that, as Vanhoozer surmises, Hodge plays down or dismisses theories, and allows that anyone can be a systematic theologian simply by assembling the facts of Scripture, without courting the danger of having those facts distorted by false theories, is a major misunderstanding.

Finally, Vanhoozer claims that in virtue of the first and second of these practices Hodge was predisposed to construe the content of the Bible as propositional teaching. This point has already become familiar to us. Well, Hodge certainly does construe the content of the Bible as propositional teaching, though interestingly enough an induction of the pages of Hodge's introductory chapter reveals that the word "proposition" is never used there. However, Hodge refers to "the truths" of the Bible, and "the facts of Scripture," and I suppose that he would not deny that these truths and facts are expressed, or are expressible, in propositions. "God was in Christ reconciling the world unto himself" is, Hodge would have said, a fact, a true proposition, a truth. Whether asserting such things "runs the risk of neglecting the larger canonical context and literary form of the biblical 'facts,' perhaps the inevitable result of biblical empiricism," as Vanhoozer claims,[52] is hard to tell. It is more than likely that Hodge, who as we noted was something of a Bible commentator, was appraised of the different literary forms

---

49. Ibid., 156.
50. Hodge, *Systematic Theology*, I:13.
51. Ibid., I:2.
52. Vanhoozer, "On the Very Idea of a Theological System," 137.

of the Scripture, capable of distinguishing between parables, narratives, and wisdom literature, and between the literal and the metaphorical. As we've also noted, he is sensitive to the fact that the Epistles of the New Testament are unique among the other books of the Bible in already providing for us examples of systematic theological reasoning.

If, finally, behind the dislike of "propositional theology" there lurks the fear of equating "propositional" with dry, detached truths located in a dry, detached theological system, then Hodge's words also allay such fears. At two places in the Introduction he noted that the Bible contains not only doctrines, or theories, or principles, or truths, but also stated "what are the effects of the truth on the heart and conscience, when applied with saving power by the Holy Ghost.... The Bible gives us not only the facts concerning God, and Christ, ourselves, and our relations to our Maker and Redeemer, but also records the legitimate effects of those truths on the minds of believers."[53] So whatever defects "propositional theology" might nowadays be thought to have, one cannot, I think, reasonably charge Charles Hodge with thinking that it is satisfactory to appropriate revealed truth in a dry or detached manner.

Vanhoozer's arguments against Charles Hodge's method turn out to be so weak that they may safely be discounted. As we have seen they are part of the retail trade of discounting Hodge and Princeton theology occurring more generally within current evangelical and Reformed theologizing. Vanhoozer uses them as part of a case for thinking of Christian doctrine and theology afresh. But his comments are inaccurate at numerous points and the overall case is seriously deficient. He is of course fully entitled to develop his novel view of systematic theology as "theo-drama," a triangulation of Scripture, church, and world, but it is wrong to use a distorted and partial account of Charles Hodge's theological method to aid him in that task. Hodge is not an untouchable icon: he shared in our common infirmities. But he is entitled to have his views fairly presented.

Interestingly, in spite of Hodge's claim that the systematic theologian proceeds calmly and smoothly in carrying out the process of collecting data by induction and devising theories on their basis, his actual practice in the body of his *Systematic Theology* is in fact rather different. His critics, who seem not to have consulted more than a few phrases in Hodge's introductory chapter, seem not to have noticed this. It is worthwhile, I think, in coming to a fair appreciation of his theological method, to see how he actually proceeds in his *magnum opus*.

---

53. Hodge, *Systematic Theology* I:11, 16. Vanhoozer notes Hodge's stress on the place of the work of the Spirit in the work of theology but cannot seem to make anything of it. Vanhoozer, "On the Very Idea of a Theological System," 157.

For example, in his treatment of providence in Volume 1, we find that he started from a conceptual discussion of the distinction between preservation and continuous creation, denying that they are the same. Then he proceeded to the biblical data. He then stated the doctrine of providence, and offered a proof of it. It is a logical consequence of the biblical doctrine of God, and he offered supporting proofs of a general kind, for example from predictions and promises, and from experience, and then restated the scriptural doctrine. He compared this view with rival views, and discussed in more detail certain features of the scriptural doctrine; for example, how providence extends to rational creatures. Finally, he drew a distinction between providence generally speaking and the influences of the Holy Spirit.

So there is a certain amount of to-ing and fro-ing here, setting up a sort of dialectic between appeals to certain basic concepts and their grounding in the text of Scripture and then to the relation of his view of providence to various other biblical doctrines as well as to contrasting views. Hodge's actual method is anything but naively inductive. This is not altogether what one is led to expect from the language of the first chapter of *Systematic Theology*, and not what the critics of Hodge have come to expect. Whatever we may think of such a dialectical method, it is certainly more than a process of naïve induction, if only because of the introduction of explicitly controversial material from the very beginning of the discussion.

Deduction

At the beginning of the chapter we considered Vanhoozer's view of concepts and propositions and noted how it puts in serious jeopardy the process of grounding theology in the text of Scripture. The same applies to deduction, but here the consequences of Vanhoozer's view are more striking. I begin by considering a case from the history of CRT.

The Puritan John Owen regarded the Trinitarian character of God to be a plainly revealed mystery, and fundamental to the development of true religion. In his view the work of redemption and reconciliation is intrinsically Trinitarian, and appreciation of this enriches our understanding and our walk with God. This general outlook can be seen in a number of Owen's works, most elaborately in his *Communion with God the Father, Son, and Holy Ghost, Each Person Distinctly, in Love, Fellowship and Consolation* (1657), but also in a smaller work, *A Brief Declaration and Vindication of the Doctrine of the Trinity* (1669).[54] Understanding and teaching the doctrine of the Trinity is vital so that "faith may be increased, strengthened,

---

54. Both these books are in *The Works of John Owen*, Vol. II.

and confirmed against temptations and oppositions of Satan, and men of corrupt minds; and that we may be distinctly directed unto, and encouraged in, the obedience unto, and worship of God, that are required of us."[55] Here also we note, incidentally, how for Owen, as for CRT more generally, the Bible is not a mere cerebral document consisting of lists of propositions, but is intended to lead to obedience and service, to faith and love.

In his short work *A Brief Declaration*, Owen's main theological idea is that the doctrine of the Trinity—that God is one God in three persons, Father, Son, and Holy Spirit, having distinct, mutual relations—is not an imposition on Scripture, or a theory about God, or a "model" of God, but found plainly in Scripture. Scripture is both clear and sufficient in the matter. Here is one place, therefore, where Scripture does not underdetermine doctrine. The scriptural portrayal of God is not misty, ambiguous, or vague. The theological formulation of the Trinity in terms of the divine essence and a Trinity of persons is not a clarification, much less an explanation, of the mystery of the Trinity. So what is it?

According to Owen, we must begin with the plain assertions of Scripture. They are our ultimate source of information about the Godhead, and our last line of defence. We find that Scripture sets forth a Trinitarian God. In our theological thinking "We produce divine revelations or testimonies, wherein faith may safely rest and acquiesce, that *God is one; that this one God is Father, Son and Holy Ghost*; so that the Father is God, so also is the Son, and the Holy Ghost."[56] We start with the text. We do not first engage ourselves in terms such as "Trinity," "substance," "persons," "properties," and the like. We first consider the Scripture. This is a clear affirmation of the sufficiency and clarity of Scripture on the matter.

And so Owen surveyed some of the biblical data respecting the oneness of God, that the Father, Son, and Holy Spirit is each God, concluding

> There is nothing more fully expressed in the Scripture than this sacred truth, that there is one God, Father, Son, and Holy Ghost; which are divine, distinction, intelligent, voluntary omnipotent principles of operation and working: which whosoever thinks himself obliged to believe the Scripture must believe.[57]

In establishing these conclusions an inductive process was used, gathering the evidence, letting it speak for itself. And this process, in the case of the biblical teaching regarding the godhead, led to a very strong, confident

---

55. Ibid., II:378.
56. Ibid., II:380.
57. Ibid., II:406.

conclusion about its Trinitarian character. But this process is not, at the same time, unthinking proof-texting. For Owen considered the context of the texts he cites. This is most apparent in the case of the data proving the deity of the Son, in which he notes that certain expressions in the New Testament are applications of Old Testament teaching. He recognized the relationship of the Testaments, and the way in which some of the language of the Psalms and the prophets was taken by Christ to apply to himself. So there is induction, but it is an inductive process that itself involves interpretation and some prior understanding of Scripture. Then there is deduction.

However, since the Scripture doctrine of the Trinity is called into question by non-Trinitarians and others we may need to use further terms not found explicitly in Scripture. In this business we may (and must) make use of "such words and expressions, as, it may be, are not literally and formally contained in the Scripture but only are . . . expository of what is so contained."[58] In any case, without such a liberty it is impossible to interpret Scripture.

> For if it be *unlawful* for me to speak or write what I conceive to be the sense of the words of the Scripture, and the nature of the thing signified and expressed by them, it is unlawful for me, also, to think or conceive in my mind what is the sense of the words or nature of the things; which to say, is to make brutes of ourselves, and to frustrate the whole design of God in giving unto us the great privilege of his word.[59]

According to Owen, the words of Scripture regarding the threeness and oneness of Almighty God have a sense, or, as we might say, a meaning. What is that sense? Can we say? If it is "unlawful" to say what the sense of Scripture is, then it is unlawful for me to conceive in my mind the sense or the meaning of Scripture in the first place. If that is so, then Scripture may be God's inspired revelation, but for me and for you and for anyone else it remains mute, a closed book. So, Owen concludes, "in the declaration of the doctrine of the Trinity, we may lawfully, nay, we must necessarily, make use of other words, phrases and expressions, than what are literally and syllabically contained in the Scripture, but teach no other things."[60]

So "divine person" may be a suitable expression with which to parse the biblical data of three distinct agencies of God; "divine nature" may parse the indivisible one-ness of God. So we can, Owen thinks, deduce the dogmatic doctrine of the Trinity from the biblical pattern of teaching respecting

58. Ibid., II:379.
59. Ibid.
60. Ibid.

the character of the Godhead. But the dogmatic apparatus is not strictly speaking essential for the statement of the doctrine.

It does not follow, even if Owen is correct on the deducibility of the doctrine of the Trinity from the original scriptural data, that every Christian doctrine has the same relation to Scripture as does the Trinity. Obviously not. An induction of the biblical data may not warrant the deduction of a doctrine in such a straightforward way. It is reasonable to conclude that there are cases in which the data of Scripture do not entail that doctrine, but probabilify that doctrine to some degree or other, entitling one to have a strong belief that Scripture teaches it, without it being reasonable to suppose that it is entailed by Scripture.

Take, for example, the idea that God exists timelessly, in a state other than that of the temporal series. One may hold that data such as Titus 1:2 and similar "before time" texts such as Ephesians 1:4, together with the assertions of Psalm 90:2 and similar, and Job 38–41 make it plausible that, or give reason to believe that, the idea of God's timeless eternity is warranted, without entailing it. There may be debates about the meaning of the original; Titus 1:2 is translated by various different versions by "before the beginning of time," "before the ages began," and "ages ago." It may be pointed out that the fact that the idea of divine timeless eternity employs concepts for which there is no equivalent in Scripture makes the idea less than totally compelling, and so on. Or when one considers a matter such as the exact mode of Christ's presence in the Lord's Supper, it is possible quickly to see that while Scripture may rule out certain views, it does not describe the Supper and Christ's presence at it in anything like the detail, and with the same polemical edge, that occurs in later theological debates. What is the relation of the brain to the mind, according to Scripture? As a general rule, one might say that the more detailed the expression of a doctrine or some other matter that is integral to the expression of a doctrine, the more cautious one ought to be in claiming that such a doctrine is entailed by the data of Scripture.

One ought not to be prematurely defeatist about this, of course. It may be that with more thought and research the scriptural basis of some theological ideas will be strengthened, while that of others be weakened. Similarly, one might extend such an argument to the treatment of the divine mysteries.[61] Such doctrines as the Trinity and the incarnation are inherently mysterious, but it does not follow that their mysteriousness might not be lessened with the employment of a new conceptuality, or whatever. Who knows? The point is that besides deductions from Scripture, such as those

---

61. For a good treatment of the epistemic status of belief in the divine mysteries, see Anderson, *Paradox in Christian Theology*.

made by John Owen respecting the Trinity, there are also many further inductions employed on the data of Scripture, of varying degrees of strength, leading to doctrinal constructions of varying degrees of convincingness.

Despite this last qualification, it is clear that Owen inhabited a very different intellectual world than that which Vanhoozer advocates. With Hodge, Owen is confident in his use of induction. But more than this, he is strikingly confident in his use of deduction in the case of the Trinity, and perhaps of other doctrines (such as the doctrine of the person of Christ), though clearly not of every doctrine.

But how do matters stand with Vanhoozer? What he has to say about the nature of a concept drastically undermines any prospect of deducing any positive conclusion from Scripture. For CRT, based upon the theologians' view of the clarity of Scripture, the meaning of Scripture is Scripture, as we strikingly see in Owen's procedure. But this is because Owen held that there are clear concepts in Scripture with a definite, stable, interpersonal meaning. But as we saw, Vanhoozer denies this. Each concept being fuzzy, my concept of sin may not be your concept of sin, and so on. It follows that what I can deduce from my concept of sin may be different from what you can deduce from yours. And in any case the meaning of what I deduce may be different from the meaning of what you deduce. As a result we each may have our own personal theologies. Note that the point is not that some concepts are vague in their meaning, as cloud, heap, and sea are vague terms. The vagueness of such is due to what the concepts mean. Some biblical concepts are inherently mysterious, for the same sort of reason. Nor is the problem that certain terms are metaphorical or analogical, for such language, though not literal, can nevertheless be used univocally, and so may find its way into inductive and deductive argument patterns. In any case, it is possible to have a clear concept of a mystery, as Owen shows in his remarks on the Trinity. On Vanhoozer's idea of a concept, no scriptural concept has any necessary consequences, and drawing inductive and deductive inferences from scriptural data becomes, if not impossible, then extremely hazardous.

This is a *reductio ad absurdum* of any public, shared enquiry about anything. But it is obvious that such interpersonal enquiries are undertaken successfully. So Vanhoozer's idea of what a concept is, and the constraints that it must place upon theological enquiry in particular, must be seriously mistaken. But his practice is better than his preaching, as can be seen from his later book, as it was bound to be.

8

Foundationalism and Its Woes

Vanhoozer believes our conceptual schemes are not derived from things as they are, as realists typically claim, but that they are formed by the human mind as it brings together perspectival aspects of reality that, though they do not correspond to reality, nevertheless successfully "render" it. He distinguishes what he calls "aspectival realism" from "perspectivism."[1]

> An *aspectival* realism is poles apart from a perspectivism that suggests that what we see is merely our own theoretical *construct*. Perspectivism holds that what we see is a function of *nothing but* the schemes or theories with which we work. To be sure, there are misleading (e.g. false) ways of looking at things; some theories are merely speculative. Yet an aspectival realism insists that theo-dramatic reality is independent of what we say and think about it, even though it is indescribable and unknowable apart from the diverse canonical forms and only partially accessible to any one form.[2]

Such aspectivalism is directly traceable to the Enlightenment, to one of its foremost philosophers, Immanuel Kant, who held that human knowledge is the joint product of the raw data of experience and the structuring powers of the mind. In his case these structures were innate. Vanhoozer maintains that they are acquired, or that at least some of them are. The theoretical world as such is inaccessible to us; we experience its phenomena, its appearances, and organize and consolidate these through the use of conceptual structures that we bring to the data. Ideally these structures are derived from the "diverse canonical forms" of Scripture. So that knowledge

---

1. For example, Vanhoozer, *The Drama of Doctrine*, 293.
2. Ibid., 289. Italics in the original.

is derived through the application of conceptual structures or frameworks. This debt to Immanuel Kant is every bit as much an Enlightenment product as is the empiricism of John Locke or the rationalism of René Descartes or the skepticism of Pierre Bayle.

Curiously, in *Remythologizing Theology*, perhaps realizing the lack of an epistemic case for his theo-dramatic approach to doctrine as developed in *The Drama of Doctrine*, Vanhoozer seems to think that the provision of a metaphysical framework, a conceptual scheme, a theology, is sufficient for epistemological purposes. Theology demands more than storytelling. "Faith that stops its search for understanding short of ontology risks falling back into mere mythologizing."[3] But, of course, the intellectual world is awash with competing metaphysical frameworks; the provision of an ontology may be "descriptive" or "revisionary" but unless, as deployed in Christian theological endeavor, it aims to depicts things as they are, it is pretty useless.

Foundationalism

In earlier chapters we have briefly discussed the nature of foundationalism and the distinction between general epistemological foundationalism and theological foundationalism. In this chapter we begin by noting the reasons why many writers on the nature of Christian doctrine and of systematic theology currently reject foundationalism. Such people now blithely talk of post-foundational or non-foundational theology. We shall then attempt to focus attention on the consequences of bidding farewell to the idea that Christian theology has foundations.

To be clearer about the territory we are attempting to traverse we need first to consider the questions, "foundational for what?" "foundations of what?" The necessary requirements for something being foundational for Christian discipleship is one thing. Is Scripture theologically foundational for that? Clearly not. A person may be a disciple while not knowing whether there be such a thing as Holy Scripture. So is Scripture foundational theologically? According to CRT, indeed it is, for that's one obvious way of understanding the principle of Scripture's necessity and sufficiency. Such necessity implies a foundational role for Scripture. The Christian church appeals to the necessity of Scripture, and its Reformed branch, having more decided convictions regarding Scripture's foundational character, also appeals to its theological sufficiency, while recognizing, as we saw at the outset, the subordinate role of councils, creeds, and confessions. Such necessity and sufficiency, expressed in a more epistemological way, appeals to a canon, a

---

3. Vanhoozer, *Remythologizing Theology*, 217. See also ibid., 222.

supreme authority or rule of faith. It is such theological foundationalism that we are now to discuss.

Why Reject Foundationalism?

We noted in earlier discussion that while foundationalist epistemology and foundationalism in theology are, naturally enough, connected, they are in fact distinct positions that may be held independently of each other. Someone may hold that there are epistemic foundations of a general kind but hold that religion, even the Christian religion, is not warranted by such foundation, but is a matter of the will. Such fideism, as we might call it, even if it is implausible, is certainly not inconsistent with a more general foundationalism. One could alternatively hold that Christian theology is based on Scripture, the epistemic authority of which is conveyed by the persuasion of the internal testimony of the Holy Spirit, like Calvin did and Alvin Plantinga does. Nonetheless it is hard to see why those human cognitive powers that are accepted by foundationalists are not part of what is at work conjointly in the internal testimony. The Spirit uses the human intellect and the senses, he does not bypass them. Grace builds upon nature. So perhaps if one is a theological foundationalist, then one must be a foundationalist more generally, though one could be a foundationalist in general without being a theological foundationalist. If one is a coherentist in regard to epistemic justification generally, then one could not be a theological foundationalist unless one had a theological foundation quite separate from that of epistemology more generally, perhaps information derived exclusively from the working of an "inner light."

But this may sound like an invitation to accept a version of double truth; at the very least it is extremely hard to see how one could avoid some such consequence unless one ventured into Gnosticism or mysticism. Such strategies are certainly rejected by CRT: for such an outlook, theological foundations sit within a more general epistemological framework of a foundational kind, even though the focus of attention is on the first of these and not on the second.

We have also noted that while CRT's attitude to theological foundationalism is fairly self-consciously worked out, via its doctrine of Scripture, its attitude to foundationalism of a more general kind is more *ad hoc*. Scripture may give an account of itself, but it does not at the same time provide us with a worked-out general epistemology. As a consequence, CRT's attitude to general epistemological foundationalism might be expressed as follows: provided one's epistemology permits the endorsement of Scripture's own epistemic claims, and its reports of others' claims, then what one's overall epistemology is is a matter of secondary importance. And so it has been usual to find a rather eclectic epistemological approach in CRT, elements of Platonism, Aristotelianism, and Stoicism, or of Cartesianism and of Reidian Common Sense Realism, being utilized in different times and places in a fairly eclectic fashion.

As far as I can see, treatments of foundationalism by "post-foundationalists" do not reflect upon the relations between epistemological and theological foundationalism in a systematic way. Nor do they pay a great deal of attention to arguments for and against foundationalism, or discuss the Chisholmian contrast between "methodist" and "particularist" epistemology.[4] Nor do they debate Plantinga's distinction between "strong" and "weak" foundationalism.[5] Nevertheless, despite a complete lack of philosophical argument, "foundationalism" in all its shapes and sizes is peremptorily rejected, but especially theological foundationalism.

So why *is* the idea of theological foundations abandoned? John R. Franke, for example, simply says that in the postmodern context, foundationalism is in dramatic retreat, "as its assertions about the objectivity, certainty, and universality of knowledge have come under fierce criticism."[6] He supports this by general discussions of context and the constructivist manner in which religion is treated by sociologists of knowledge such as Peter Berger. He goes on to note that it is asked whether such knowledge is possible, and indeed desirable, and sharply negative answers are implied: no, it is not possible, and in any case it is not desirable. Further, foundationalism seems to be thought of as invariably a way of securing and mastering the knowledge of God, a form of theology by philosophical works. Perhaps it is regarded as an irreligious way of buttressing personal faith so as to eliminate or lessen its riskiness. One might suppose, even so, that a sympathetic hearing might be given to Plantinga's weak foundationalism. But though it is occasionally noticed, its merits are not aired. Theological foundationalism is thus thought to be a symptom of a more general malaise, that of succumbing to the rationalistic climate of the Enlightenment, as well as being inveigled into a kind of intellectual idolatry. It is because of a deep conviction that theology has in these ways become contaminated that foundationalism is dismissed with the wave of a hand.

---

4. Chisholm, *Theory of Knowledge*, chapter 4,
5. Plantinga, "Reason and Belief in God."
6. Franke, *The Character of Theology*, 27. For a discussion of Franke and postmodernism, see Trueman, "It Ain't Necessarily So."

This does not mean that the non-foundationalist may not have strong convictions. "It simply maintains that all such convictions and commitments, even the most long-standing and clear, remain subject to on-going critical scrutiny and the possibility of revision, reconstruction, or even rejection."[7] But the fallibilism of CRT, and epistemological fallibilism more generally, say more or less the same thing.

There also appears to be a general suspicion of epistemology as the study of how we justifiably believe and know things, because it is held, in true postmodern fashion, that claims to knowledge are oppressive. The claim to possess knowledge enables the persuasive claimant to gain and exercise power over others, to determine what they may believe and what is to count as knowledge. So there is thought to be an immorality about claims to knowledge, which is at odds with the non-oppressive human relations that a Christian should foster. These factors clearly create a climate in which serious epistemology will not be pursued vigorously by the theologian, nor theology exposed to epistemic scrutiny.[8]

But can this avowed post-foundationalism be sustained by Christian theologians in practice? Surely Vanhoozer's canonical linguistic approach to Christian theology implies that the canon of Scripture is the theological foundation? He distinguishes between the church's having a foundation, in the canon, or in Christ, from being foundationalist. He writes that "The canon is a foundation but not the type that characterizes classical foundationalism."[9] But we are not further enlightened, except that we see that foundationalism is rejected for theological reasons, because it privileges propositions and disregards the different literary genres of Scripture.[10]

We have seen Vanhoozer making such a charge against CRT and also seen how weak it is. Efforts to generate theological conclusions are, according to CRT, subject to all manner of pitfalls, not the least of which are the workings of the noetic effects of sin. For Charles Hodge at least, Christian theology is not an easy task. Further, why classical foundationalism is alleged to privilege abstract propositional truths is not at all clear. Maybe foundationalism privileges concrete propositions, like "Jesus Christ came into the world to save sinners." A Chisholmian particularist in theology may be thought to do just that, to have a set of particular propositions such as "Christ Jesus came into the world to save sinners" forming part of the foundations of his noetic structure of belief.

---

7. Franke, *The Character of Theology*, 78.
8. Vanhoozer, *The Drama of Doctrine*, 303; Franke, *The Character of Theology*, 19.
9. Vanhoozer, *The Drama of Doctrine*, 293.
10. Ibid.

Despite the protests against foundationalism, the appeal to the foundationalist character of the canon of Scripture is striking. Perhaps what Vanhoozer has in mind is not that Scripture provides foundationalistic assertions for the theologian but that the canon is the privileged *source* of data. That would certainly be foundational, and the appeal to a canon of books of diverse genres seems to be something like this. But if so, in virtue of what, epistemically speaking, does the canon have this privilege? As far as theology is concerned, two things are rather puzzling about this. The first is that the foundationalistic pattern in Christian theology predates the foundationalism of the Enlightenment. It was not called by that name, but the thing itself is present in Christian theology from its beginning, and regarded as vital for it. Connected with this, it is important to note that not all foundationalisms connect with the rationalist strand of the Enlightenment. A word on each of these.

Earlier, in chapter 2, we saw that in CRT grace builds on nature, and so nature has, in this sense, a "foundational" character. The stress before the Enlightenment is on reason and the senses as foundational *instruments*, not on the foundations as sets of propositions (or sensations) established by the reason from which we derive other sets of propositions in the superstructure. So Turretin, for example, writes

> Reason is taken either materially for the kind of doctrine derived from the light of reason, or formally for the manner of delivering it which is commonly called the mode of instruction. But in neither senses can it be called the principle of theology; not in the former sense because theology is neither built upon reason nor resolvable into it; not in the latter sense because although it is in this sense an instrument (as has been said), yet it cannot be considered as the principle.[11]

So reason is ancillary in theology, but it is a divine gift, as aspect of human nature.

> The question is not whether reason is the instrument by which or the medium through which we can be drawn to faith. For we acknowledge that reason can be both: the former indeed always and everywhere; the latter with regard to presupposed articles. Rather the question is whether it is the first principle from which the doctrines of faith are proved; or the foundation upon which they are built, so that we must hold to be false in things of

---

11. Turretin, *Institutes of Elenctic Theology*, I:27.

faith what the natural light of reason cannot comprehend. This we deny.[12]

Reason is the instrument through which we understand the sentences and clauses of the revelation and draw inferences from them. But it is not the foundation of the faith, nor does it supply the criteria for what is to be believed. It is an instrument of faith, but not the foundation of faith.

Similarly with the senses.

> The question is not therefore whether the testimony of the senses is in every case to be regarded, so that we should grant nothing except what the senses can seize. For we grant there are many mysteries to which reason and much less the senses cannot rise, such as the mysteries of the Trinity, of the incarnation, etc. Rather the question is when the senses judge of an object belonging to them and do not go beyond their proper sphere, must their testimony be rejected or admitted? The question is whether faith may be opposed to a well-directed judgment of the senses and overthrow it. This we deny.[13]

So here is a rather different sense of foundationalism employed in CRT, before the Enlightenment, in which the reason and the senses are "foundational" within their (carefully delimited) spheres of operation.

Further, as far as theology is concerned, it is obvious that, as a matter of history, Protestantism and particularly CRT has its cognitive basis in what came to be referred to as the necessity and sufficiency and perspicuity of Scripture, or as the sole or primary authority of Scripture in matters of faith and practice. The conflict with the Church of Rome was, *inter alia*, a conflict over cognitive authority, and "authority" here is simply a rather older-fashioned term for "foundation," in this case "theological foundation."

Word and Spirit

In CRT in particular, the recognition of this cognitive basis has a strikingly self-conscious character. For the authority of Scripture is based upon itself, on its self-authenticating or self-attesting power to evidence itself to the believer as the word of God, through the ministry of the Holy Spirit. The "foundational" character of Scripture is not itself referred to some more basic epistemic authority, even though the general reliability of the senses and the intellect are assumed. So the Bible authenticates itself to the believer

---

12. Ibid., I:24.
13. Ibid., I:35.

through her appreciation of its material content as the Word of God, the gospel of Jesus Christ, an appreciation engendered by the enlightening activity of the Holy Spirit.

So we find Calvin making the following appeal:

> Let this therefore be held as fixed, that those who are inwardly taught by the Holy Spirit acquiesce implicitly in Scripture; that Scripture carrying its own evidence along with it, deigns not to submit to proofs and arguments, but owes the full conviction with which we ought to receive it to the testimony of the Holy Spirit. Enlightened by him, we no longer believe, either on our own judgment or that of others, that the Scriptures are from God; but, in a way superior to human judgment, feel perfectly assured—as much so as if we beheld the divine image visibly impressed on it—that it came to us, by the instrumentality of men, from the very mouth of God.[14]

In writing about how the doctrine of divine inspiration and sufficiency of Scripture functions, Charles Hodge says:

> Besides, we have the witness in ourselves . . . in like manner the soul receives and appropriates the truths of Scripture as the atmosphere in which alone it can breathe and live. Thus in receiving the Bible as true, we necessarily [because of what it teaches about itself] receive it as divine. . . . After all Christ is the great object of the Christian's faith. We believe him and we believe everything else on his authority.[15]

And Bavinck says:

> Not the church but Scripture is self-authenticating (*autopistos*), the judge of controversies (*judex controversiarum*), and its own interpreter (*sui interpres*). Nothing may be put on a level with Scripture. Church, confession, tradition—all must be ordered and adjusted by it and submit themselves to it. The Remonstrants charged that the Reformed, by their use of the confession, failed to do justice to the authority, sufficiency, and perfection of Holy Scripture. But the Reformed, though deeming a confession a necessity in this dispensation of the church in order to explain the Word of God, to turn aside heresies, and to maintain the unity of the faith, denied with the utmost emphasis that the confession had any authority apart from Scripture. Scripture alone is the norm and rule of faith (*norma et regula*

---

14. Calvin, *Institutes*, I.7.5.
15. Hodge, *Systematic Theology*, I:167.

fide et vitae). The confession deserves credence only because and insofar as it agrees with Scripture and, as the fallible work of human hands, remains open to revision and examination by the standard of Scripture.[16]

Of course there are differences as well as similarities between this idea of a Christian foundation based upon the self-authenticating witness of the Spirit to the truth of the evidence of Holy Scripture, and epistemic foundationalism. One obvious difference is that the foundations, for Descartes, for example, notably the *cogito*, were incorrigible truths, propositions that once understood could not be denied, and for Locke they were incorrigible sensations. Scripture has not been claimed by CRT to be self-evident in this sense; its meaning as well as its truth-claims are all too readily deniable, and denied. And related to this, according to CRT the work of the Holy Spirit in illuminating the mind to the evidence of Holy Scripture is particularistic: it is not an endowment of every rational person, but a gift of God's grace to some and not to others. This last point will be taken up later on.

The Consequences

Whatever the reasons post-foundationalist theologians have for doing so, they have moved away from such an epistemic structure in theology, and we now must examine some of the consequences of their doing so. I shall argue that despite their intentions they cannot consistently hold to non-foundationalism. Or, that if they do so, the entire character of Christian theology is imperilled.

I shall first take as an example of the consequences of this what Kevin Vanhoozer has to say in *The Drama of Doctrine* about foundationalism and the difficulties that attend it. Then look at greater length at John R. Franke's views in *The Character of Theology*. As previously, we are looking at these thinkers from within the Reformed tradition for purely illustrative purposes, as indicative of a trend that is sharply at variance with CRT.

Vanhoozer on Post-Foundationalism

Vanhoozer distinguishes his post-foundational position from that of those who think of knowledge in coherentist terms, as a web, net, or mosaic of belief.[17] This is because, he claims, in such configurations no belief is more

---

16. Bavinck, *Reformed Dogmatics*, I:86.
17. Vanhoozer, *The Drama of Doctrine*, 293.

important than another. (This does not seem very strong; a web may have a core, which if it is disturbed affects the periphery, but not *vice versa*.) But he is also against imputing "basicness" to a community or tradition, which many other non-foundationalist accounts, such as Lindbeck's, welcome.[18] So some beliefs are more important than others, but none is foundational.

His position is that, while a metaphysical realist, he acknowledges (a rather powerful epistemological term, incidentally) the provisional, contextual, and fallible nature of human reason. (This language is taken from F. LeRon Shults, quoted by Vanhoozer with approval.) The argument here is: since all our data are theory-laden, none of them can be basic in the required foundationalistic sense. "Nevertheless, thanks to aspectival realism, we may say that some filters allow true knowledge to get through."[19] That is, (I think) that the aspects may connect with (though not be what the language pictures or corresponds to) the theory-laden language in which they are appraised.

An analogy for knowledge of the Vanhoozerian kind is neither that of a building with foundations nor a web with a center, but a map, a guide for us in our walk towards the truth and the life. Theologically speaking, the map is the canonical text; in fact, the text is an atlas of maps.[20] So, it would seem, the canonical text, the atlas, is (after all) the epistemic foundation, and this would be consistent with the priority that Vanhoozer gives to the canon throughout the *Drama of Doctrine*. But is this another case merely of one word being substituted for another, "map" for "foundation"? Does the possession of a "fiduciary framework" not function as an epistemic foundation?

The relationship between canon and the maps that have it as their source is not so clear, though. Certain things that Vanhoozer says suggest that the imagination is, or ought to be, one element of such cartography.[21] And while it may be true that the chief purpose of a map is to be useful, it can be useful only to the extent that it provides the map-reader with accurate information, and the map-reader knows where she is on the map, if anywhere. So the polarization between informing and living presents us with a rather false dichotomy. "Knowledge of God begins with trust in what we have been told about God by God, and this means taking the canon as the beginning of theological knowledge, the interpretative framework for understanding God, the world and ourselves."[22] But is a beginning not a

18. Ibid., 293, citing Grenz and Franke.
19. Ibid.
20. Ibid., 294.
21. Ibid., 377.
22. Ibid., 295.

foundation? And is not what we are told about God by God propositional? Still, the emphasis on trust rather than on belief has a fideistic look about it. So this may be fideism, an adherence to the canon by an act of the will, the maps being subordinate to this, the aspectual product of intellect, emotions, and will.

Yet for all the attempt to distance himself from foundationalism, Vanhoozer's alternative proposals look pretty foundationalistic after all. The canon is the beginning of a framework. For he also says that this is trust in what we have been told by God about God, and this surely amounts to a core of knowledge, or of knowledge claims, or the reliable basis for knowledge claims, even if the knowledge has more to do with wisdom than with belief. We know what the map is about, and we take it that it is accurate, before we begin to use it. And yet "maps are not mirrors of reality; they do not literally reflect the way the world is.... A map is an interpretative framework, not a foundation of basic facts."[23] Of course a good map is not a literal mirror of reality; but if nevertheless such a map, with the help of a set of conventional signs, accurately represents the terrain it does so in ways that have elements of projection and picturing.

It is ironic that having protested against the picture theory of meaning Vanhoozer should choose the analogy of a map. If it is possible to be a tentative foundationalist, then perhaps Vanhoozer is one.[24] Mapping by the canon has all the virtues: coherence as a canon, correspondence in multiple modes to the one reality through discernment of its literary content. So theology's task is to make explicit the nature of these multiple modes, which are implicit in Scripture.[25]

Part of the reader's problem here is that Vanhoozer provides a series of imaginative proposals with little or no attempt to show how these work in approaching the text of Scripture. As we have already noted, one of the great drawbacks in Vanhoozer's project is that he does not provide any instances of doctrines being redrawn or reworked as a result of the adoption of a theo-dramatic outlook. Nevertheless, the general impression one has is of a position that, as regards the issue of foundationalism, is somewhat unstable. This is not the confident theological foundationalism of CRT. But nor is it the wholesale abandonment of foundationalist ways of thinking. This canonical "foundation" is polyphonic[26] and aspectival, and the results

23. Ibid., 296.
24. Ibid., 298.
25. Ibid., 301.
26. Franke uses the same word in "Nonfoundationalism, Truth, and the Knowledge of God," 299.

of consulting it are tentative, furnishing many different accounts of the one divine reality mapped out through different literary genres, and so the prospect for a theology that is genuinely systematic, clear, consistent, and interconnected seems dim. Yet it seems that Vanhoozer overstates the real as opposed to the merely verbal novelty of what he proposes. For some of the expressions he uses look to be mere variants of traditional ways of speaking of theological language and its epistemic status.

Franke on Foundationalism

In common with many contemporary Christian revisionists, John R. Franke also turns his back on epistemic foundationalism, claiming that it cannot provide the appropriate theological method. He stresses his rejection of "strong" or "classical" foundationalism like this:

> At the heart of the foundationalist agenda is the desire to overcome the uncertainty generated by the tendency of fallible human beings to err and the inevitable disagreements and controversies that follow. Foundationalists are convinced that the only way to solve this problem is to find some universal and indubitable means of grounding the entire edifice of human knowledge.[27]

These are remarks about epistemic foundationalism in general, of course, but they are applied by Franke to theology alone. He says or implies that theologians have previously asserted that the knowledge claims of the Christian faith are grounded in universal and indubitable criteria, in universally accessible universal beliefs. But Franke names no names. So it is hard to fathom who he has in mind. But as we have seen, and shall see again, CRT is guarded about such a grounding, but for different reasons than those that have persuaded Franke.

Franke holds that theology cannot be an edifice in which the various doctrines and dogmas of the Christian faith—the superstructure—are grounded in a set of "indubitable beliefs that are accessible to all individuals." He stresses (as we saw) that the *objectivity*, the *certainty*, and the *universality* of the knowledge that foundationalism claims to provide have been fiercely criticized in the contemporary culture.[28] Franke accepts the current critique of foundationalism without going into it in any detail. But drawing on Merold Westphal, he grounds his anti-foundationalism in the twin creaturely

27. Franke, *The Character of Theology*, 26.
28. Ibid., 27

incapacities of finitude and sin, which in turn engender the hermeneutics of finitude and the hermeneutics of suspicion.[29] Quoting Westphal, Franke claims that: "The hermeneutics of finitude is a meditation on the meaning of human createdness, and the hermeneutics of suspicion is a meditation on the meaning of human fallenness." He comments "In other words, many of the concerns of postmodern theory can be appropriated and fruitfully developed in the context of the Christian doctrine of creation and sin."[30] So the challenges to foundationalism are not only philosophical, but they also emerge from the material content of Christian theology. But, he claims, the recognition of these incapacities leads not to skepticism, but to fallibilism. As we have repeatedly stressed, fallibilism has always been recognized, and has even been stressed, by CRT.

There is some paradox here if these two incapacities are intended to have a dominant epistemic role. For on what epistemic grounds can he appeal to these distinctively Christian incapacities? As Christian ideas, certainly, but also as truths? If finitude and sin so severely compromise our ability to know things, do they not also cramp our ability to know about the theological categories of creatureliness and sin that they connect with?

Franke runs together three quite different ideas: the *certainty*, *objectivity*, and *universality* of knowledge. Each of these embodies a different epistemic claim. In the remainder of this chapter we shall be chiefly concerned with the issue of certainty, reserving objectivity and universality for the next chapter.

It is clear from what he writes that Franke rejects epistemic foundationalism in any form. At one point he notes that Plantinga's Reformed epistemology offers a vigorous defense and affirmation of truth as well as a telling critique of modernity.[31] This is true, at least in that phase of Plantinga's work to which Franke is alluding, but he fails to note that the Reformed epistemologists do so by utilizing a version of foundationalism, what Plantinga calls "weak" foundationalism, based not upon indubitable truths recognized by any rational person but upon the "proper basicality" of certain beliefs that may be recognized only by some. This means that it is rational to accept certain propositions without basing that acceptance on any other beliefs or propositions. This is not a mandatory foundationalism, setting up a universal requirement for rationality, but a permissive foundationalism that entitles or warrants basic beliefs that may not be held universally, and

29. Franke, *The Character of Theology*, 27.

30. Quoted in Franke, "Reforming Theology," 9. Cf. Franke, *The Character of Theology*, 80–81.

31. Franke "Reforming Theology," 5.

that may contradict basic beliefs held by others. It is therefore a form of foundationalism that undercuts the textbook Enlightenment view of rationality. Weak foundationalism is able to function like this because, Plantinga argues, strong or classical foundationalism is self-referentially incoherent.[32] That is, the criteria that classical foundationalism sets for belief-worthiness it itself fails to meet.

Franke is concerned with more than the failings specific to classical foundationalism. He has a principled objection to the foundationalist thinkers as a whole. But although he refers to the "entire edifice of human knowledge" it seems that he is particularly objecting to the edifice of Christian theology being founded on a set of indubitable foundations. So we shall understand him in the following way: that in rejecting the very idea of foundationalism he is principally interested in constructing a non-foundational Christian theology. As we have noted, his understanding of the cultural contexts in which human cognizers operate is distinctly constructivist.[33] So, with theology specifically in view, he bids farewell to foundationalism.[34]

According to Franke, a non-foundationalist method in Christian theology is one in which no element of the theological enterprise is privileged, but which consists in an inter-play between a number of different epistemic concerns that exist in parity with each other. Franke initially defines theology very generally as "the orderly study and investigation of the truths of the Christian faith."[35] As he develops his view, paying particular respect to the context in which all theology is inevitably situated, he offers the following working definition:

> Christian theology is an ongoing, second-order, contextual discipline that engages in the task of critical and constructive reflection on the beliefs and practices of the Christian church for the purpose of assisting the community of Christ's followers, in their missional vocation to live as the people of God in the particular social-historical context in which they are situated.[36]

This is quite a complex set of claims. There is a noticeable emphasis on the community whose beliefs and various activities provide the first-order data on which the reflective theologian engages. Two further things about them are noteworthy. The reference to "the truths" of the Christian faith made in the earlier more general definition disappears and is replaced by

32. Plantinga, "Reason and Belief in God," 59f.
33. Franke, *The Character of Theology*, 113.
34. Ibid., 85f.
35. Ibid., 40.
36. Ibid., 44.

"beliefs." This may be thought to be a slip, but in view of what follows it has great significance. Franke later on denies that his non-foundationalist approach presupposes a denial of truth, and distinguishes between ontological foundations (or sets of truths) and epistemological foundations—that is, our beliefs that may or may not be true. "While non-foundationalist theology means the end of foundationalism, it does not signal the denial of foundations or truth."[37] There are objective truths, but theology does not build on any of these so much as aim for them. Such truth-claims must be accessed by non-foundational methods. We may note a similarity here with Vanhoozer, a commitment to realism but not to the acquisition of objective knowledge, but of a regulative ideal, and to sets of beliefs that are provisional in the sense that there's a real chance that all of them will be modified or rejected. For all our attempts at knowing are skewed and distorted by the fact that our truth claims are aspectival and infected with subjectivity (Vanhoozer) or are contextual, as well as being the product of mechanisms that are finite and sinful (Franke).

But the critical theological question for both Vanhoozer and for Franke is, does the Christian, and the Christian church, have reliable access to these ontological foundations, these sets of truths? If they are accessible only to a limited degree, as Franke seems to claim, then according to him non-foundationalist theology is a never-ending quest to gain access to these truths in the particular, varied situations in which all theologizing must take place. These "situations" are particular social or cultural contexts. In this quest, considerable prominence is given by Franke to "context" (there are two references to context in his definition), to cultural situatedness.[38] This is one reason, I believe, why the focus of his discussion is on belief rather than on truth. Nevertheless, despite the various caveats, according to Franke, non-foundationalist theology aims at truth. Truth is not merely a matter of social or cultural consensus. So theology is a contextual discipline endeavoring to help the Christian community to form true beliefs about its faith in its particular socio-historical context. These beliefs are not simply the regulative rules of the Christian community, for they aim at truth, but with the clear prospect of achieving only the limited success that we have noted.

Besides the problem that Franke has with the idea of privileging certain truths as foundational, he has another difficulty:

> Attempts on the part of humans to seize control of these relations [viz. our epistemic relations with God] are all too common throughout the history of the church and, no matter how well

37. Ibid., 80.
38. See also Vanhoozer, *The Drama of Doctrine*, 292–93, for the same emphasis.

intentioned, inevitably lead to forms of oppression and conceptual idolatry.[39]

As we noted earlier when discussing Vanhoozer, such claims are characteristic of the postmodern view that knowledge claims are a form of cultural oppression or hegemony, unwarrantable attempts to pressure people into intellectual allegiance. However, on a closer examination, the words are not altogether clear. They appear to be empirical, historical claims, but Franke does not offer any evidence for their truth. Perhaps, since he holds that seizing epistemic control of our relation to God inevitably leads to forms of oppression, he does not see the need for evidence. But it would be rather rash to adopt such an attitude. And part of what he claims seems unclear. For example, why *must* the claim to know something lead to idolatry, to the worship of concepts? What is it to worship a concept? There is neither a necessary nor a sufficient connection here, surely. There are plenty of other sources of oppression, and plenty of examples of claims to knowledge leading to self-denial and service. Nevertheless such language serves to underline the fact that Franke seriously intends to call into question any idea of there being foundations in theology that lead to knowledge, or to certainly-true belief. We must now explore his case for doing so.

Theological Foundationalism

Franke's chief claim is that foundationalist theology makes exaggerated epistemic claims because it neglects the cognitive importance of contexts. Or, to put the point positively,

> The adoption of a non-foundationalist approach to theology accents an awareness of the contextual nature of human knowledge and mandates a critical awareness of the role of culture and social location in the process of theological interpretation and construction[;] . . . [it] envisions theology as an on-going conversation between Scripture, tradition, and culture through which the Spirit speaks in order to create a distinctively Christian "world" centered on Jesus Christ in a variety of local settings.[40]

> [It] seeks to nurture an open and flexible theology that is in keeping with the local and contextual character of human knowledge while remaining thoroughly and distinctly Christian. It also

---

39. Franke, *The Character of Theology*, 81.
40. Ibid., 79.

provides a conceptual theological framework for the maintenance of the reforming principle.[41]

Several matters are worth noting about these various descriptions. First, according to Franke, one prominent consequence of this non-foundationalist approach to Christian theology is that it sets up a three-way conversation between God's revelation in Christ, the church (in its local expression), and the cultural context in which the church is situated. Secondly, some of these descriptions, such as the first cited, are so general that no Christian could dissent from them. Who could reasonably complain about the statement that no human perspective is adequate to do full justice to the truth of God's revelation? Who could deny that all our convictions remain subject to on-going critical scrutiny? This has been the staple position of Christian thought—including CRT, as well as the wider Christian tradition—throughout the centuries. It arises out of the inability of the finite human mind fully to comprehend the nature of God and of his ways, and the need to critically scrutinize new proposals made in the history of the church as to how Scripture is to be read and understood. But finitude may be consistent with having some knowledge, creaturely knowledge of God and his purposes, even though errors occur, and sinfulness leads to self-deception and distortion, and even though omniscience is impossible. The only alternative to this would be a form of skepticism. Thirdly, and most crucially, Franke's proposal is characterized largely in terms of its outcomes rather than its procedures or methods. The reader is told much more about what a theology that arises from the three-fold conversation that Franke proposes will achieve, but little or nothing about how it will achieve it. Nevertheless, it is clear where Franke wants to go. Theology is a refining activity, taking account of the distorting effects of tradition and culture. The important question is, how can the outcomes that Franke identifies be ensured without the help of a foundation for Christian belief?

Take, for example, Franke's central idea of a three-way conversation. Human conversations are notoriously open-ended and unpredictable. Who knows where they may lead? In the conversation held by the three conversation-partners, Scripture, tradition (i.e., local church tradition), and culture, who knows in advance what the outcome will be?[42] In chapter 2 of *The Character of Theology*, Franke takes some pains to set out the subject of theology, which is the Triune God,[43] and earlier we noted his defini-

---

41. Ibid., 80.

42. Compare at this point Vanhoozer's proposal regarding the "triangulation" of Scripture, church and world in, "On the Very Idea."

43. Franke, *The Character of Theology*, 46f.

tions of theological method. The intention is to be thoroughly and distinctively Christian. But once the three-way conversation gets going, how can anyone be confident that this will remain its ambition? Why may not the conversation drift away from this? For one factor that Franke stresses is that there is parity between the conversation partners. "Neither gospel nor culture can function as the primary entity in the conversation between the two in light of their interpretive and constructed nature; we must recognize that theology emerges through an ongoing conversation involving both gospel and culture."[44]

Because the gospel is interpreted, and constructed into a theology by theologians in a culture, how can Franke be so sure that the theology will continue to be Christian theology? Why may not a different theology emerge? How can he "recognize," that is, know, that what will emerge from such a conversation will have a distinctively Christian character? For neither gospel nor culture is allowed to operate as the "primary entity," and the reason for this is clear. If one of them did operate as primary, then they would take up a privileged position akin to that occupied by an epistemic foundation. If Franke really means this (and, as we are seeing, it looks to be contradicted by other things that he says about the gospel), then the gospel may be swamped by the culture, be taken over by it and imprisoned within it.

Suppose that during the conversation, the conversation-partners are led to the conviction not that the glory of God is revealed supremely or exclusively in the face of Jesus Christ, but that (in John Hick's phrase) God has many faces. Then, as far as I can see, on Franke's paradigm of theological method, that is the way things must go. We must follow our theological method wherever it leads, even if it leads in presently unforeseen and unacceptable directions. So here's the dilemma: if Franke says that things could not go in such a direction, then he is committed, after all, to a foundationalist position, whatever the exact character of that may be. But if he says that we must follow the conversation wherever it leads, then that is certainly more consistently non-foundationalist, but at the cost of offering up the uniqueness of Christian theology in the interests of advocating a particular contextual theological method.

For who knows whether or not tradition will succeed in radically reinterpreting the claims of Scripture, or the culture succeed in neutralizing the claims of tradition? Apparently, Franke knows, for as he describes this conversational process he specifies an outcome. Despite its open-endedness

44. Ibid., 103.

it remains "thoroughly and distinctly Christian."[45] He might appeal to the canonical character of Christian theology, as Vanhoozer does,[46] but then (as we noted) the idea of a canon, a rule, has a foundationalist look to it. But in a situation in which such conversations could go anywhere, how can he be sure in advance that the outcome will be consistently Christian? These questions are accentuated when we remind ourselves of the logic of non-foundationalism. A non-foundationalist theology is one in which there are no foundations. No position, whether this is characterized in terms of starting points or of outcomes, is privileged.

The problems that Franke has are beautifully illustrated by something from Karl Barth, which he cites with approval.

> On this basis, Karl Barth concludes that the focal point and foundations of Christian faith, the God revealed in Jesus Christ, determines that in the work and practice of theology "there are no comprehensive views, no final conclusions and results. There is only the investigation and teaching which take place in the act of dogmatic work and which, strictly speaking, must continually begin again at the beginning in every point. The best and most significant thing that is done in this matter is that again and again we are directed to look back to the center and foundation of it all."[47]

Franke does not seem to spot the irony of these remarks, their inconsistency with his overall position. Karl Barth appeals directly to the center and foundation of all theology, the foundational character of God's revelation in Jesus Christ. Franke endorses this, but in the course of promoting a non-foundational theology! But if he endorses what Barth says, then there *is* a foundation after all. And this foundation acts or ought to act as the controlling material principle in Christian theologizing. Franke may wish to retort: "What Christian theology is, is what Christian theologians do." But this is hardly satisfactory unless we can somehow specify some distinctive feature that makes someone a Christian theologian in the first place.

Further, non-foundational theology presumably amounts to something more than the need for Christian theologians to be cautious and modest in the way in which they treat the divine mysteries. That note has resounded through the long centuries of Christianity, though perhaps it has not been heeded as often as it ought to have been. Perhaps theologians have been over-confident, over-dogmatic, in claiming or implying that theirs

---

45. Ibid., 80.
46. Franke, "Reforming Theology," 13f.
47. Franke, *The Character of Theology*, 81.

is the final word. It is certainly possible to have different, reasonably held views on the formulation of the revealed mysteries. Protestants above all Christian people have a stake in affirming human fallibility, including human theological fallibility.

First-order and Second-order

Here I wish to consider one further feature that both Vanhoozer's and Franke's theology have in common. Each regards Christian doctrine and theology as a second-order discipline that organizes the first-order data, canonical data, or on Franke's view the beliefs and practices of the local church community. Vanhoozer's entire project is based upon the belief that formulating doctrine is a second-order discipline. Other views, such as those of Lindbeck and Hodge, are seen as promoting competing second-order proposals. There is Scripture, a canon of diverse literature, and then a doctrinal portrayal of Scripture (as in *The Drama of Doctrine*), and then there is theology, as proposed in *Remythologizing Theology*. The theologian provides a conceptualization of the *mythos*. Scripture is not, as Scripture, theological, not even to the extent of giving priority to some of the literature over the other, as the provider of the theological framework or presupposition of the entire canon.

For Hodge, along with CRT more generally, the dominical and apostolic teaching interprets the rest. For example, we learn of the nature of the Old Testament, its theological character, from the Letter to the Hebrews and Paul's Letter of the Galatians, say, as well as from Christ's teaching about his fulfilment of the law. Scripture is not simply theological raw data, but it is already theology-laden. In the case of Franke, part of his answer to the questions that arise in his idea of a three-way conversation is to stress that theology is also a second-order activity, though it has (he claims) a distinct subject matter, for it is indelibly Trinitarian.[48]

The doctrinal, theological, and confessional formulations of theologians and particular communities are the products of human reflection on the primary sources, teachings, symbols, and practices of the Christian church. Therefore these formulations must be distinguished from these "first-order" commitments of the Christian faith. For example, theological constructions and doctrines are always subordinate to the content of Scripture and therefore must be held more lightly.[49]

48. Ibid., chapter 2.
49. Ibid., 104.

Is theological activity distinct from the discourse of Scripture? According to Franke, the answer is: yes and no. There are two discourses, and in that sense they are separate. But at any one time, if the second-order discourse of theology is taken seriously, then it informs the church what Scripture means, or proposes revisions to some current understanding. It is the doctrinal and theological interpreter of the first-order material, the gospel that the church confesses in its preaching and worship. For this reason it must be held more lightly than the first-order material, not because what Scripture says may trump what the theologian says, but because Scripture is the first-order material on which the Christian theologian works and to which he must defer. But can the second-order material never direct the conversation?

Scripture is the basis of Christian theology, and such theology, as Franke puts it, "has as its goal the setting forth of a particular understanding of the framework of meaning and the mosaic of beliefs that are at the core of the Christian community."[50] But can he consistently say this? The figure that characterizes the shape of theology has now changed: it is not longer based on foundations, but as with Vanhoozer earlier, it is a framework,[51] it has a core, though this is a feature of a sociological entity, the beliefs of the local church. It may indeed be helpful to think of Christian belief in this way: like an apple, it has a core and outer flesh. It may be possible, in a relatively neutral manner, to discern a central set of claims, a framework of beliefs at the core of the Christian community. These give the church its identity.

But Franke has to mean more than this. For as we saw in our discussion of Charles Hodge's appeal to induction, at the center of the church's confession there are beliefs drawn from Scripture, and these already have theological significance. The core of the confession is not a vague adherence to Jesus Christ (to which the theologian gives meaning) but something that already has meaning. The CRT theologian does not give this core of sentences—drawn from Scripture, and giving the church its Christian character—a meaning that it does not already have, but by his exegetical and systematizing activities he vindicates this meaning, setting it in relation to other parts of Scripture and other elements of Christian theology, and in doing so he influences the beliefs of the Christian community, confirming or modifying them. That, at least, is how theology has classically been understood in the Reformed tradition.

A "core," a "framework"—despite himself (and rather like Vanhoozer) Franke continually returns to the distinctive character of the Christian faith,

---

50. Ibid., 105.
51. Vanhoozer, *The Drama of Doctrine*, 295.

for these changes, from foundation to framework to core, seem to be merely verbal. The essential point is not affected by making one word, "core," do for another word, "foundation." To say that confessions of faith are activities through which the church binds itself "to the truth and hope of the gospel of reconciliation and redemption" and thus that such "confessional statements and formulas function as servants of the gospel"[52] is to think foundationally. On the one hand, there is "the gospel of reconciliation and redemption." On the other hand, there is the work of confessing that gospel, involving the fallible, revisable, on-going theologizing of the church, which "serves" the gospel.

It is only in virtue of the meaning that the gospel possesses that we become aware that it is a gospel of reconciliation and redemption, which then controls and adjudicates the thinking of the Christian theologian, or ought to. Because this meaning is fixed, though open to further exposition and application, as the theologian relates one aspect of this content to another, and to the vagaries of the culture, it makes theologizing much more difficult than Franke seems to appreciate. Theology is not simply a three-sided conversation that has its own impetus. Something holds up the conversation, getting in its way, namely the gospel. The gospel is a difficult, awkward conversation-partner. That's because it has a foundational character, or at least a permanent priority in theological construction. It is this fact, that at all points the Christian theologian has to test his affirmations by "the gospel" that makes systematic theology (in Charles Hodge's words) "no easy task."

How is this authority of the gospel recognized and owned? In common with many who propound post-conservative or post-evangelical theologies, Franke has little or nothing to say about this, though he implicitly recognizes that the theologian does not by his activity confer authority on Scripture, for Scripture already has that authority in the church. But is the fact that Scripture has this authority of merely sociological significance, or is the Christian church justified in acceding to this authority above all others? As we have seen, CRT emphasizes that in fact God himself gives recognition to the authoritativeness that is already present, as he witnesses by his Spirit to the spirits of his faithful people. This recognition comes to the people of God in the form of an instinct, a gut-like instinct of recognition that God speaks in the words of Scripture. And how does this come about? Not by a fideistic leap of faith, nor in unquestioning acquiescence to the quasi-political authority of the church, but by the Spirit's testimony to the words and works of God as they are found in Scripture. So it is intrinsic

---

52. Franke, *The Character of Theology*, 105.

to the recognition of the authority of Scripture that it witnesses to its own God-given character of the good news to which it testifies. The Holy Spirit ratifies that testimony to believing minds and consciences. The Bible has first-order meaning, which is the meaning that the Spirit witnesses to as the very truth of God.

Franke may think that because theology is, in his view, "an ongoing, second-order, contextual discipline,"[53] this somehow preserves the integrity of the first-order discourse of Scripture, allowing it to continue to speak in its own right and to exercise its own authority over the church. He sometimes seems to write like that. It may be that he thinks that whatever the theologian may make of this first-order material while developing a second-order discourse about it, the first-order material remains intact. In a sense this is true. The first order-discourse remains physically there, on the page, whatever the theologian makes of it. Yet on Franke's view of the theological task, that first-order discourse has no prospect of being foundational for the work of the Christian theologian. Furthermore, the understanding of that discourse is constantly changing as the second-order discourse develops. For the second-order discourse, arising from the church and the culture, tells the theologian what that first-order discourse means, or at least what it means for the time being.

So the very idea of theology as a second-order activity, a common theme in Vanhoozer and Franke, goes sharply against the stance of CRT. As we have seen, for CRT Scripture is self-attesting not because of its formal properties, such as the grandeur of its style, but because of its cognitive content and what follows from this. What came to be called the *notae* of Scripture—clarity, sufficiency, and so on—are theological in character. It is otherwise impossible to see how Scripture could have this character and be (as CRT claims) the supreme judge of theological opinion in the church. Scripture is clear and sufficient at the theological level. It is not simply a resource from which the imaginative and resourceful theologian can construct various theological "models." Theology works from Scripture downwards, not from Scripture upwards, for its task is subordinate to Scripture, not superior to it.

Culture and Context

A final factor that makes the task of theology much harder than Franke thinks is the need to make a sharp distinction between what is the case and what ought to be the case, between facts and values, descriptions and

---

53. Ibid., 84.

prescriptions. He hardly seems to recognize the need for such a distinction. But without it, when one bears in mind the heavily contextual and cultural emphasis that Franke makes, sociology will invariably triumph over theology. In fact, in such a situation theology becomes sociology. I shall illustrate the dangers of not observing this distinction from what Franke says.

In his section "The Contextual Nature of Theology,"[54] Franke points to the obvious fact that all forms of thought are embedded in social conditions; they are "situated." Christian theology is no exception. That's true of anything about anything, and so true of everything about Christianity, including the incarnation itself and the emergence of the books of the New Testament. But then Franke immediately follows this with something rather different. "It is not the intent of theology simply to set forth, amplify, refine, and defend a timelessly fixed orthodoxy."[55] This claim, whether or not it is justified, does not at all follow from the point about situatedness. From the fact that theology is situated, inevitably situated, it does not follow that it may not have the objective or the goal of setting forth a timelessly fixed orthodoxy and that it may not, in a measure, realize that objective. What is to stop it from doing this? It is obviously no answer for Franke simply to repeat the point about situatedness, nor to elaborate this point from the facts of Christian history, as in fact he proceeds to do. For from the incarnation, an event situated in first-century Palestine, permanently available health and blessing flow. As we argued earlier, in pointing out the Utterance Fallacy, apostolic and other teaching is not restricted to the time of its first occurrence, so the situatedness of a doctrine does not prevent it having a permanent or fixed meaning for humankind. Whether or not this is regarded as "timeless," it is permanent.

As Franke says, Christian theology has taken shape from, and has been revised by and navigated through a number of cultural transitions in its history. But unless "theology" is simply the name of an activity, such as whistling, then some distinctive cognitive content must have endured through these various vicissitudes.[56] Otherwise Christian theology is a wax nose, or a mere collection of ideas without either truth or internal structure. It is the fact that this phrase refers to an enduring body of beliefs that ensures that the theology that endures is Christian theology and not the theology of some other god or gods. Christian theology is *trans*cultural.

Sometimes Franke appears to think that "contexts" are temporally and geographically confined, and fairly impermeable. In his approach to the task

54. Ibid., 84f.
55. Ibid., 84.
56. Ibid., 84–85.

of theology, he emphasizes that theology is "local," though it cannot be pursued at this level in a way that is in isolation from the universal church.[57] Yet, paradoxically, his discussion of Origen (c. 185–254 AD) is rather at odds with such a heavily contextual emphasis. Franke clearly believes himself to have access to the thought-world of Origen. Among several other things, he tells us that Origen's work *On First Principles* "is an ordered and systematic account of Origen's theological and philosophical positions concerning God, creation, Jesus Christ, the Logos of God, and salvation."[58] If this is true, then it must be possible for someone in one historical and cultural context to have access to the products of another context, to gain true beliefs about them, and to be able to criticize Origen, for example (as many have), for the way in which he over-accommodated his Christian thought to his own Hellenistic setting.

In the light of his various reflections on Origen, Franke asks, "Have we too readily conformed our conception of the Bible and its interpretation to the assumptions and aspirations of our culture? Further, given our participation in our culture, on what basis are we able to make such an assessment?"[59] These questions are pretty rich coming from someone who wishes to invest so heavily in postmodernism! But, more importantly for us, the questions reveal that, despite what Franke elsewhere says, it is an exaggeration to suppose that each of us is cocooned within the particularities of his or her own culture and that we cannot be addressed by saints and doctors of the church from other times and places. And it is an equal exaggeration to suppose that today's non-Christian culture cannot be addressed in a similar way.

But Franke goes further. It is not simply that our context differs from Origen's. Rather, every understanding of the Christian message is "particular."[60] As he sees things, we too readily assume a Christian constant or universal that "then functions as the foundation for the construction of theology, even though it will need to be articulated in the language of a particular culture."[61] This way of thinking of the relation between culture and the gospel is condemned by Franke because it is foundational. For presumably there is some "given" that requires translation. He returns to his familiar theme: "Neither gospel nor culture can function as the primary entity in the conversation between the two in light of their interpretive and

---

57. Franke, *The Character of Theology*, 119.
58. Ibid., 93–94.
59. Ibid., 99.
60. Ibid., 103.
61. Ibid.

constructed nature; we must recognize that theology emerges through an on-going conversation involving both gospel and culture."[62] So he favors an "interactive model" of theologizing.[63]

It is tempting to reverse the argument: translation occurs, therefore translation is possible. We translate the writings of Aristotle, Origen, or Augustine. Do we translate every nuance? Clearly not. Are the translations faithful? Some are, some are not. How do we know which is which? By repeatedly consulting the original and anything we can find out about it. The attempt to translate Origen, for example, has met with some success, as Franke clearly shows. Why may we not enjoy similar success with the New Testament?

We might ask how Franke can be so confident about this approach to culture. How does he know that cultures are "particularities" in this sense? How does he know that cultures can be separately identified and counted like beans? What counts as one culture, what as two, or more? Isn't it much more likely that a new cultural force is a blend of several earlier cultural influences? We might press all these questions. But it is sufficient for our present purposes to dismiss this appeal to cultural particularity by noting that his discussion of Origen is a *reductio ad absurdum* of his own tentativeness or skepticism induced by his emphasis on the impermeability of "contexts."

What Is and What Ought to Be

Yet without doubt Christian theology is contextual, which raises the following questions: In any situation in which Christian belief is being assessed or evaluated, what elements of that belief ought we to accept because they cohere with, illuminate, and vindicate the sense of the sentences of the Bible? What ought we to reject because they compromise that sense from being over-influenced by some feature of the context in which those beliefs were formulated and expressed? Some contexts and cultures are supportive of the Christian faith, others oppose it. For while all our activity is inevitably contextual, it by no means follows that we cannot attempt to minimize the effects of one kind of context, and maximize that of another, or evaluate the culture in terms of the Christian gospel.

Take, for example, moral contexts. Some contexts are deeply morally evil, others less so, while others are morally good. How do we assess the moral values of a particular culture, such as our own culture? Suppose we can. We note that it has various moral aspects or elements, some of them

62. Ibid..
63. Ibid.

in conflict with some others: for example, rights may conflict with duties and responsibilities. Which of these aspects ought we to indulge and allow to condition our theological thinking? The language of rights or the language of duties? Which ought we to resist because they cut across our present understanding of Christian theology? More pointedly, which ought the church to minimize the influence of by her present understanding of Christian theology? Obviously, she ought to attempt to minimize the effect of those that, it is believed, undermine the gospel.

Are there Christian moral values, set forth in Scripture, which have become lost to our culture, or obscured by it, or which as a matter of fact our culture has never recognized? Why can't the gospel judge the morals of our culture? Wasn't the judging of the culture a vital aspect of the ministry of Jesus, and of the teaching of Paul and the other apostles? When Paul writes to the Corinthians about their beliefs and their behavior, he is of course writing to them from a particular context. His readers are, perhaps, in another context. Paul has beliefs, a place and a time, as do the Corinthians. Nevertheless, he does not scruple to criticize both their beliefs (about the resurrection of the dead, say) and their behavior (at the Lord's Table) by what he calls "my gospel." Of course, the Christian church lacks Paul's apostolic authority. Nevertheless, he sets a precedent and a pattern of judging the context by the gospel. Is this an easy task? No, most certainly not. There are numerous pitfalls. Is it impossible? No, most certainly not. It cannot be. For if it were impossible, then the church would be forced to accept that the culture, our situatedness, will invariably swamp the gospel, and what *is* (that is, her context) becomes merged with what *ought to be* (that is, the church's Christian commitment). The gospel then becomes a plaything of the culture.

Or take epistemological contexts. Some are more affected than others by skepticism, or cynicism, or relativism. In these circumstances, what is the Christian theologian to do? He could go with the curve of the culture, and willingly become infected. He may hear it is said that for us human beings there is no such thing as pure objectivity or infallible certainty. We may grant this. But then the question is, granted our imperfections and fallibilities, what ought the Christian theologian, and the Christian church, to do? Ought they simply to conform to the culture, or aspire to become as objective as it is possible to be? There is no such thing as perfect justice, but what ought the judge and jury to do? To rest content with bias, partiality, or unfairness, or to seek, as far as is humanly possible, to make their verdicts equitable and fair based on the facts before them?

We have argued earlier that, according to CRT, although its propositions may not be "timeless," the gospel and the theology that it gives rise to, and ought continually to be informed by, is *permanent*. The "core" of the faith remains through time, giving theology its distinctively Christian meaning. It is this balancing act between the abiding "orthodoxy"—the "form of sound words," the foundation that cannot be replaced by any other foundation—and its varied and on-going expression in a variety of contexts, that makes the practice of theology no easy task. Franke does not seem to appreciate this. Jesus Christ is the same yesterday, today, and forever. The faith is once delivered to the saints. There is "no other name." "For no one can lay a foundation than that which is laid, which is Jesus Christ" (1 Cor 3:11), and besides this, there is the "foundation" (in the light of our discussion, an interesting New Testament word) of the apostles and prophets, and of Jesus Christ the cornerstone (another interesting word). And Paul makes plain that this foundation is accessible to us, for it may be built upon, as well as noting that some do a better job of building on it than do others.

Theology or Sociology?

A familiar fallacy must be avoided at this point. Let us grant, once more, Franke's point that our present understanding of the Christian faith is "situated." To give an account of such situated understanding—of how people come to understand these things as they do in this time and this place—is to engage in the sociology of knowledge. But nothing follows from the fact that our present stock of beliefs can be studied sociologically and certain valid sociological inferences can be drawn from how the present-day Christian community has come to hold its beliefs, to a conclusion about whether this understanding of the Christian faith is the true one. The question of truth is not settled by noting sociological facts about how the church (or any other body) has come to have the beliefs it has, but rather by determining whether or not they are beliefs that (in the case of the Christian church) faithfully—although no doubt fallibly—reflect the truth of the gospel. If there is no opportunity to ask this non-sociological question, then theological skepticism or relativism must follow. For since all human knowledge claims of whatever kind are embedded in a culture, the claims of the sociology of knowledge included, that fact alone cannot be used to adjudicate the truth or otherwise of any knowledge claim.

Is it "docetic" to maintain that the Christian faith is transcultural? Is such faith fully divine but only seeming to be human? Does this downplay and even ignore the reality of culture? Are we making insufficient allowance for the "incarnational" character of the revelation? The One who was incarnate had a situation too. He was divine, and also human. But according to

CRT in deed and word he was nevertheless God's revelation. The situatedness of the gospel is real, but so is its transcultural character. We shall return to these themes in the next chapter.

9

Knowing and Believing

We shall now take further the main reason that representative post-foundationalists such as Kevin Vanhoozer and particularly John Franke offer for rejecting foundationalism, that is, for rejecting the possibility of theological knowledge as *certain, objective,* and *universal.* We shall continue our consideration of the idea of theological epistemic certainty by looking at the way in which the degree of certainty with which the church has historically confessed her faith is imperilled by the repeated claim that theologians do all their work fallibly and tentatively and in a particular cultural context that may have different presuppositions and procedures from other cultures. We have already seen, in chapter 2, the attitude of CRT to the issue of knowledge and belief. What Bavinck says is typical.

> According to Scripture, this faith [viz. Christian faith] brings its own certainty with it, it is the assurance of things hoped for and the conviction of things not seen (Heb 11.1), not because it is inherently solid and firm but because it is grounded in God's testimony and promise, as the sequel of Hebrews 11 clearly teaches.[1]

And Turretin

> The Scriptures do not posses metaphysical certainty; otherwise the assent which we give to them would bespeak knowledge, not faith. Neither do they possess simply a moral and probable certainty; otherwise our faith would not be more certain than any historical assent given to human writings. But they have a

---

1. Bavinck, *Reformed Dogmatics,* I:573.

theological and infallible certainty, which cannot possibly deceive the true believer illuminated by the Spirit of God.[2]

Turretin does not claim that an infallible certainty can only be based on what is explicitly understood about Scripture, because that would require knowing what every detail means. Rather, such a reader of Scripture is convinced that, through reading it and attending to what it says, he has in his hands the word of God, and has faith in it, even though, where there is a failure to understand the meaning of some aspect of Scripture, the faith in it will be correspondingly implicit. The one is certainty arising from self-evidence and valid inferences based on it; the other, certainty based upon divine testimony recognized as such.

In the last chapter we noted the importance for CRT of the self-attesting character of Scripture in conveying its authority to us, and saw that such an instinct or conviction is regarded as the product of the Spirit's work testifying to the truth explicitly evidenced in Scripture. So CRT theologians are not exclusively epistemological naturalists; they do not hold that we may only know what our sense and reason alone tell us. They are also epistemological supernaturalists. They are supernatural evidentialists. Features of the objective and human mind-independent creation are in principle and in fact accessible to us. But in addition, God has revealed himself in a similarly objective way in Scripture. There are barriers to that knowledge, but these are chiefly in the sin-conditioned minds of us all. While they are fallibilists, they are not skeptics. It may be logically possible that the whole of life is a dream, but we have no reason to think that it is. Despite the fall, our senses and intellects have a high degree of reliability.

Right Reason

The postmodern tendency involves an overstressing of the presence and of the legitimacy of subjective and contextual factors in acquiring knowledge. It is strange that at the same time that postmodern theologies, even those from within the Reformed stable, neglect almost entirely the place that the state of the subject plays in acquiring the knowledge of God, or of failing to acquire it, and the way in which that knowledge should affect his self-knowledge. The knowledge of God involves a coming together of objective states of affairs, the teaching of Scripture, and the state of mind of the subject, his self-knowledge. One might have thought that these themes would be congenial to the postmodern theological mind.

2. Turretin, *Institutes of Elenctic Theology*, I:68.

It is not easy to account for this almost total neglect of the subjective in the need of the human mind for the Spirit's illumination. It is as if the currently more fashionable sense of subjectivity involved in the particularity of each person's situation swamps it. In the case of Vanhoozer, subjectivity is concerned with the place of the will and emotions (to fill the void left by the purely cerebral theology of Hodge and his tradition) and the practice of the virtues. The idea that being confronted by God's revelation of himself may and should result in greater or better self-knowledge is missing. Calvin's words, the opening sentences of the *Institutes*, which concern the knowledge of God and of ourselves, are largely ignored.

It is true that Franke begins *The Character of Theology* by quoting the words of Calvin from the beginning of the *Institutes*. But then he says,

> Calvin's observation continues to provide a helpful model for reflecting on the character of theology and suggests that we must always be attentive not only to the knowledge of God but also to the knowledge of ourselves as human beings if we hope to practice an approach to theology that leads to wisdom. . . . This suggests that in the discipline of theology we must take account of the particular social and intellectual settings in which we engage in theological reflection and exploration.[3]

Then follows what is by now an all-too-familiar *apologia* for the need for us to be postmodernists in theology, to take account of context, and the like. Despite this nod in Calvin's direction, this is a radical misunderstanding of what the Reformer is saying. Calvin is not stating that when we do theology (which concerns the knowledge of God) we are to be aware of the social and cultural setting in which we, as human beings, are placed (the knowledge of ourselves). This is a point almost too obvious to be worth noting. After all, the opening words of Book One of the *Institutes* are preceded by an elaborate *apologia* for the Reformation addressed to King Francis the First of France. When it comes to being a contextual theologian (which all theologians are now urged to become) John Calvin was certainly no dunce. Unfortunately, Franke has missed Calvin's distinctive twist, even though he quotes the very words that express it.

The objective and subjective emphases are kept in a balanced, mutually dependent relationship by Calvin. Where does that emphasis on the twofold knowledge, of God and of ourselves, in this particular formulation emerge from? I suggest that it was one of the very many things that Calvin learned from St. Augustine, from the *Confessions*, and the *Soliloquies*, and no doubt from elsewhere.

3. Franke, *The Character of Theology*, 14.

But Calvin gives this Augustinian emphasis his own distinctive twist. The relationship between the knowledge of God and of ourselves is *immediately reciprocal*. Through word and Spirit, in coming to know God we at once begin to gain true knowledge of ourselves, and in knowing ourselves we are at once led to know God. There is, so to speak, no choice in the matter. It is not that there are two distinct subject matters—God and ourselves—that it is wise to bring into some kind of positive relationship. No, the knowledge of the one immediately leads to the knowledge of the other; the knowledge of the second leads immediately to the knowledge of the first. The knowledge of God and of ourselves is "joined by many bonds," but that "which one precedes and brings forth the other is not easy to discern." If we look on ourselves, then we immediately turn our thoughts to the contemplation of God. For our "mighty gifts" are clearly not of our own creation. Further, it is our "miserable ruin" that especially "'compels us to look upward.'" He goes on, "Thus, from the feeling of our own ignorance, vanity, poverty, infirmity, and—what is more—depravity and corruption, we recognize that the true light of wisdom, sound virtue, full abundance of every good, and purity of righteousness rest in the Lord alone." "We cannot seriously aspire to him before we begin to become displeased with ourselves." So, "the knowledge of ourselves not only arouses us to seek God, but also, as it were, leads us by the hand to find him." "Man never achieves a clear knowledge of himself unless he has first looked upon God's face, and then descends from contemplating him to scrutinize himself." Our innate pride is such that unless we look to the Lord, the sole standard of righteousness, we shall not be convinced "of our own unrighteousness, foulness, folly, and impurity."[4] As far as I can see Franke misses all this. These emphases in Calvin become reduced to the now familiar concern with social and cultural context.

Besides the prominence that is given to the knowledge of the self, CRT is concerned with the state of the observer in a more general epistemological sense. While the normally equipped enquirer can come to understand the teaching of Scripture through his senses and his judgment, he will not be apt to discern its personal significance for him or others without the illuminating and regenerating influence of the Spirit. In CRT the result of this influence is the development of what is sometimes referred to as a "new sense."[5] It is best to understand this not as the acquisition of a sixth sense,

---

4. These sentences are taken from Calvin, *Institutes* I.1.

5. See, for example John Owen *The Reason of Faith*, *Works*, IV:64, "He [the Holy Spirit] gives unto believers a *spiritual sense* of the *power and reality of the things believed.*" Such language was later adopted by Jonathan Edwards in his *Religious Affections*, "The sensation itself is totally diverse from all that men have, or can have, in a state of nature." (Part III.1).

but as the gaining of a new range of sensibility, using "sense" as we talk of a "sense of humor." Similarly with the noetic effects of sin. This can be seen, for example, in the way the *Westminster Confession of Faith* summarizes the activity of faith: "yielding obedience to the commands, trembling at the threatenings, and embracing the promises of God for this life and that which is to come."[6] Faith accepts, receives, and rests on Christ. It may be weak or strong, it may lose assurance or gain it.

The distinction between reason as corrupted and restored as "right reason" runs like a refrain in the writings of Reformed theologians. So Turretin distinguishes between "sound enlightened reason" and "corrupted and blind reason," "reason rightly instructed" and reason "slippery and fallible," "reason as corrupt and in the concrete may be at variance with theology, but not reason as sound and in the abstract," "not reason as blind and corrupted by sin . . . reason as healed by grace," "not that which is blind and corrupted by sin but that which is restored and enlightened by the Holy Spirit," and "the darkness of the human intellect does not hinder sound reason from judging of the truth of connections and so contradictions."[7]

Epistemic Strength

We saw in the last chapter that there is a strong tendency amongst postfoundationalist Reformed theologians such as Franke and Vanhoozer to weaken the epistemic strength of any theological claim. The clarity of Scripture seems to be permanently imperilled. This is due to overstating the epistemic influence of the situatedness of our knowledge, expressed in terms of "context" in the case of Franke, and of the epistemological doctrine of aspectivalism and of the influence of personal bias and other sources of fallibility, in the case of Vanhoozer. Occasionally Vanhoozer offers a different judgment than Franke. For example, he holds that there is need to cultivate the "sapiential virtue" in order to avoid being overcome by contextual concerns.[8] But the two are essentially making the same point. That point is that knowledge claims are skewed, denied, or misunderstood by others, so as to make them not generally reliable.[9] Though, very surprisingly, some knowledge manages to get through. Fallibility, which is also to be found in CRT, ought to occur only when there is a good reason for it. As

---

6. *Westminster Confession of Faith*, XIV.21.

7. These phrases occur in Turretin, *Institutes of Elenctic Theology*, I:27–33. See also the data assembled by Heppe in his *Reformed Dogmatics*, chapter 1.

8. Vanhoozer *The Drama of Doctrine*, 335.

9. Ibid., 302.

a result, the characteristic theological posture of present-day revisionists is tentativeness. Using the terminology of an earlier era, Christian theological claims are nothing more than sets of *opinions*, none of which does or can constitute certainty. This is a good thing, say the post-foundationalists, for (as we have seen) claims that knowledge is "objective" and claims to have such knowledge lead inevitably to idolatry and oppression by the claimant.

Knowing and Believing

Let us now test such an emphasis on fallibility against some data. We noted in chapter 2 how Francis Turretin, for example, makes the point of stressing the place that the senses, as well as the reason, have in theology. He cites the words of Jesus to doubting Thomas. "Put your finger here, and see my hands, and put out your hand, and place it in my side" (John 20:27). This is hardly a case of Jesus teaching his disciples some epistemology, it is more a case of what Jesus is assuming, that under normal conditions touch and sight are reliable. Perhaps it is to such a case that Charles Hodge is referring when he states that "lest we should misinterpret our own consciousness and the laws of our nature, everything that can be legitimately learned from that source will be found recognized and authenticated in the Scriptures."[10]

Of course this is part of a ramified epistemological framework that it is possible to discern in the New Testament. There is the reliability of sight and touch in the confirming of faith, as we have noted, but there are also instances where what is revealed is not straightforwardly a case of "flesh and blood"; our senses are in general reliable, but they may be deceived. For it is possible to follow "cleverly devised myths," being deceived by them, just as it is possible to have things "made known" (2 Pet 1:16). The puzzle is why post-foundationalists do not show any interest in such data. It is surely pertinent in discussing knowing and believing in theology. Jesus knows that he has wounds, and he invites Thomas to know this too.

But let us turn from Jesus's practice to aspects of his teaching that involves believing and knowledge.

- If you abide in my word, you are truly my disciples, and you will know the truth, and the truth will set you free (John 8:31–32).
- If anyone's will is to do God's will, he will know whether the teaching is from God or whether I am speaking on my own authority (7:17).
- If I am not doing the works of my Father, then do not believe me; but if I do them, even though you do not believe me, believe the works, that

10. Hodge, *Systematic Theology*, I:11.

you may know and understand that the Father is in me and I am in the Father (10:37–38).

- I do as the Father has commanded me, so that the world may know that I love the Father (14:31).

These assertions are taken almost at random from the Gospel of John. They arise from one particular context, one that is pretty distinct (and distant) from our own. Yet we seem to be able to understand what is being asserted. There may be nuances to "truth" and "knowledge" as used here that escape us, of course. Nevertheless, we can take it that the writer is not offering us a perfect equivocation here. Nor is he trying to persuade us of something that is not true. So we may gain a fair understanding of these ideas. More importantly, it seems that, if what John says (or what Jesus says through John) is true, then by God's grace men and women may come to understand certain things, believing some of them and knowing others. And unless we are going to think of these words as having a meaning and an application wholly confined to that original context, other people who live in other contexts may likewise understand, believe, and know. There is the presumption, that is, that terms like "belief," "truth," and "knowledge" are not here being used in secret, stretched, or technical senses,[11] and that they can be communicated at large, achieving a similar measure of understanding, knowing, and believing in those who receive them.

But what must post-foundationalist theology make of such assertions? As noted, they originally occur in a very different context from the one we occupy, presumably, and so our understanding of these words, and our trust in them, must be seriously qualified. Perhaps the words "know," "truth," and "understand" ought to be given the standard post-foundationalist treatment. Is it not presumptuous for us to appropriate them? Ought not our claims to be suitably tentative? Ought not the fallibility of these claims of Jesus to be emphasized? Would it not be "docetic" to do otherwise? At the very least, the fallibility of our own understanding of them ought to be emphasized. To make this clear, perhaps we should place inverted commas around the relevant words. Not "know the truth" but "'know' the 'truth'" and so on. Of course, the result of doing this would be to seal us off from the words of John or Jesus, placing them in a kind of theological museum, which confines them to the original context of utterance. That would hardly be a satisfactory state of affairs as far as Christian theology is concerned.

But if not that, then what? If not that, ought not post-foundationalism to accept such statements at face value, as part of the canon, the "core" or "fiduciary framework" or "foundation of truth" of the Christian faith? Perhaps

---

11. Notwithstanding Jesus' statement "I am . . . the truth" (John 14:6).

we can accept them as the words of Jesus, while being unsure about what they mean? Perhaps we ought to maintain a high degree of implicit faith in them.

We might ask, more directly: Does Franke really mean to say that because there are many different contexts in which these words may be understood, including the context in which they were originally uttered and written down, we cannot, in our present epistemic context, understand these words of Jesus, when he talks to his followers about understanding and knowing and believing? The fact that it is possible to gain more and more understanding of the words, as the scholars pore over the text and then tell us what they've found, cannot be discounted. But do we not have a basic grasp? And doesn't that basic grasp depend on our grasp of our own uses of those words? Doesn't this grasp include, for instance, such things as; it is possible to understand something without believing it, and it is possible to believe something without knowing it? I understand the claim that the moon is made of green cheese but I don't believe it; and I may believe that there will be a full moon three weeks on Thursday without knowing it. If we know something, then isn't what we know true? Isn't there a basic, accessible sense to Scripture—or to much of Scripture, particularly to the New Testament writings—that establish the identity and mission of the church and are therefore so important for her life and work? And isn't this true, despite the fact that their original setting is fast receding into the past, and we are suffering from (as we are continually told) "rapid cultural change"? And may not Christians too have a basic confidence that what Jesus is saying is true? Unless our faith is wholly implicit, what alternative ways of establishing such confidence are there, except to use every reasonable means in an endeavor to understand what Jesus means by what he says?

CRT has traditionally held that it may reasonably claim a high degree of certainty about the meaning and truth of many biblical claims and that it may strive, partly by adopting practices familiar from non-theological areas, to increase the degree of certainty that it is possible to gain of them. We may use familiar ways of checking and testing. If this is so, then it is a short step to see that to the degree to which the meaning of some biblical statement is certain, it is objectively certain. However, not unequivocally and objectively certain to everyone, just like that. Yet such certainty, when it is present, is not, on the other hand, just a feeling of confidence, but a belief that is grounded in an understanding of the language of Scripture so that it may be the basis for action. That is, the certainty that Christians and others may have that what Jesus said is true is inter-cultural, or inter-contextual, in the same sort of way in which the Great Commission may be said to have inter-cultural implications. What Jesus teaches may mean the same in different cultures, and so people living in these cultures may have the same beliefs. The words may express the same truth for them that it presently does for us.

Certainty and Objectivity

The church holds that biblical claims such as the ones we cited are objectively true, really true and not merely true for me or true in their original setting. The internal testimony of the Holy Spirit does not leave the meaning of Scripture to the mercy of the merely subjective personal preferences of the reader. By continuous efforts at Bible exposition and theological reflection upon the words, we may attain an understanding that attains a closer and closer approximation to the truths as originally given and, it may be, warrant a correspondingly clearer and perhaps firmer belief in their truth. No doubt there are times of upheaval and reformation in the church, when the meaning, and hence the truth, and hence the certainty of some significant interpretation of Scripture, is seriously called into question by some fresh proposal. And there may be periods of personal doubt, when a person's beliefs, what they are personally certain of, are rocked by some new theory or new finding, or some personal tragedy, or by the onset of a skeptical mood. But the point of principle remains, and the history of the church bears witness to it.

According to CRT, the objectivity of the truth of Scripture is not to be understood merely in terms of some scholarly or popular consensus, or the results of an opinion poll. If theologians took that line then once again they'd be treating theology, or hermeneutics, as a branch of sociology. It is understood and believed as a result of the recognition of its God-given character. Such objectivity is conferred on our theological statements to the extent that they reflect the meaning of Scripture, but given our inherent fallibility our reflections may not have objectivity to the degree that the sentences of Scripture themselves do. As we have seen, we may deduce certain statements from Scripture, and we may, by induction, come to believe that Scripture teaches such and such with differing degrees of confidence. However, the objective truth, as the church confesses it, does not consist in the agreement of a group of people, each of whom has their own private or subjective certainty. For the objective truth confessed by the church may be as certain for Jim as it is for Joanna if Jim has the reasons, or similar reasons (or perhaps has no reason to deny the reasons) that make Joanna certain.

The same thing may follow if two people are in the same or a similar certainty-conferring environment. If it is certain for Jim that Jesus Christ came into the world to save sinners, then it may become similarly certain for Joanna. Would gaining more evidence from Scripture for the truth of that interpretation make it more certain than it is? Of course it could. Because this evidence would provide more reasons for confirming earlier beliefs, making them stronger. Could the consideration of more evidence make it become less certain than it is? It may, of course, because sometimes, and paradoxically, we may come to know less by becoming aware of more, as happens in periods of doubt induced by the challenge of new theories or new facts. But these are the purely logical consequences of the fact that certainty ought to based on evidence, and that evidence typically comes in degrees, and sometimes ebbs, and sometimes flows. So with certainty, not the mere feeling but the grounded conviction, comes the recognition of the objective truth of various claims, not the objectivity of mere human consensus but the objective truth of what is asserted, whether we like it or not, or believe it or not. The question is never: could we, as a matter of logic, be mistaken? but rather, do we presently and in the foreseeable future have any reason for thinking that we are in fact mistaken?

Knowledge, Power, and Control

In contrast to this, what Vanhoozer and Franke seem to be endorsing, besides their recurrent stress on fallibility and tentativeness, is a moral suspicion of knowledge claims. This is the postmodern thesis that claims to knowledge are attempts to seize power, and that attention to the context in which knowledge claims are made effectively neuters such attempts and is itself an exercise in Christian humility. As we have already seen, Vanhoozer also makes the now-familiar connection between knowledge claims and power, though perhaps in a less dogmatic form than Franke, who endorses Merold Westphal's remarks:

> If our thinking never merits the triumphalist title of Truth *and* there is no other knower whose knowledge is the Truth, then the truth is that there is no Truth. But if the first premise is combined with a theistic premise, the result will be: The truth is that there is truth, but not for us, only for God.[12]

The claim to possess the truth is apparently always triumphalist. When mother returns home from the hospital with the news that father has inoperable cancer, whom, one wonders, is she triumphing over? The jigging about with the word "truth," now capitalizing it, now not, is a bit confusing,

---

12. Quoted in Franke, *The Character of Theology*, 80. Emphasis in original.

though perhaps it is not as confusing as it ought to be. For we might ask, does Westphal know that there is no Truth for us, only truth; or does he Know it? For perhaps Westphal (and Franke) are saying that whereas God Knows the Truth, you and I can only ever "know" the truth. At the same time, we may *realize* (a near synonym of "come to know," presumably) that "there is truth, but not for us, only for God." And where does that leave us? If one does not Know the Truth but only knows the truth that "there is truth, but not for us, only for God," are there any truths that one Knows, or do we only ever have beliefs, never Knowledge? And so is the lower case "know" nothing other than a synonym for "believe"? Alternatively, the capitalizing of the words could be a rather irritating way of making the standard theological observation that God's knowledge, being archetypal, is different in quality and extent from our human, ectypal knowledge.[13] Adopting this distinction would be quite consistent with the claim that human beings know truths, including truths about God, though not in the way in which God knows them. Or, finally, Westphal could be making the claim, familiar to students of absolute idealism, that it is impossible to possess any of the truth unless one has the Whole Truth, and that it is only God, or the Absolute, that possesses, or embodies, the Whole Truth. But somehow I don't think that Westphal is claiming either of these last things. Rather, it amounts simply to the claim that sinful, finite creatures cannot possess objective knowledge about God. But does no one see that such a thesis seriously imperils the Christian faith?[14]

Certainly Franke, with Westphal at this point, is also committed to this: if someone knows (but does not Know), then such knowledge, particularly if the person believes that his knowledge is Knowledge, is oppressive.

> Attempts on the part of humans to seize control of these relations [viz. epistemic relations with God] are all too common throughout the history of the church and, no matter how well intentioned, inevitably lead to forms of oppression and conceptual idolatry.[15]

But if they are all that common then maybe Franke's and Vanhoozer's epistemologies are oppressive too, pressuring believers into holding their Christian faith with much less certainty and conviction than they previously thought they were entitled to do. Who oppresses whom, and what instruments of oppression are employed, are merely sociological questions.

13. For discussion this distinction in CRT, see Bavinck, *Reformed Dogmatics*, II:107f.
14. For discussion on this, see Westphal, *Ontotheology*, 80.
15. Franke, *The Character of Theology*, 81.

Now let us consider the case of Jesus himself. Christians confess that he is God the Son who has assumed human nature. He is situated in a context, first-century Palestine. Does he know, or Know? If he merely knows, then, according to Franke, such knowledge leads inevitably to forms of oppression and conceptual idolatry. This is hardly an acceptable consequence. But if, alternatively, Jesus Knows, then it seems that Franke will have to say that Jesus did not have a context, or that he transcended his context, or was somehow able to neutralize its epistemological ill effects. But an altogether different conclusion is possible, surely: that contexts do not have the enormous epistemological significance currently invested in them.

Whether or not these knots can be untied, I take it that Christians (including Franke) want in the main to say that claims to knowledge, if they are from the lips of Jesus, are not simply claims to knowledge that are made in order to seize power, but are rather more than that. However we characterize Jesus's own epistemological position, his claims to know (which must be more than mere claims) are not and cannot be oppressive claims to power or instances of conceptual idolatry. But it's not clear how, under Franke's auspices, we may consistently say this. For on his view, to know that Jesus Knows, and to know what Jesus Knows, is not to pay respect to Jesus's Knowledge, it is to demote it.

This postmodern charge about the connection between knowledge, power, and control is especially odd when levelled against CRT. For in one of the central theological motifs of CRT, "word and Spirit," the two elements can only be linked rather uneasily together. The reason is this: matters to do with "the word" can be humanly organized. But matters to do with "the Spirit" are divinely sovereign and free, out of human hands. Matters to do with the word may be dispensed through secondary, creaturely agency alone, but matters to do with the Spirit cannot be dispensed in the same way. The idea that they could be is, for CRT, the root failure of the sacramentalism of the Papacy. People can be trained for the Christian ministry, study the Bible, and preach it. Churches can be set up, pastors, teachers and deacons appointed, the sacraments may be administered, people catechized, and the unruly disciplined. All this can be undertaken in a routine, institutional way and some of these institutional powers could no doubt be wielded in a power-hungry way.

But in the case of "the Spirit" there is a dramatic difference. For God the Spirit, though he attends the word, is free not to do so. CRT does not maintain that the linkage between word and Spirit is automatic or necessary, or that God is under an obligation always to accompany the word with the salvific influence of the Spirit. God has covenanted to accompany his word by his Spirit, but the exact distribution of the Spirit's saving influence is still at his disposal. As Calvin expressed it:

> But who, I ask, can deny the right of God to have the free and uncontrolled disposal of his gifts, to select the nations which he may be pleased to illuminate, the places which he may be pleased to illustrate by the preaching of his word, and the mode and measure of progress and success which he may be pleased to give to his doctrine—to punish the world for its ingratitude by withdrawing the knowledge of his name for certain ages, and again, when he so pleases, to restore it in mercy?[16]

In the case of the authority of Holy Scripture, while it is possible for human agencies to educate people in what the Bible means, it is not possible in a similar way for them to convey the internal testimony of the Holy Spirit to anyone. This reminds us that CRT is concerned not only with the status of the objective pole of theological knowledge, divine revelation, but also with the state of the knower in a more general epistemological sense.

Of course, if the thesis about the oppressiveness of knowledge claims has any validity, then it extends to *all* knowledge claims, including those of CRT theologians and post-conservative theologians alike, which are also claims to have some grasp of the truth and are therefore to that extent potentially oppressive. After all, to draw men and women into participation or to give a local church instruction on how it should relate its faith to its "context" may also be exercises of social control. But maybe the point that the post-foundationalists are making is that beliefs, if they are sufficiently tentatively expressed, cannot be oppressive or idolatrous. But if so, what is the argument for this? Presumably, the more convincing the argument, the greater the danger of being oppressed! At all events, the reader may conclude that what exactly Franke and Vanhoozer are claiming and what they are denying about the nature of theological knowledge and belief is not altogether clear, even though their confidence-undermining effects are very clear.

Downplaying Knowledge Claims

As we have already noted, according to Franke, postmodernism critiques the modernist project's quest for certain, objective, and universal knowledge.[17] So it follows that postmodern theology will play down such

---

16. Calvin, *Institutes*, II.11.14.
17. Franke, *The Character of Theology*, 15.

knowledge claims, replacing them with something more "situated," and so more suitably tentative or provisional, or perhaps abandon the activity of making knowledge claims altogether. The latter is one possible corollary of our earlier discussion. But if this corollary is to be taken seriously, then according to CRT this also would fatally compromise the faith. Let us see why.

Let us suppose that the "quest for certain, objective, and universal knowledge" is an accurate characterization of the Enlightenment "quest." To abandon the quest, as Franke bids us to do, for the reason he gives, is far too clumsy and indiscriminate a reaction. When would that quest be finished? When every knowledge claim was certainly, objectively, and universally known to be either true or false? Obviously not. This would be to forget that the Enlightenment, or certain figures within it, set out an ideal, a program of positive epistemology, just as other Enlightenment thinkers, such as Bayle and Hume, were skeptics.[18] But according to some, that positive program has failed, even in science. But what of the Christian faith? How do its claims measure up?

Universality

It is important to be clear that the three epistemological goals—certainty, objectivity, and universality—are logically independent of each other. For example, a proposition may be known, but not known by everyone; it may be an objective claim, but not certain, only tentative. An objective claim may be made by some but not by others. And so on. In particular, it is of crucial importance to the integrity of Christian theology that there is knowledge that need not be immediately accessible to everyone, or even to anyone. The Christian church, including those nineteenth-century Reformed theologians such as Charles Hodge who were allegedly in thrall to the Enlightenment, have routinely claimed that this is so.

> The external foundation of the Christian religion is not the general revelation of God in nature, but a special revelation of God in Christ. The internal principle must correspond to the external principle. The mind of the "natural" [unspiritual] person is

18. Perhaps this is the place to note how naively uncritical such theologians are of the secularist and rationalist historiography of the Enlightenment. Descartes, Locke, and Leibniz (to look no further) were men of strong religious convictions. Locke's project in his *Essay Concerning Human Understanding* was to find a way of settling religious differences in terms of using the senses to make judgments of probability. See Wolterstorff, *John Locke and the Ethics of Belief*. And Descartes' epistemology can plausibly be regarded as being in the Augustinian tradition of seeking knowledge of God and the soul. See Menn, *Descartes and Augustine*.

not equipped to discern the things of the Spirit of God. God can only be known through God. They who are of God hear the words of God.[19]

Knowledge of what is specially revealed is not innate, or immediate, and the conditions for knowing are, as we have seen, partly objective, partly subjective. Perhaps everyone could *in principle* acquire such knowledge, but not everyone does *in fact* have it. Consider an elementary example of such a case. I know that I now have a sore throat. But unless I tell you, and you believe me in a way that justifies your belief, you don't know it, and perhaps never shall. I am certain that I have the soreness now, and that knowledge is objective (in at least one sense of that slippery term), since Helm's having a sore throat now is a fact about the world and I know that fact. Of course there are differences in the manner of my knowing that I have a sore throat and knowing that the piano is against the wall. You may see the piano for yourself but you cannot have my sore throat for yourself. But no issues of epistemological principle are raised by these nuances. So there can be knowledge that is certain and objective without its being universal. Otherwise it would be impossible for anyone ever to make a discovery. There was quite a time during which Captain Cook knew much more than his friends back home in England, and Madame Curé knew more than her baker. And perhaps I can know such facts without being certain that I know them; being of a retiring disposition, or dreading that the soreness of my throat may be a tell-tale symptom of cancer of the throat, I might well know that I have a sore throat but be reluctant to claim with confidence that this is so. So it would be unwise to welcome the characterization of the Enlightenment as the search for "certainty, objectivity, and universality" in knowledge with the handshake of the postmodernist. A good deal more discernment is called for.

In particular, it would be unwise for a Christian theologian lightly to dismiss the possibility of obtaining objective knowledge, because such knowledge, the knowledge of what God has revealed, is intrinsic to his project, at least to the project of CRT. Some awareness of the character of that knowledge is a *sine qua non* for attempting Christian theology in the classical sense. If this is surrendered, and we proceed to think of theology merely as the systematization of the beliefs that Christians in church happen to have, then once again theology is reduced to anthropology or sociology, to some branch or other of religious studies. In reflecting on the character of epistemology at this point, the Christian theologian must have in mind the fact that Scripture testifies that there is knowledge that is not universally

---

19. Bavinck, *Reformed Dogmatics*, I:587.

possessed or acquired, at least not without adding to it a set of strong conditions about the manner in which such knowledge is obtained. Such cases are not confined to religion. They are perfectly familiar in situations where people have mental or intellectual "blocks," or failures of empathy or insight. In such situations a person may not realize another's distress, or be aware of the hurt that he himself is causing. Could he come to realize such things? Perhaps he could, unless the insensitivity or self-deception is deeply embedded and remains so. The accepting or rejecting of the knowledge claims of the Christian faith may have a similar structure, or may sometimes have it, a structure familiar to us from moral and aesthetic contexts more generally.

"To you it has been given to know the secrets of the kingdom of heaven, but to them it has not been given" (Matt 13:11). Both the modernist and the postmodernist are likely to be turned incandescent by the particularism of such knowledge claims, even when those claims were uttered by Christ himself. Here Jesus is not saying that his disciples simply thought that they knew, nor that "knowledge" is an honorific term, or a kind of persuasive definition uttered by Christ in order to bind himself and the band of his disciples more tightly together. In a very straightforward way, which does not owe anything to Gnosticism, nor require a mastery of what counts as the justification of a belief, Christ says that his disciples *knew* what others did not know; in fact, what they knew included what some of those others dismissed as fairy stories. And they knew these things because it had been "given" them to know them, willingly disclosed to them but not to everyone else.

As far as Jesus's own appreciation of the situation was concerned, it appears that the fact that some may dismiss as fairy-stories what others claimed objectively to know to be the mysteries of the kingdom did not affect the reality of the disciples' knowledge. (Here we must once again resist the temptation to reduce theology and epistemology to sociology by defining an objective truth in terms of what everyone or some social group holds to be true. This was never a part of the Enlightenment project!) Behind Jesus's claim, then, is another claim both about the objectivity of truth, and also in the case of some of such truths, their particularity. There are secrets of the kingdom. That's an objective epistemic claim that Jesus makes, whether we believe it or not. It is possible for some to know the secrets; and (according to Jesus) he and his disciples did know them. On the standard account, the objective truth of what is known may have been a part of the Enlightenment *quest*, at least of those who were not skeptics, but it was most certainly not an Enlightenment *invention*.

When we discussed Franke's views about culture in the last chapter, we noted that the fact that some goal—such as perfect objectivity or perfect justice—is unattainable does not mean that we should not strive to approach it as nearly as possible. Similarly, it is one thing to hold that the quest for objective knowledge is not achievable, quite another thing to maintain that we ought not to strive for it. The fact that we are all biased does not undermine the quest, for we know that bias can be reduced and, in some obvious cases, that it can be eliminated. Despite all my biases, I can know that there's a piano against the wall.

No doubt the elimination of disease, or hunger, or war are also unattainable goals. But we do not and ought not to allow that fact to excuse a fatalistic attitude to the onset of disease, or to abandon the challenge of making provision for the starving, or of striving for peace. Rather, we should do all that we can to cure and to feed and to reconcile. So it is with the objectivity of our knowledge claims. We are all to some degree or other biased, lazy, self-deceived, and self-serving in our attempt to understand and learn, particularly, perhaps, to learn about ourselves. But there are ways of mitigating the effect of such factors. We may check one belief against others, others of our own, or others of members of the community. We may take objections to our views seriously when they are raised. We may learn to distinguish between an important and a trivial objection to what we hold. We may proportion our beliefs to the evidence. And so on. But the result of employing such methods to mitigate error is not that we should become equally skeptical or reserved about all our beliefs, but that we are able to cultivate the ability to distinguish those that are well-grounded from those that are not.

Fallibility

As we've noted, epistemic fallibility is inherent in Protestantism. Historically, this is due to the claims of the Roman Church to possess an infallible *magisterium*, as well as to the belief, a matter of common awareness, that human beings are ignorant and biased and open to various forms of epistemic failure. Fallibility gives due acknowledgement to human finitude and sin, and also to the fact that error may arise through wilfulness and ignorance. Protestantism, and especially its Reformed segment, has willingly confessed that God alone is infallible. If Scripture is inspired by God, then no doubt that infallibility transfers to the word of God, but it does not transfer further to all human interpretations of it. It cannot do so since these interpretations may and do conflict. Such fallibility is also recognized in much modern epistemology, not simply the epistemology of postmodernity but also, say, Popperian philosophy of science with its strong emphasis upon the search for empirical falsifications. So in drawing attention to human fallibility, and to its epistemological significance, postmodernism is doing nothing new.

Yet although this recognition of our all-too-human fallibility may be unsettling, we must put that fact in proportion, or keep it there. We are most certainly fallible, but it does not follow from this fact that general skepticism is warranted.[20] Being fallible, we are inclined to err, but fallibility—or on the other side, certainty—comes in degrees, as can be seen from some simple examples. I am fallible, but I know that I have a head; fallible, but pretty confident that this piece is being written in the United Kingdom; fallible, and less confident that the emission of carbon dioxide is responsible for current global warming than that I am presently in the United Kingdom; fallible, and not at all confident that I shall live to be a hundred. Certainty—not only the mere subjective feeling, but certainty-on-evidence—comes in degrees. Some claims may be highly certain and thus more certain than their opposites, and so they may be strongly believed: I know that I have a head, and I thus am justified in confidently rejecting the claim that I am headless; I am quite sure that I am writing this piece in the United Kingdom, and so can confidently reject the claim that I am writing it in Antarctica. How these degrees of certainty ought to be measured, whether by a probability calculus or in some other way, is a separate and more contentious matter. But the fact that there are degrees of certainty, or fallibility, cannot be doubted, any more than can the fact that there ought to be degrees of belief.

So there are some things about which we can be very certain. Could it be that among these are the assertions of divine special revelation? The fact that there are religious matters that we are uncertain of, or that not everyone agrees about religion, or that religious toleration is a virtue, do not at this point alter anything that is of any epistemological significance. Nor does the necessary situatedness of all human believing and knowing, or the travails of having to deal with the various aspects and perspectives of the "differentiated reality" of Scripture.

Contrast this with Vanhoozer's procedure. In discussing fallibilism and epistemic rationality, he writes in terms of the development of intellectual virtues.[21] But the virtues that he commends, honesty and humility, are curiously one-sided. Honesty and humility are certainly among the virtues, but what about tenacity and confidence? And honesty cuts more than one way; honesty may make a person tentative, but it may also make him firm and strong in upholding his beliefs. In the case of humility, we certainly ought to

---

20. Wolterstorff notes that the denial of strong foundationalism does not entail skepticism. "Nothing I have said requires the profession of cosmic agnosticism." *Reason within the Limits of Religion*, 56.

21. Vanhoozer, *The Drama of Doctrine*, 303–4.

be humble in the face of evidence to the contrary, but not necessarily to be humble in the face of popular or scholarly consensus. Tenacity may also be a virtue. When Paul confessed "I know in whom I have believed . . ." or Luther said "Here I stand. I can do no other," were they not also displaying virtues?

Those virtues privileged by Vanhoozer are all on the side of the exploratory, the tentative, and the conditional. Even so his procedure is curious. In setting up his view of cognitive or intellectual virtue, like Franke and Westphal he appeals to the doctrine of creation and fall (characterizing these in rather de-dramatized form, it must be said), but such an appeal raises a further question. These, he says, "lend support" to reliabilist and fallibilist epistemologies.[22] "The doctrine of creation serves as a powerful warrant for affirming the reliability of human cognition and the rationality of believing testimony."[23] But then our knowledge of creation and of the fall must be correspondingly firm in order to be able to function in this way. So there's the looming prospect of epistemic circularity here, or at least of the presence of a dilemma: either Vanhoozer knows these doctrines to be true, or they are only reasonable beliefs he holds with a high degree of confidence. For they provide the reasons why we may have confidence in the reliability of our beliefs, and similar confidence in our own fallibility, in which case these beliefs must in some way be epistemically privileged, even "foundational." Alternatively, if they share the characteristic tentativeness of our other beliefs they cannot reliably ground less tentatively held epistemic claims.

Aspectival Realism

The sources of Vanhoozer's epistemic caution at such a point are rather different from Franke's. They are not so much social as textual, for due regard has to be taken of the many genres of Scripture, its polyphony. This inevitably leads to aspectivalism, the building of a multi-dimensional model. This is always "framework-filtered and theory-laden." There is a "differentiated reality"[24] that calls for a "pluriform testimony."[25]

This is one example of a feature that we have noticed about the epistemology of postmodern or post-foundational theologians such as Franke and Vanhoozer. We might call it an "epistemology of convenience." On the one hand, each stresses, in characteristic postmodern fashion, the impact of subjectivity, of bias, of the hermeneutics of suspicion and of finitude, the

22. Ibid., 303.
23. Ibid., 302.
24. Ibid., 289.
25. Ibid., 286f.

effect of context and of the multiple genres of Scripture. In addition there is the assertion that even to claim knowledge is a bid for power and authority over others' lives. Taken together, the presence of these factors makes the claim that one knows something or other a precarious business. The call is for tentativeness of conviction, of "knowledge" claims rather than "Knowledge claims." The firm convictions that have undergirded CRT are replaced by an emphasis upon fallibility and caution, a mood of self-distrust.

And yet, and yet. There is the clear impression of an awareness that such an attitude cannot be carried through consistently. For example, Franke pivots his epistemological caution on the ideas of human finitude and sin. But these are not just religious ideas. Rather they function (presumably) as *firmly held* beliefs, even as what Nicholas Wolterstorff has called "control-beliefs,"[26] for they play a kind of basic or presuppositional role in the way that Franke, in this case, formulates Christian theology. What warrants this confidence? Why does not bias make its malign influence felt in the case of *these* basic convictions? How, consistently, can a postmodernist theology have a clear Christian character? In the case of Vanhoozer we have noted the unintentionally amusing way in which he writes of postmodernism in the all-too-familiar fashion: "Knowledge on this view is neither immediate nor indubitable; it is rather mediated via interpretative frameworks. No set of data is ever foundational because the data is always framework-filtered and theory-laden." And yet, to our collective relief, no doubt, "Nevertheless, thanks to aspectival realism, we may say that some filters allow true knowledge to get through. The post-foundationalist thus enables the epistemological lion to lie down with the hermeneutical lamb."[27]

Just when we needed some knowledge, not too much, just enough, a gap appears in the wall of cloud and some "true knowledge" shines through, enough to keep us in business, so to speak. How this is "enabled," how "aspectival realism" achieves such a timely rescue is not made clear, I think, any more than how it is that we could or do know that this was the fact of the matter. There are no arguments. As we saw in the last chapter, aspectival realism is the thesis that reality, the real, objective world, is conveyed to us by different, complementary points of view, thus avoiding naive realism, the realism of the monologists' world described exclusively by propositions.[28] According to Vanhoozer, aspectival realism is different from perspectivism, which is constructivist in character.[29] Aspectival realism enables us

---

26. Wolterstorff,, *Reason within the Limits of Religion*, 70f.

27. Vanhoozer, *The Drama of Doctrine*, 293.

28. Ibid., 289.

29. Ibid. Incidentally, Vanhoozer has a tendency to get entangled in his own terminology of aspects and perspectives. Here there is a clear distinction between aspects

to access the theo-dramatic reality that is independent of what we say and think about it. For it is "obvious"[30] that there is a plurality of literary forms in Scripture. (Vanhoozer sees no incongruity in having steps in his argument in favor of a tentative epistemology he takes to be obviously true.) How do we know that aspectival claims are not themselves infected with the usual diseases of postmodernism—bias, self-deception, finitude, and a lust for the controlling others?

Very conveniently, aspectival realism provides us not with as much knowledge as we might wish for, but with enough to enable us to make an appropriate response. But how do we know that our imaginations are not deceiving us, that what we "see, feel, and taste" is there to be seen and felt and tasted?[31] Are these cases of knowledge, just as the fact that the Bible has a diversity of literary forms is obviously true? If so, what has happened to the postmodern thesis that knowledge claims are power plays? Has it been possible to turn off this particular malign influence? How? There is an absence of argument here which is alarming, and a convenient absence of self-criticism that give Vanhoozer's account something of the character of a "Just So" story.

Running throughout the religious epistemologies of Franke and Vanhoozer is another tension: between what *is* the case and what *ought* to be the case, the *de facto* and the *de jure*. As we have noted more than once, the postmodernist temper of the times leads them, Franke in particular, in the direction of treating epistemology as a branch of sociology, as the study of what people in fact believe and how their circumstances generate these beliefs. Our postmodern world is characterized by cultural and epistemic diversity. Equally sincere, intelligent, and well-motivated people have radically different beliefs about fundamental matters. As a result there is a strong tendency to sociologize knowledge, to provide an account of these differences in terms of culture, starting point, history, tradition, community, and their respective cognitive influences. We have found that the postmodern theology of Franke and Vanhoozer is strongly affected by this current.

(realist) and perspectives (constructivist). But we also identify reality through "multiple perspectives," "a plurality of perspectives" in order to gain knowledge of the theo-drama (290). In the later work, *Remythologizing Theology*, there are sources of further complication, between "simple perspectives" and "three agent perspectives" (347 fn. 24). Perhaps there is yet a further a distinction being made between "perspectivalism" (constructivist) and "perspectivalism" (realist). As far as I have been able to discover, there is no one place where these distinctions are set out and explained clearly.

30. Vanhoozer, *The Drama of Doctrine*, 289.

31. Ibid., 291

Testimony and Tradition

Both Vanhoozer and Franke make appeals to the past, and so must place some reliance upon human testimony. No one can sensibly deny the important place that testimony plays in human affairs, for example, in the authority of the expert scientist or the historian. The question is whether human testimony is nothing more than a convenient shorthand for what each of us may, with sufficient time and energy, find out for ourselves. Or is there a more principled distinction between what we can know for ourselves and what we know only on the say-so of others? This is another area in which some Enlightenment and postmodern attitudes differ sharply from those of CRT.

On the pre-Enlightenment Christian view, tradition and testimony were essential ingredients in human knowledge. It was recognized that we each depend upon them for the most elementary pieces of knowledge, such as the knowledge of our birthday and early life. In respecting the past in this way, it comes to exercise control over the present, our present beliefs. We cannot dispense with the historical record and substitute our own investigations from scratch for the simple reason that we cannot go back in time. So we have no alternative but to rely upon the testimony of those whom we have good reason to think lived at earlier times.

So Augustine, for example, says,

> I considered the innumerable things I believed which I had not seen, events which occurred when I was not present, such as many incidents in the history of the nations, many facts concerning places and cities which I had never seen, many things accepted on the word of friends, many from physicians, many from other people. Unless we believed what we were told, we would do nothing at all in this life. Finally, I realized how unmoveably sure I was about the identity of my parents from whom I came, which I could not know unless I believed what I had heard.[32]

Augustine says that such trust of another person is not something that one *could* gain from experience but is itself a pre-condition of experience. I cannot gain the knowledge from experience that Ronald and Lottie are my parents. In the same way, it is an illusion that one might, even in principle, personally verify everything that one believes.

The Christian faith essentially involves having beliefs about the past; in the case of the Christian tradition, beliefs about the fairly remote past; about

---

32. Augustine, *Augustine's Confessions*, 95.

Scripture itself, the conciliar and confessional teachings, the writings of the great doctors of the church, and so on. The theological content of these beliefs, the classical Christian "spine" on which CRT has built, may and must exercise authority over the present, for this tradition is *normative* for the formation of doctrinal teaching. Such normative authority of the past over the present presupposes that one can gain reliable access to the past.

So in thinking about the place of tradition in the light of the attitudes of modernity, the first issue is not whether the tradition ought to exercise, or ought to continue to exercise, *de jure* authority over those who are within it, but whether it can. Here there is need to distinguish between the *de facto* view of tradition, tradition as what has in fact happened in the past and our recollection of it, and *de jure* tradition, tradition that exercises or should exercise normative influence upon our present belief-formation. A *de facto* tradition is merely what is believed or done over time; what makes it a tradition is that the same thing (or same sort of thing) is believed or done over time, the same beliefs are handed down. Thus a person or a family may have a tradition of going to Clacton for their holidays, or playing golf on Sunday afternoons. This is a *de facto* tradition; nothing requires them to maintain or carry it on. In the case of a *de jure* tradition, however, the tradition itself provides rules for present action or truths presently to be believed. The point of the difference can be brought out by noting the ambiguity of the English expression "as a rule"; a family may go on holiday to Clacton as a rule, but they may not hold a rule to the effect that they must or should go to Clacton. The first sense of "rule" is simply the rule formed from the past regularity of behavior, and it does not amount to a prescription requiring them to take their holidays in a particular place. The purely *de facto* does not license the counterfactual; *if I were to choose a place for a holiday, then I must choose Clacton*. The *de jure* sense of "as a rule" does; because if I have a rule to the effect that I must always go to Clacton for my holidays, then it is true that if I were to choose to go on holiday, Clacton must be the place that I would choose.

By contrast, the Enlightenment philosopher David Hume, for example, while recognizing the importance of human testimony, holds that it must be evaluated or assessed solely by our own present beliefs; never *vice versa*. In his famous discussion of miracles he writes:

> There is no species of reasoning more common, more useful, and even necessary to human life, than that which is derived from the testimony of men, and the reports of eye-witnesses and spectators . . . our assurance in any argument of this kind is derived from no other principle than our observation of the

veracity of human testimony, and of the usual conformity of facts to the reports of witnesses . . . and as the evidence, derived from witnesses and human testimony, is founded on past experience, so it varies with the experience, and is regarded as a proof or a probability, according as the conjunction between any kind of object has been found to be constant or variable . . . the ultimate standard, by which we determine all disputes, that may arise concerning them, is always derived from experience and observation.[33]

On Hume's view, historical testimony is shorthand for what we ourselves could have witnessed, "our observation of the veracity of human testimony," assuming we had sufficient time and energy. For historical testimony must be evaluated by the present. Indeed, everything about the past must be evaluated by the present. This is, of course, a characteristic "modernist" outlook. Let us call this the *reductionist* view of testimony.[34]

So in "the enlightened ages," which according to Hume he now occupied, the past must be judged by the present, or by a certain sort of account of the present. This realization of our epistemic authority over the past, the recognition that we must take up a "critical" attitude to it, is what makes the present "enlightened." In order to make a compelling case against belief in miracles Hume has to describe such as have borne uncritical testimony to them as lacking in good sense, education or learning, or as lacking in integrity, or as in some other way being deficient in epistemological *bona fides*. They are not "enlightened."

Such a view is not only a reductionist view of the epistemological worth of human testimony, it may also be a reductionist account of divine testimony. If one takes the view that miracles do not occur in one's own day (as Hume notoriously did), and if one is a Humean reductionist, then one must take the view that miracles have not occurred in any period; hence any supposed divine testimony to miracles will either have to be rejected or at best re-interpreted. The miracle stories are then perhaps hyperbolic, vividly fictional ways of presenting abiding moral truths. The consequences of such a view for the Christian tradition are radical. If one comes to adopt this view of human testimony, as Hume came to adopt it, then one's understanding of that tradition must change radically.

---

33. Wollheim, ed., *Hume on Religion*, 207–8.

34. Hume then reverses the argument; since this testimony is uniformly against the occurrence of miracles, one ought not, given that testimony, to believe the evidence of one's own senses that a miracle has occurred, since in such a case it is overwhelmingly likely that one's senses are deceiving or deceived.

It is only so far as I have confidence in memory and the testimony of others that I can gain knowledge, particularly any knowledge of the past. Such credence is, so to speak, a primitive feature of the human cognitive situation, one that is not reducible to any other, and certainly not a shorthand or shortcut for one's own first-hand cognitive endeavors. We must certainly attempt to evaluate the claims about the past that various "authorities" make, but it is a fallacy to suppose that we can do this in such a way as not to rely on any authority in doing so.

How might we express this more exactly? Perhaps as follows: that testimony as a source of knowledge is not inferential in character. Hume maintains, on the contrary, that it is; that any appeal to testimony depends upon the acceptance of a major premise about the trustworthiness of the one who is the source of the testimony. Of course, it is not in dispute that some cases of the evaluation of testimony depend upon inference, but not all, as a matter of logic, can do so.[35]

In the light of all this, let us remind ourselves of the central place that testimony and tradition play, and must play, in the pages of *The Drama of Doctrine* and of *The Character of Theology*. For example, central to both works is the doctrine of the Trinity, a sophisticated and mysterious conceptual structure that crosses the centuries and arrives intact into our contemporary context, or contexts. Neither Vanhoozer nor Franke provides us with any help as to how this is possible in the light of their own epistemological theories and attitudes, theories that have the opposite effect, that of breaking down our confidence in past testimony, and in testimony of any kind. All the help we receive are Vanhoozer's brief remarks about the reliability of testimony in the course of which, as it happens, he invokes Thomas Reid, so helping himself to a portion of Enlightenment epistemology! Nevertheless he tells us in the same breath that "cognitive foundationalism is rotten to the core."[36]

Then, for Vanhoozer especially, there is the idea of the canon of Scripture, integral to his "canonical linguistic" approach to Christian doctrine. Appealing to the canon, to its history and to its material content, has to be reasonably secure if it is going to function as the "theo-dramatic script"[37] and perform the role of directing the theo-drama that Vanhoozer assigns to it. Then there is the importance that he attaches to church tradition, to creedal and confessional theology. Creedal theology, we remember, is what

---

35. Dummett, "Testimony and Memorr," in *The Seas of Language*, 419.

36. Vanhoozer, *The Drama of Doctrine*, 30. For a similarly insouciant appeal to tradition, see Franke, "Scripture, Tradition and Authority."

37. Vanhoozer, *The Drama of Doctrine*, 133.

he calls the "history of great performances," confessional theologies are "great performance-responses to their own historical context that contain lessons for the rest of the church as well."[38]

I shall not comment on how far-fetched such claims are, but instead raise a final question or two about the nature of tradition if we take the proposals seriously. Are these great performances in any way normative for the Christian theologian today? Are they *de jure* traditions? Such great performances are exemplary, but are they directive for us? It is not clear that they need to be for Vanhoozer, since a new generation might notice new features of the canon not noticed by even the greatest performers of the past, and past performances may simply be regarded as passé. Such a possible outcome is of the essence of "polyphony." It is surely a real possibility that we cannot access the past with sufficient reliability for it to function as the bearer of a *de jure* tradition. Yet whatever doubts one has about the normativity of the great performances, it cannot be denied that for Vanhoozer the canon is a rule, the rule. So it has to be normative, in at least the sense that it is the original exclusive source of theo-dramatic authenticity. And so it has to be accessible. But Vanhoozer's epistemology has made the success of such accessibility a rather precarious business.

However, let us give Vanhoozer the benefit of the doubt at this point, and allow that both the doctrine of the Trinity, the canon, the creeds, and the confessions are reliably accessible and so each may have a normativity of descending importance. The question then is, on what grounds are we to believe that we have knowledge of the past sufficient to convince us that there is a canon and creeds and confessions? We have noted that in order to provide his theo-dramatic view of doctrine within a Christian framework, his work has to be parasitic on the propositionalist theology that he is otherwise so eager to dismantle. The knowledge of the doctrine of God the Trinity, and creation, the canon, the creeds, to look no further, are presupposed as part of the dramatic framework. We find a similar parasitism in his epistemology, in the way that, without argument, and with the skill of a conjuror, he attributes to "aspectival realism" just that degree of epistemic success that he requires, no more and no less. In a more pervasive sense he has to be able to carry out an operation that relies upon the reliability of that testimony, which is so crucial to the very idea of the theological importance of Trinity, canon, and the creeds, without providing us with a single argument to justify such reliance.

38. Ibid., 452.

CONCLUSION

10

CRT and the Future

That's my case against these particular examples of current "post-foundationalist" and "post-conservative" Reformed theology. For all the skill, imagination, inventiveness, and sheer graft shown by the authors we have looked at, their work represents, alas, a step back from the creedal and confessional tradition of CRT, and of Christian theology more generally, and the methods used to exhibit it. The ambition to go beyond the standard patterns of doing theology is misplaced, for such theology does not suffer from the ills that allegedly beset it. And what is offered in its place is either substandard in the critique offered against CRT, or has been found to be anticipated by CRT. The old is better.

I do not offer this as a merely negative conclusion, nor as a reaffirmation in either a complacent or an antiquarian spirit. The work of CRT is not to be preserved as a museum piece. For its work is never done. New cultural situations continually call for new presentations of theology, and Reformed theology is no exception to this. To show that I really mean this, I close the book by mentioning two or three areas where CRT will in future, in my judgment, need to pay attention.

To begin with, however, it needs to be stressed that CRT now persists at a time of academic specialization that would have astonished our forbears. The result of this specialization is that systematic theology has come to be one option among many in the curriculum. The bearing that systematics ought to have on the interpretation of a passage of Scripture in teaching and preaching is these days left to the individual student or minister to work out for themselves. The historically important idea that Christian hermeneutics is *theological*, with its foundational place for our understanding of the overall divine revelation and purpose, tends to fall into the gaps between the options of the curriculum. There is urgent need to reinstate the theological unity of Scripture, and hence the overarching importance of systematic theology and especially CRT as the synoptic presentation of the Christian faith.

For the system of theology is not an end in itself, fascinating though engaging in debates about theology may be. It does not exist as an end in itself, to be worshipped and idolized. It is true that theology deals with the study of realities and therefore can be defended as worthwhile in itself. What is more worthwhile than the study of God and his ways? If systematic theology at its best is a case of *scientia* then nevertheless, as Thomas Aquinas insisted, *scientia* must lead to *sapientia*, to what John Calvin called "true wisdom." Nor is systematic theology the only thing that matters, out-doing and out-thinking the Bible itself. A supremely good knowledge of the bones of the human frame is no substitute for hearing a sob or a seeing a smile or listening to a song. Systematic theology is like a skeleton, no more, but no less.

In his chapter on justification in the *Institutes* John Calvin conducts a series of discussions with various theologians, ending in a sharp critique of the Lutheran theologian Andreas Osiander over how we receive Christ as our justification. Osiander took the view, according to Calvin, that this reception takes the form of an "essential union." Calvin strongly demurs, and indicates why this is in an intricate discussion of the relation between justification and union with Christ, the sort of topic that is grist to the systematic theologian's mill. Reading this, the first-time reader of the *Institutes* will be brought up short by the title of the next chapter, "Necessity of Contemplating the Judgment Seat of God, in Order to be Seriously Convinced of the Doctrine of Gratuitous Justification."[1] The importance of justification is not exhausted simply by gaining an understanding of it and a true estimate of its place in systematic theology, but (for Calvin) its value is only recognized when the reader is faced with the prospect of divine judgment. This to-ing and fro-ing between getting the doctrine as clear as we can, and valuing its religious importance, is characteristic of Reformed Theology, a way of working that theologians no doubt took from the Apostle Paul.

Systematic theology points to those realities and mysteries that are the life of faith and obedience. A system of theology, however grand, is but a framework. Such a system does not explain, or explain away, the mysteries of the faith. It endeavors to provide a grammar for us to think and talk about them. How are we to think of the Trinity? We are to think in such a way as to preserve the distinction of the persons, and yet their indivisibility. How are we to think of divine sovereignty and human free will? In such a way as to preserve the holiness and the complete sovereignty of the creator, decreeing

---

1. Calvin, *Institutes*, II.11–12.

all that comes to pass yet so as not to be tainted by evil, and the responsibility and culpability of men and women for the evil that they do or allow. And so on. So constructing the elements of a systematic theology is not a project of philosophical rationalism, discarding all that is mysterious and ironing out all the rest in terms of a system of "clear and distinct ideas."

Systematic theology must also keep abreast of particular challenges that the Christian church faces from the surrounding culture, and new religious developments. Take, for example, the renewed prominence of Islam. Ought not a modern systematic theology engage with Islam? "Do Christians and Muslims worship the same God?"; "Christian providence or Muslim fate?" Ought not covenant theology to be considered in the light of the respective different positions of other "Abrahamic religions"?

As we noted at the outset, the form in which Christian theology is cast—catechetical, elencthic, or locus, patterned on the Apostles' Creed or the Epistle to the Romans—is varied, and there is no *a priori* reason to suppose that this list is closed. But new proposals of ideas or patterns should not make the task of conserving the faith once delivered more difficult. Maybe information technology will result in interactive styles, a repristination of the catechetical tradition.

There is the perennial danger of triumphalism. It is obvious to us nowadays that there are degrees of certainty and of belief. This applies to the body of Christian doctrine; some doctrines are more unambiguously embedded in the revelation of Scripture, other have more of the status of conjecture, of opinion. The epistemic status of the theology of the church is rather like a web, or webs, with individuals and churches having differently shaped webs from the fixed center and the more mobile periphery. Traditionally, systematic theologies have been written in a fairly uniform tone of certainty. In the case of the Reformed theology the impetus to such an attitude was no doubt the need to provide a theology that matched the certainties of Rome, a Protestant *magisterium*.

But such uniformity does not reflect the degrees of belief that the individual theologian or Christians may have. The Trinity is no doubt in the center of the web, but what about the mode of presence of Christ at the celebration of the Supper, or the relation of extra-ecclesiastical institutions to the church? The great differences of opinion over such matters no doubt owes a great deal to denominational tradition, but it also reflects, surely, the more tenuous exegetical basis in the New Testament. The wise systematic theologian, or the wise theologian of any other kind, should proportion his belief (and the tone of his voice) to the evidence.

Bibliography

Adams, Marilyn M. "Praying the *Proslogion*." In *The Rationality of Belief and the Plurality of Faith*, edited by Thomas Senor, 13–35. Ithaca, NY: Cornell University Press, 1995.
Adams, Robert M. "Idealism Vindicated." In *Persons, Human and Divine*, edited by Peter Van Inwagen and Dean Zimmerman, 35–54. Oxford: Oxford University Press, 2007.
Alston, William. *A Realist Conception of Truth*. Ithaca, NY: Cornell University Press, 1996.
Anderson, James. *Paradox in Christian Theology*. Paternoster Theological Monographs. Milton Keynes, UK: Paternoster, 2007
Anselm. *Anselm of Canterbury: The Major Works*. Edited and introduced by Brian Davies and G. R. Evans. Oxford: Oxford University Press, 1998.
Aquinas, Thomas. *Summa Contra Gentiles. Book One: God.* Translated with an introduction and notes by Anton C. Pegis as *On the Truth of the Catholic Faith*. Garden City, NY: Image, 1955.
———. *Summa Theologiae*. 9 vols. Reprint. London: Catholic Way, 2014.
Audi, Robert. *The Cambridge Dictionary of Philosophy*. Cambridge: Cambridge University Press, 1995.
Augustine. *Augustine's Confessions*. Translated by Henry Chadwick. Oxford: Oxford University Press, 1992.
———. *On Nature and Grace. Writings against the Pelagians.* Translated by Peter Holmes. *The Nicene and Post-Nicene Fathers* V. Edited by Philip Schaff. Grand Rapids: Eerdmans, 1971.
Austin, J. *How To Do Things With Words*. Oxford: Clarendon, 1962.
Bavinck, Herman. *Reformed Dogmatics*. 4 vols. Translated by John Vriend. Edited by John Bolt. Grand Rapids: Baker Academic, 2003–8.
Berkhof, Louis. *Systematic Theology*. Grand Rapids: Eerdmans, 1941.
Brakel, Wilhelmus à. *The Christian's Reasonable Service*. Translated by Bartel Elshout. Orlando, FL: Soli Deo Gloria, 1992.
Breckinridge, Robert J. *The Knowledge of God, Objectively Considered, Being the First Part of Theology, Considered as a Science of Positive Truth, Both Inductive and Deductive*. New York: Carter and Bros., 1858.
Calvin, John. *Commentary on Isaiah*. Calvin Translation Society. Reprint. Grand Rapids: Baker, 1979.
———. *Institutes of the Christian Religion*. Translated by Henry Beveridge. Reprint. Peabody, MA: Hendrickson, 2008.

Charnock, Stephen. *Discourse upon the Existence and Attributes of God*. London: Bohn, 1853.
Chisholm, Roderick M. *Theory of Knowledge*. Englewood Cliffs, NJ: Prentice Hall, 1988.
Clark, David. *To Know and Love God*. Wheaton, IL: Crossway, 2003.
Cooper, John W. *Panentheism: The Other God of the Philosophers*. Grand Rapids: Baker Academic, 2006.
Craig, William Lane. *Time and Eternity*. Wheaton, IL: Crossway, 2001.
Crisp, Oliver D. *God Incarnate: Explorations in Christology*. London: T. & T. Clark, 2009.
Dolezal, James E. *God without Parts: Divine Simplicity and the Metaphysics of God's Absoluteness*. Eugene, OR: Pickwick, 2011.
Dummett, Michael. *The Seas of Language*. Oxford: Clarendon, 1993.
Edgar, Robert McCheyne. "Christianity and the Experimental Method." *Presbyterian and Reformed Review* 22 (1895) 201–23.
Edwards, Jonathan. *Religious Affections*. Edited by John E. Smith. New Haven: Yale University Press, 1959.
Edwards, Jonathan. *Observations on the Trinity*, in *Treatise on Grace and Other Posthumously Published Writings*. Edited with an Introduction by Paul Helm. Cambridge: James Clarke, 1971.
Franke, John. R. *The Character of Theology: A Postconservative Evangelical Approach*. Grand Rapids: Baker Academic, 2005.
———. "Nonfoundationalism, Truth, and the Knowledge of God". *Philosophia Christi* 8 (2006) 295–304.
———. "Reforming Theology: Towards a Postmodern Reformed Dogmatics." *Westminster Theological Journal* 65 (2003) 1–26.
———. "Scripture, Tradition and Authority: Reconstructing the Evangelical Conception of Sola Scriptura." In *Evangelicals and Scripture: Tradition, Authority and Hermeneutics*, edited by Vincent E. Bacote, Laura C. Miguelez, and Dennis L. Okholm, 192–210. Downers Grove, IL: InterVarsity, 2004.
Fretheim, Terence, E. "The God Who Acts." *Theology Today* 54 (1997) 6–18.
Geach, P. T. *Providence and Evil*. Cambridge: Cambridge University Press, 1977.
Gerrish, B. A. *Continuing the Reformation: Essays on Modern Religious Thought*. Chicago: University of Chicago Press, 1993.
———. *The Old Protestantism and the New: Essays on the Reformation Heritage*. Chicago: University of Chicago Press, 1982.
Grenz, Stanley J. *Renewing the Center: Evangelical Theology in a Post-Theological Era*. Grand Rapids: Baker, 2000.
Grenz, Stanley J., and John R. Franke. *Beyond Foundationalism: Shaping Theology in a Postmodern Context*. Louisville: Westminster John Knox, 2001.
Helm, Paul. *Eternal God*. 2nd ed. Oxford: Oxford University Press, 2010.
———. *Faith and Understanding*. Edinburgh: Edinburgh University Press, 1997.
———. *John Calvin's Ideas*. Oxford: Clarendon, 2004.
———. "Revealed Propositions and Timeless Truths." *Religious Studies* 8 (1972) 127–36.
Helseth, Paul Kjoss. *"Right Reason" and the Princeton Mind: An Unorthodox Proposal*. Phillipsburg, NJ: Presbyterian and Reformed, 2010.
Henry, Carl F. H. *God, Revelation and History, III: The God Who Speaks and Shows*. Waco, TX: Word, 1979.

Heppe, Heinrich. *Reformed Dogmatics*. Translated by Ernst Bizer. London: Allen and Unwin, 1950.
Hodge, Charles. *A Commentary on the Epistle to the Ephesians*. 1856. Reprint. London: Banner of Truth, 1964.
———. *A Commentary on the Epistle to the Romans*. 1886. Reprint. Grand Rapids: Eerdmans, 1963.
———. *Systematic Theology*. 1875. Reprint. London: James Clarke, 1960.
Horton, Michael S. *The Christian Faith: A Systematic Theology for Pilgrims on the Way*. Grand Rapids: Zondervan, 2011.
———. *Covenant and Eschatology*. Louisville: Westminster John Knox, 2002.
Kelsey, David H. *The Uses of Scripture in Recent Theology*. London: SCM, 1975.
Kretzmann, Norman. "A General Problem of Creation: Why Would God Create Anything At All?" In *Being and Goodness: The Concept of the Good in Metaphysics and Philosophical Theology*, edited by Scott MacDonald, 229–49. Ithaca, NY: Cornell University Press, 1991.
Kuyper, Abraham. *Encyclopedia of Sacred Theology*, Vol. II. Translated by J. Hendrik de Vries. 1898. Published as *The Principles of Sacred Theology*. Grand Rapids: Eerdmans, 1954.
Lindbeck, George A. *The Nature of Doctrine: Religion and Theology in a Postliberal Age*. Philadelphia: Westminster, 1984.
Luther, Martin. *The Bondage of the Will*. 1525. Translated by J. I. Packer and O. R. Johnston. London: James Clarke, 1957.
Marsden, George. "The Collapse of American Evangelical Academia" In *Faith and Rationality*, edited by A. Plantinga and N. Wolterstorff, 219–64. Notre Dame, IN: University of Notre Dame Press, 1983.
McCormack, Bruce L. *Orthodox and Modern: Studies in the Theology of Karl Barth*. Grand Rapids: Baker Academic, 2008.
McGowan, A. T. B. *The Divine Spiration of Scripture*. Nottingham, UK: Apollos, 2007.
McGrath, Alister, E. *A Passion for Truth: The Intellectual Coherence of Evangelicalism*. Downers Grove, IL: InterVarsity, 1996.
Menn, Stephen. *Descartes and Augustine*. Cambridge: Cambridge University Press, 1998.
Mitchell, Basil. *How to Play Theological Ping Pong: Collected Essays on Faith and Reason*. Edited by William J. Abraham and Robert W. Prevost. London: Hodder & Stoughton, 1990.
Muller, Richard. A. "*Ad fontes argumentorum*: The Sources of Reformed Theology in the Seventeenth Century." In *After Calvin: Studies in the Development of a Tradition*, 47–62. New York: Oxford University Press, 2000.
———. *Calvin and the Reformed Tradition*. Grand Rapids: Baker Academic, 2012.
———. "'Duplex Cognitio Dei' in the Theology of Early Reformed Orthodoxy." *Sixteenth Century Journal* 10 (1979) 51–61.
———. *Post-Reformation Reformed Dogmatics*. Grand Rapids: Baker Academic, 2003.
———. *The Study of Theology*. Grand Rapids: Zondervan, 1991.
Murphy, Nancey. *Beyond Liberalism and Fundamentalism: How Modern and Postmodern Philosophy Set the Theological Agenda*. Valley Forge, PA: Trinity, 1996.
Owen, John. *Works*. Edited W. H. Goold. 1850–63. Reprint. Edinburgh: Banner of Truth, 1966.
Packer, J. I. "*Fundamentalism*" *and the Word of God*. London: InterVarsity, 1958.

———. "Introduction: On Covenant Theology." In *The Economy of the Covenant between God and Man Comprehending a Complete Body of Divinity,* by Herman Witsius, 1–77. 1693, translated 1763. Reprint. Escondido, CA: den Dulk Christian Foundation, 1990.
———. "Justification." In *The New Bible Dictionary,* edited by J. D. Douglas, 683–86. London: InterVarsity, 1960.
Piper, John. *The Future of Justification.* Wheaton, IL: Crossway, 2007.
Plantinga Alvin. "Augustinian Christian Philosophy." In *The Augustinian Tradition,* edited by Gareth B. Matthews, 1–26. Berkeley, CA: University of California Press, 1999.
———. "Reason and Belief in God." In *Faith and Rationality,* edited by Alvin Plantinga and Nicholas Wolterstorff, 16–93. Notre Dame: University of Notre Dame Press, 1983.
Rowe, William L. *Can God Be Free?* Oxford: Oxford University Press, 2004.
Russell, Bertrand. *The Philosophy of Logical Atomism.* Peru, IL: Open Court, 1985.
Shedd, William G. T. *Dogmatic Theology.* 1888. Reprint. Grand Rapids: Zondervan, 1969.
Sparks, Kenton L. *God's Word in Human Words.* Grand Rapids: Baker Academic, 2008.
Stump, Eleonore. "The Problem of Evil: Analytic Philosophy and Narrative." In *Analytic Theology,* edited by Oliver D. Crisp and Michael C. Rea, 251–64. Oxford: Oxford University Press, 2009.
———. *Wandering in Darkness: Narrative and the Problem of Suffering.* Oxford: Clarendon, 2010.
Sudduth, Michael. *The Reformed Objection to Natural Theology.* Farnham, UK: Ashgate, 2009.
Turretin, Francis. *Institutes of Elenctic Theology.* 1679–85. 3 vols. Translated George M. Giger. Edited by James T. Dennison Jr. Phillipsburg, NJ: Presbyterian and Reformed, 1992–97.
Trueman, Carl R. *The Claims of Truth: John Owen's Trinitarian Theology.* Carlisle, UK: Paternoster, 1998.
———. "It Ain't Necessarily So." *Westminster Theological Journal* 65 (2003) 311–25.
Van den Brink, Gijsbert. *Philosophy of Science for Theologians.* Frankfurt am Main: Lang, 2009.
Vanhoozer, Kevin J. *The Drama of Doctrine: A Canonical Linguistic Approach to Christian Theology.* Louisville: Westminster John Knox, 2005.
———. "Lost in Interpretation? Truth, Scripture and Hermeneutics." In *Whatever Happened to Truth?* edited by Andreas Köstenberger, 93–129. Wheaton, IL: Crossway, 2005.
———. "On the Very Idea of a Theological System: An Essay in Aid of Triangulating Scripture, Church and World." In *Always Reforming* edited by A. T. B. McGowan, 125–82. Leicester, UK: Apollos, 2006.
———. *Remythologizing Theology.* Cambridge: Cambridge University Press, 2010.
Vermigli, Peter Martyr. *Lectures on the Nicomachean Ethics.* Edited by Emidio Campi and Joseph C. McLelland. The Peter Martyr Library 9. Kirksville, MO: Truman State University Press, 2006.
Vos, Geerhardus. *Biblical Theology.* Edinburgh: Banner of Truth, 1974.
———. "The Idea of Biblical Theology as a Science and as a Theological Discipline." In *Redemptive History and Historical Interpretation: The Shorter Writings of*

Geerhardus Vos, edited by Richard B. Gaffin Jr., 3–24. Phillipsburg, NJ: Presbyterian and Reformed, 1980.

———. *The Letters of Geerhardus Vos*. Edited with an Introduction by James T. Dennison Jr. Phillipsburg, NJ: Presbyterian and Reformed, 2005.

Warfield, B. B. "Dr Charles Hodge as a Teacher of Exegesis." In *Selected Shorter Writings of B. B. Warfield*, edited by John E. Meeter, 437–40. Phillipsburg, NJ: Presbyterian and Reformed, 1971.

———. "The Idea of Systematic Theology." In *Studies in Theology*, 49–87. New York: Oxford University Press, 1932.

———. "'It says' 'Scripture says' 'God says.'" In *Revelation and Inspiration*, 283–332. New York: Oxford University Press, 1927.

———. "The Task and Method of Systematic Theology." In *Studies in Theology*, 91–105. New York: Oxford University Press, 1932.

Westphal, Merold. *Ontotheology: Towards a Postmodern Christian Faith*. New York: Fordham University Press, 2001.

Witsius, Herman. *The Economy of the Covenant between God and Man Comprehending a Complete Body of Divinity*. 1693. Translated 1763, 1771. Reprint. Escondido, CA: den Dulk Christian Foundation, 1990.

Wittgenstein, Ludwig. *Tractatus Logico-Philosophicus*. London: Kegan Paul, 1922.

Wollheim, Richard, ed. *Hume on Religion*. London: Collins Fontana, 1963.

Wolterstorff, Nicholas. "Divine Simplicity." *Philosophical Perspectives 5. Philosophy of Religion*, edited by James M. Tomberlin, 531–52. Atascadero, CA: Ridgeview, 1991.

———. *John Locke and the Ethics of Belief*. Cambridge: Cambridge University Press, 1996.

———. *Reason within the Limits of Religion*. 2nd ed. Grand Rapids: Eerdmans, 1984.

Wright, N. T. *The Last Word: Scripture and the Authority of God: Getting beyond the Bible Wars*. London: SPCK, 2005.

Wright, Tom. *Justification: God's Plan and Paul's Vision*. London: SPCK, 2009.

Index

À Brakel W., 27
abstraction, 36
accommodation, 145, 159
Adams, M. M., 120
Adams, R. M., 49
Alston, W., 155
Anderson, J., 22, 204
Anselm, 120
Aquinas, T., 72, 117, 136, 140–41
Apostles' Creed, 174, 176
Aristotle, 128, 158, 164
aspectivalism, 156, 160, 162, 206, 216, 253f. 255
    and perspectivalism, 254–55
assertion, 137
Augustine, 25, 128, 237
    and nature and grace, 60f
    testimony and the past, 256
Austin, J. L., 132, 135, 147, 175

Bakhtin, M., 125, 168
Barth, K., 2, 80, 224
Bavinck, H., 17, 18, 35, 41, 43, 51, 53, 66, 184, 235
    on definition, 31
    on God's immutability, 122
    on God's timelessness, 171
    on Hodge, 185f.
    on Scripture, 213–14
Bayle, P., 248
belief
    degrees of, 265
Bellarmine, R., 127
Berger, P. 209
Berkeley, G., 49

Berkhof, L., 11, 173
    on definition, 30f.
biblical theology, 78
'bundle' of properties, 104–6, 130

Calvin, J., 11, 12, 19, 25, 208, 264
    and accommodation, 145
    and Augustine, 237–38
    and definition, 34, 124
    and effectual calling, 81
    and God's freedom, 247
    on God in himself, 90
    on Hezekiah's sickness, 148f.
    and narrative, 149
    on Pharoah's hardening, 126–27
    on religion vs. theology, 164
    and Scripture, 213
    on the two-fold knowledge of God, 40, 56 f., 237
canon, 215–16
causality, language of, 114
certainty, 235f.
    and objectivity, 243f.
Charnock, S.
    on the essence of God, 104
    on God's goodness, 132
Chisholm, R. M., 67, 209, 210
Christianity and the past, 257
cerebral theology, 131f., 136f.
Cicero, 97
cognitivism
    exclusive cognitivism, 163
    and expressivism, 86, 88
cognitivist attitude, 144
communicative force, 81

communitarianism, 56
complementary descriptions, 156, 160
connectedness, 24f., 30
  organic, 30
consequences, 18, 20
consistency, 20, 21, 22, 24
constructivism, 49–50
context, 220f., 228f., 231, 242
conversion, 83
  passivity in, 82
Cooper, J. W., 109
covenant faithfulness, 106
covenant theology, 12, 13
Craig, W. L., 171
creedal language, 89f.
creeds and confessions, 86
Crisp, O., 96
culture, 222f., 228, 233
curriculum, 263

de-dramatization, 72, 138, 181, 253
deduction, 2, 201f.
definition, 30f., 124
  and explanation, 31
  and mastery, 30–31, 34–35
  real, 34
Demiurge, 115
Descartes, R., 214
dichotomy, 196
distinctions,
  logical and temporal, 79–80
doctrine and application, 100f.
doctrines 24
  as public, 65
dogma and modality, 95, 98, 99–100
drama
  participation in, 72f.
  and real time, 75

Edgar, R. M., 185f.
Edwards, J., 49
  on communication, 114–15
effectual calling, 80f., 113
empiricism, 51

Enlightenment, the, 44, 52, 53, 211, 248, 250
  and foundationalism, 67
  and theological foundationalism, 209
entailment, 25
epistemic strength, 239f.
essence, 84–85
  and accident, 28
evidentialism
  supernatural, 67
expressivism, 85–86

fact and theory, 183
faith, 239,
  and understanding 39f.
fallibilism, 218f.
fallibility, human, 44–46, 251–52
  and Protestantism, 251
fideism, 40, 208, 216, 227
finitude, 218, 222
  and knowledge, 222
'flattening,' 151
force
  illocutionary, 133
  perlocutionary, 91, 133
foundationalism, 207f.
  and the canon, 211
  as permissive, 218f.
  and Scripture, 208f., 212
  and theology, 52f.
Franke, J. R., 4, 47, 55, 182, 209, 216
  on Calvin, 237
  on conversation, 222f.
  on context, 219, 229f.
  on culture, 230, 232
  on epistemic caution, 264
  on foundationalism, 217f.
  on knowledge, 218f.
  on theology, 219f. 221
  on truth, 220
  and understanding Scripture, 242
Free will or free grace, 128
Frege, G., 180
Fretheim, T. E., 89f.

genre, 18, 22, 144f.
Gerrish, B. A. 2
Gnosticism, 63, 208
God
    as 'bundle' of properties, 104f.
    communicative activity of, 117f.
    as Creator, 119
    decrees of, 172
    descriptions of, 77
    doctrine of, 84
    essence of, 84
    essential properties of, 121
    and evil, 125f.
    freedom of, 25
    in se and *quoad nos*, 159
    knowledge of, 12
    promises of, 43, 109
    righteousness of, 106f.
    timeless statements about, 91f.
    titles of, 77
    trustworthiness of, 123–24
    and truth, 41
    unknowable, 106
    what he is and what he does, 108f.

Hanson, N. R., 184, 197
Helseth, P., 193
Henry, C. F. H., 131, 141
    on genre, 145
Hick, J., 223
history and dogma, 95f., 97
    as normative, 98
Hodge, C., 29, 66, 86f., 112f., 136, 140–41, 155, 173, 183f., 225f., 240, 248–49
    on the bible and theology, 199
    on biblical language, 145 f.
    on definition, 34–35
    on facts, 187
    on induction, 183, 188f., 192f.
    on internal relations, 197–98
    method in theology, 187
    on the mind, 40–41
    and propositions, 183, 199
    on religion, 66f.
    on Scripture, 213
    on singing, 162
    spirituality of, 166
    on virtues and duties, 167
Holy Spirit
    as enlightener, 59
    testimony of, 46
Horton, M., 4
Hume, D., 53, 248
    on historical testimony, 257–58

idealism, 49
identity and identification, 78, 116
illocutionary force, 72, 135, 147
imagination, 161
indexicality, 138f., 174
    and occasions of utterance, 138
infallibility and Enlightenment, 44
informational content, 161
intellectual structure, 14
Islam, 265

justification, 35, 264
    and sanctification, 29

Kant, I., 2, 46, 49, 206
Kelsey, D. H., 142, 169
know
    and 'Know,' 245
knowledge
    barriers to, 236
    and belief and truth, 241f.
    of God and ourselves, 40–41
    of God, partial 44
    objective, 43, 249
    and universality 249
knowledge claims
    and oppression, 210, 221, 244
    and power and control, 168, 244f.
    and sociology, 250
Kretzmann, N., 119
Kuyper, A., 184. 188f.

Lakatos, I., 184

Lindbeck, G., 56, 85–86, 88, 112, 179, 225
Locke, J.,
　on foundations, 214
locution, 133, 135, 147
logic, 16–17
logical and temporal distinctions, 79f.
Luther, M., 126, 133

meaning
　and picturing, 157
metaphysics of theo-drama, 112
method
　thematic, 12
　topical 12
miracle stories, 258
Mitchell, B., 55
McCool, G. A., 11
McGowan, A., 150f.
McGrath, A., 22–23
modalities, 84
　and doctrine, 100, 118, 121f.
monergism, 127
Muller, R. A.,1, 2, 56, 90, 91, 147
mystery, 22, 32, 204, 264

narrative 4, 6
　and configuration, 134
　how it borrows, 75
　how structured, 74
　narrative theology, 71, 74f.
　and neglect of creation, 61
　and participation, 100
natural law
　resistance to, 61
natural theology
　senses of, 66
nature
　and Christian theology, 63
　and general revelation, 56
　nature and grace, 56f., 208, 211
　senses of, 60f.
necessity
　hypothetical, 27
　of kinds, 28

neologisms, 117
New Testament
　and the senses, 64f.
non-foundationalism, 210
non-narrative framework, 76
non-realism, 86

objectivity
　and sociology, 243
omnipresence, 31–32
Origen, 230
Osiander, A., 264
Owen, J., 12, 23, 25
　on deduction, 201f.
　on new sense, 238
　on the sense of Scripture, 203
　on the Trinity, 202 f.
order, 12

Packer, J. I., 13, 18–19
panentheism, 103, 109, 113
parasitism, 260
participation, 73, 87, 101, 124
past and present, 53, 256f.
perfect being theology, 98f.
　Biblical basis of, 99
performance, 73
performative, 132
　justification as, 132
perlocution, 133
perlocutionary effect, 136
permanent truth vs. permanent force, 172, 174
person-to-person relations, 80f.
personal vs. coercive, 83
perspectivalism, 206
Piper, J., 106f.
Plantinga, A. C., 47, 65, 208, 209, 218
Popper, K. R., 184, 251
post-conservatives, 3
　suspicion of knowledge-claims, 42, 210, 239
post-foundationalism, 3, 209
　and receptivism, 51
post-Kantianism, 50

post-modernity
    and Spirit's illumination, 237
    stress on context and
        subjectivity, 236
post-propositionalist theology, 131
proof-texting, 143
proposition,
    limits of, 153
    meanings of, 137
propositional content, 136, 141, 154
propositional theology, 125, 131, 200
    as exclusively cognitive, 163f.
    and mastery of divinity, 163
    as 'static,' 131
    as timeless, 137
propositionalism, 131, 155
'Propositionalist Fallacy,' 161
propositions, 130f.
    and assertion, 131f.
    and de-dramatization, 136
    and 'flattening,' 150f.
    and knowledge, 158f.
    and reductionism, 142
    and speech acts, 136f.
    as timeless, 169
    and truth, 155, 156f.

Quine, W. V. O., 65

realism
    and anti-realism, 47
    epistemological, 160
    metaphysical, 6, 48f.
reason and the senses, 57f.
reasoning, 23
reasons, 20
referential success, 54f.
Reformed orthodoxy, 1
Reid, T., 193, 259
relativism, 22, 46f.
    forms of, 47
representation, 157
right reason, 236f., 239
Rorty, R., 46
Rowe, W., 117

Russell, B. A. W., 157

sapientia, 15
Schleiermacher, F. D. E., 50, 185
scientia, 15
Scottish Common Sense Realism, 50, 65
Scripture
    authentication of, 212, 236
    and foundationalism, 52
    and knowledge, 39
    as 'lists of propositions,' 140
    as polyphonic, 110
    and speech acts, 133f.
self-deception, 48
Seneca, 97
senses, 50, 63–64
sensus divinitatis, 40
Shedd, W. G. T., 11, 191–92
Shults, F. L., 215
sin, 218
    noetic effects of, 40
sinlessness and impeccability, 96, 98
skepticism, 45–46
sociology
    and theology, 233f., 243, 250
speculation, 22
speech-acts, 55, 139
    as events, 135
    and genre, 134
    and grammar, 133
    vs. propositions 131
Stoics, 65
Stump, E., 76, 153
subject-object dichotomy, 183, 196
systematic theology
    as abstract, timeless, 75f.
    and biblical theology, 77f.
    as a body of divinity, 33
    a circle, 77
    and epistemology, 39
    justification of, 14–15
    meaning of, 16
    organic nature of, 26

tabula rasa, 51

teaching and application, 146f.
testimony
    and post-conservatism, 258–59
    reliable, 53f., 256
    and tradition, 257f.
theater, 72
theo-drama, 4,6, 71f., 85f.
    and doctrine, 87f.
    metaphysics of, 110f.
    parasitic on systematic theology, 88–89, 90
theo-dramatic projection, 111
theological autonomy, 54
theological method, 5
theology
    biblical 14, 15–16
    and consistency, 21
    exegetical, 14
    as foundational, 208f.
    as grammar, 32
    historical 14,
    humane discipline, 58
    as monologic, 110
    personal or mechanical? 114f.
    as propositionalist, 86
    and remythologizing, 111f.
    as second-order, 225f., 228
    and sociology, 48, 227, 229f.
    systematic, 37
    and theo-drama, 110
theory-ladenness, 182, 183, 197–98
timelessness, 169f., 204
    as permanence, 174f.
tradition, 2–3, 19
Trinity and theology, 113
triumphalism, 265
true and 'True,' 245f.
Trueman, C. R., 25, 209
truth
    as correspondence, 156–57
    permanence of, 172f.
    as representation, 41
    value, 137
    never exhaustive, 52
Turner, P., 86
Turretin, F., 12–13
    on certainty, 235f.
    on effectual calling, 127–28

on faith, 165
and first principles, 58
and the senses and reason, 59, 211f., 240
two-fold knowledge, 59

'Utterance fallacy,' 91f., 161

Van den Brink, G., 185
Vanhoozer, K. J., 61, 71f., 90, 95f. 104f, 113, 116, 244
    on Aristotle, 159
    on concepts, 179–80, 205
    and canonical theology, 162, 210, 215
    on creation, 115–16, 124, 149
    on deduction, 205
    on definitions, 180
    on effectual calling, 80f.
    as foundationalist, 216
    on Hodge, 195f.
    on intellectual virtues, 252f.
    on knowledge as a map, 215–16
    on knowledge-claims, 247, 254
    on language, 182
    a metaphysical realist, 15
    on propositions, 180
    on reason, 215
    on time, 170
    on truth, 155f.
Vermigli, P. M., 128
Von Balthasar, H. U., 4
Vos, G., 76f., 189f., 191
    on biblical and systematic theology, 190

Warfield B. B., 11, 26, 66,155, 169
    on Hodge, 167f.
    on the Bible as speech, 138
    theology and exegesis, 15
    on theology as organic, 26
Westphal, M., 217f., 244f.
Witsius, H., 12, 13
Wittgenstein, L., 46
Wolterstorff, N. P., 106, 252, 254
'Word and Spirit,' 65, 127, 212f., 246
Wright, T., 106f., 124

www.ingramcontent.com/pod-product-compliance
Lightning Source LLC
Chambersburg PA
CBHW022001220426
43663CB00007B/904